DRAWING ARCHITECTURE

DRAWING ARCHITECTURE

CONVERSATIONS ON CONTEMPORARY PRACTICE

EDITED BY
MARK DORRIAN, RIET EECKHOUT
AND ARNAUD HENDRICKX

CONTENTS

INTRODUCTION
7 Drawing Conversations
  Mark Dorrian, Riet Eeckhout
  and Arnaud Hendrickx

ESSAY
9 Dialogical Entanglement:
  Conversation as Close Encounter
  Riet Eeckhout

PART 1: DRAWING AS MATERIAL PRACTICE

ESSAY
12 Talking Drawing
  Mark Dorrian

TRANSCRIPTS
18 Michael Webb
  The Impossible Journey
28 Peter Cook
  Knitting It
40 Neil Spiller
  Prerequisites for Discovery
54 Smout Allen
  Dynamic Drawings

KEYWORD PHRASES
68 Michael Webb
69 Peter Cook
70 Neil Spiller
72 Laura Allen and Mark Smout

PART 2: METHODS AND MODES OF WORKING

ESSAY
76 Mediating Drawing Practice: Curatorial
  Reflections on Encounter and Dialogue
  Carole Lévesque and
  Thomas-Bernard Kenniff

TRANSCRIPTS
80 C.J. Lim
  Two-and-a-Half Dimensional Drawings
91 Shaun Murray
  Drawing for Potential
98 Riet Eeckhout
  Sequential Depositions of the Image

KEYWORD PHRASES
111 C.J. Lim
112 Shaun Murray
114 Riet Eeckhout

PART 3: THE AGENCY OF DRAWING

ESSAY
118 Inquisitive Drawings
  Nat Chard

TRANSCRIPTS
122 Bryan Cantley
  Media-specific Impregnation:
  the Drawing as Subject
134 Perry Kulper
  Multiple Languages of Representation
146 Natalija Subotincic
  Stabilising the Evanescent Thought

KEYWORD PHRASES
158 Bryan Cantley
160 Perry Kulper
162 Natalija Subotincic

PART 4: THE LIMIT CONDITIONS OF DRAWING AND OTHER DISCIPLINARY CONSIDERATIONS

ESSAY
166 Spectral Mediums
  Michael Young

TRANSCRIPTS
170 Mark West
  Estrangement is Critical
184 Michael Young
  The Speculative Territory Between
  Image and Drawing
196 Metis: Mark Dorrian + Adrian Hawker
  Between Drawing and Model
208 Nat Chard
  Drawing Instruments

KEYWORD PHRASES
220 Mark West
220 Michael Young
222 Mark Dorrian and Adrian Hawker
224 Nat Chard

227 Biographies

Introduction
Drawing Conversations

Mark Dorrian,
Riet Eeckhout and
Arnaud Hendrickx

This book has its origins in a research project that was initiated at KU Leuven in Belgium by Riet Eeckhout and Arnaud Hendrickx with the intention of exploring, debating and exhibiting practices of contemporary architectural drawing. Titled 'Drawing Architecture', it aimed to investigate the work and approaches of contemporary authors who pursue architectural research through speculative acts of graphic inquiry.

In 2019, a cohort of architects, critics and curators met in a series of symposia to present and discuss their ongoing work in relation to current drawing practices and modes of production. These events were structured in relation to drawings or drawing-related artefacts produced by the participants, around which a dialogue was developed. Beyond the usual representational imperatives that often constrain discussions of architectural drawing, the group focused upon its status as a site of emergence and of imagination.

The word 'conversations' of the title of this book – *Drawing Architecture: Conversations on Contemporary Practice*[1] – is intended to carry a double meaning, referring both to the presentation of the drawings themselves, which, through their collection and positioning in this volume, are put into dialogue with one another, and to the interactions of the authors in extended discussion, affording readers a dynamic insight into the way they articulate and think about their work. The authors' conversations are presented in 14 edited transcripts developed from recordings made at the three symposium events. These are presented in four sections – 'Drawing as Material Practice', 'Methods and Modes of Working', 'The Agency of Drawing' and 'The Limit Conditions of Drawing and Other Disciplinary Considerations'. The transcripts are printed together with key drawings by the various contributors, who include Laura Allen, Bryan Cantley, Nat Chard, Peter Cook, Mark Dorrian, Riet Eeckhout, Adrian Hawker, Perry Kulper, C.J. Lim, Shaun Murray, Mark Smout, Neil Spiller, Natalija Subotincic, Michael Webb, Mark West and Michael Young.

Augmenting the transcripts, specific content-related phrases featured in the conversations are elaborated in short reflective commentaries by the authors. These work as 'keyword' essays, in which specific terms and phrases that have a particular conceptual and/or operative value for the authors are highlighted and reflected upon. Taken together, they form an accumulating glossary that runs through the volume.

Finally, the book includes a sequence of interpretative framing essays by Nat Chard, Mark Dorrian, Riet Eeckhout, Thomas-Bernard Kenniff and Carole Lévesque and Michael Young, which reflect on the materials and themes contained in the book and on issues to which they give rise, situating them within an expanded cultural-historical and theoretical context.

We believe that the significance of this publication lies not only in the way that it collects and presents drawings by its contributors but also in its documentation of ways of thinking – how the different authors interpret their work, the way they see it in relation to that of others, and

'Drawing Architecture' symposium, London, October 2019. Left to right: Mark Dorrian, Peter Cook, Mark West and Michael Young.

what they understand to be at stake in it. The small number of crossings in space and time that the book records through its transcripts were events that continually implicated larger histories, which are refracted and negotiated with in different ways by the various voices in the discussions. But, importantly, the meetings were also future-orientated and, in that spirit, our aspiration is that this book will play its part in extending these 'drawing conversations' beyond their initial settings into a wider sphere, where, we hope, they will animate and inspire the work of others.

1 A related exhibition, *Drawing Conversations*, was held between September and November 2022 at the Design Centre, Montréal, Canada (Director: Louise Pelletier; Exhibition Curators: Carole Lévesque and Thomas-Bernard Kenniff; Exhibition Design: Arnaud Hendrickx).

Dialogical Entanglement:
Conversation as Close Encounter

Riet Eeckhout

When 14 architectural practitioners decide to gather in a closed, intimate setting and unroll their drawings across the table to engage in a conversation, it results in long hours and even days of intense dialogue. When these practitioners subsequently decide to do this on a regular basis, the persistent exchange — of seeing, phrasing, questioning, answering, hesitation and rephrasing — starts to shed light on a dynamic and shifting landscape of thought.

When and where do we encounter the core of spatial thinking? Engaging in conversation about the intuitive and operative heuristics of these practitioners compels a close encounter that reveals traces of reflection in action.

Through inquiry into the circumstances of the drawings, their intent, and their methodological and representational implications, the limit conditions of normative understandings are revealed. It becomes clear, as conversations gain momentum, that there is no singular way in which to comprehend the work. Instead, the conversation rather seems to open doors to a richer and more refined understanding, triangulating between the experience of the actual work, its internal logic and intent, and the manner in which one is moved to talk about it.

The actual work, the actual drawing, the actual produced artefact in hand, materialised and present on the table, has a power of voice of its own. Artefactual agency is manifested by its presence. The work substantiates the particular knowledge, to be sensed, seen and experienced first-hand, there and then. One might describe it as a 'stepping into the drawing', where the space between the observer and the work evaporates, enabling an immersion in it. The American architect and educator John Hejduk referred to such action as '*a flight of no substance* collapsing space in its wake'.[1]

Through their presence, the drawings operate as conversation pieces, giving rise to an in-depth exchange about their material and intellectual concerns, methods and modes of operation, every time instantiating a connection between intellectual reasoning and the sensed material agency of the work. Allowing this kind of physical proximity to the work to give rise to, and interweave with, conversational threads, generates, each time, articulate reconsiderations of spatial notions.

The characteristic rhythms with which one speaks or questions, the impetus and insistence — sometimes hectic, sometimes poetic and inaccessible, sometimes controlled and with well-attuned phrasing — bear traces of the relentless search and consideration from which the work originates.

This inevitably entangled environment of knowledge-in-process that gives access not only to the work, but to the thought-worlds from which it has emerged, is documented through the array of materials — images, writings and discussion transcripts — that comprise *Drawing Architecture: Conversations on Contemporary Practice*.

[1] John Hejduk, 'Evening in Llano', in Elizabeth Diller, Diane Lewis, and Kim Shkapich (eds), *Education of an Architect* (New York: Rizzoli, 1988), pp 340–41 (italics in original).

DRAWING AS MATERIAL PRACTICE

12

Talking Drawing

Mark Dorrian

DRAWING ARCHITECTURE

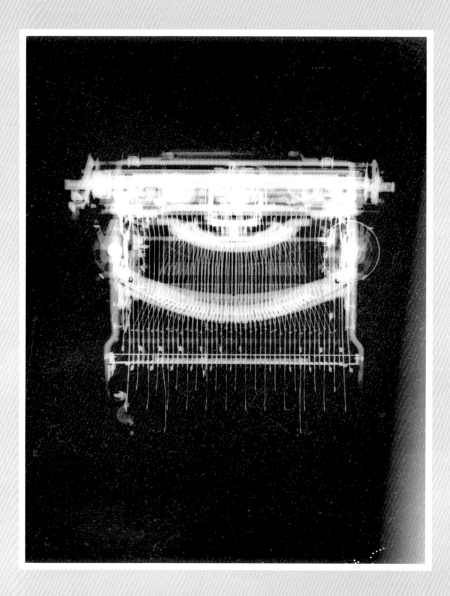

Typewriter X-ray
Nick Veasey/
Science Photo Library

The series of meetings convened by Riet Eeckhout and Arnaud Hendrickx, and recorded through the transcripts and images in this book, were unusual in the way they brought together a group of architects, known for their graphic practices, to present and discuss their work with one another, specifically in relation to questions of drawing. The transcripts give us rich insight, not only into what the various participants do, but also into the ways in which they think about their work and how they articulate it, both monologically, through spoken presentation or commentary, and dialogically, through conversation – and these can turn out to be a little different from one another. Reading through the material, we learn of preoccupations and obsessions; of ways of working and approaches developed at specific points, sometimes in response to new technologies of visualisation and fabrication; of anecdotes that are told to exemplify something, perhaps something that can't be otherwise stated, and that confer practice with an orientation; of investments in, and attachments to, particular words, which go beyond any straightforward signification and maybe even become incantatory; of references and relations, real and imagined (but what might the difference be?), with other practices and works; of principles, convictions and commitments to particular ideas or modes of thinking; and more …

What is at stake in talking drawing? Why should be we be interested in it, and is what is being talked about self-evidently drawing anyway? Good questions, and not necessarily easy to answer. Certainly, the fact of the involvement of the participants in the events suggests that they understand what they do to be in some way 'drawing', and that the term itself continues to be meaningful for them – and perhaps also, though I may be getting ahead of myself here, that the use of the word is important to sustain. A sceptical view might be that we have entered a more complicated and multimodal epoch of image-making and transmission, and that a continued adherence to a concept of drawing is anachronistic, serving primarily to retain attachments to an ideal of practice that is solitary, withdrawn, self-consciously profound and even quasi-mystical. But another could be that the technological development of diverse forms and processes of representation has, as these have expanded, involved and conveyed procedures and attributes that we would recognise as 'belonging to' or being characteristics of drawing, as it has historically been conceived.

Media theorists have commented on the way that technological development tends to bring to the fore conditions that have always been present, although latent and unthematised, making them explicit and newly recognisable. Seen in this way, the contemporaneity of LIDAR scanning, to take one example, with its point-based mapping of surfaces, is highly differentiated. On one hand, it re-performs a long-standing technique of image construction and transference that runs through the pricking of cartoons to map images on to wall surfaces to the spot heights of topo- and hydrographic surveying, whose establishment allows contours to be drawn. On the other, the quantitative density of the data produced, as visualised in the 'point cloud', and the manipulability of its visual construction enabled by computational technology, gives us something that seems quite new. And that newness turns out to open the possibility of reintegrating the data recorded with specific historical regimes of representation – of seeing and spinning the point cloud in perspective and, in doing so, discovering (or constructing) an unexpected resemblance to earlier visual forms, such as X-rays or spirit photography.

It seems to me that something common to the diverse practices presented in this book is an alertness to, and willingness to engage with, this kind of complexity – which is to say, this sort of re-finding, or intensification, or re-assignment of attributes or processes of drawing, which are now also distributed across different agencies, including machinic ones. We could talk about an 'expanded field of drawing' here, which might be understood, in part at least, as an outcome of drawing's confrontation with its own histories, as they are embedded in contemporary technologies, as well as in the material tools we fabricate and use. This can give rise to procedures that don't necessarily look like acts of drawing, but also extend — via image capture and tracking technologies, for example — the ways that other actions might be thought of as, and might produce, kinds of drawing. Equally, the logic of digital fabrication produces devices that start to appear as so many drawing machines — laser cutters and three-dimensional printers that track tool paths, which seem entirely predefined but that can produce unexpected outcomes and effects in contact with diverse materials.

The complexity that I see these practices entertaining is reflected in their non-hierarchical and non-teleological character, which allows materials, procedures and techniques to be de-sedimented and shuffled into different sequences. Things are made to work upon one another, and means are found of doing things, in ways that scramble expectations built on the familiar narratives of historical media development. What was before comes after — although it returns with a difference and is likely orientated toward other ends. And this, I think, is why the staging of the drawing, the 'scene' of its production, comes to the fore as such a central issue for many — something has to be constructed in advance before the drawing can emerge, a construction that sets up the terms of this interaction, puts a series of relations in play, and opens a kind of field of visibility. We see this concern running in various forms through the approaches: in the spatial, material and technological configuration of Riet Eeckhout's projection of sequential digital video stills and her manual redrawing of these on a vertically orientated Mylar surface; in Shaun Murray's combination of projection, from above, and re-sequencing of layers of tracing paper sheets, from below, to edit what is seen on the active surface of drawing; in Nat Chard's construction of devices for producing contingent acts of projection and his recording of those; in C.J. Lim's collaborative scene of 'quilting' for his Venice drawings; in Neil Spiller's appropriation of a scarred cutting mat to produce an atmosphere of marks that is both the drawing itself and an environment in which it can emerge; in the role of the 'room' and the presences that animate it in Natalija Subotincic's dreamworks; in Mark West's discussion of visual distances in the development of his drawings and how things are set up to 'get right with chance'; and so on.

These intense interests and concerns with the construction of the conditions within which drawing takes place reflect what seems to be a generally shared commitment to the idea of drawing as a site where things are encountered and found, and an oscillation set in motion between discovery and invention. In this light, the assorted stagings of drawing that we find described here are displacement strategies that enact a complex play of control and its loss. A controlled situation (itself inevitably not outside the realm of improvisation) is set up that enables control to be lost, at least lost in the right way — and it would be interesting to think at length about what that might mean for the various practices discussed. All this is also to say that these constructed arenas of navigation and disorientation are ways of shifting the relation between the author and the work, transforming it into one of interlocution and endowing the materials of drawing, thought in their widest sense, with a newly-active agency. The 'conversations' of the title of this book turn out to be as much about things talking to people, as they are about people talking to one another.

    So, now the question of what is at stake in 'talking drawing' is refocused. The various conversations recorded in this book are motivated by a faith in drawing as a zone of inquiry, discovery and exploration that entails risk and uncertainty, and the efforts to express and articulate the importance of this act to maintain the openness of drawing to which they are dedicated. Related to this, I am struck by a certain tone in the conversations — a kind of modesty or tentativeness in the advancing of ideas or arguments about the works. For when working in this way, while one might have clear ideas about what one is pursuing or the processes undertaken, nobody commands the final word on what has been produced. Instead, there is always the sense that the things being discussed are never absolutely identical to what is said about them, and that offering them for conversation is a process of expanding the understanding of what has been done.

    Why is the word 'drawing' so important in all this, as opposed to, say, 'image'? Maybe it is to do with the quality of time that 'drawing' conveys, with its double aspect of noun and verb, of object and process, allowing a sense of lingering with something that unfolds temporally. But also, I think it is important that — at least, as I understand it — drawings might be images but they are not always so, which entails the possibility of the passage of something that had hitherto been purely a 'mark', or an array of marks, to the condition of an image with some sort of referential attachment. For it is through the movement back and forth between these — or perhaps, at times, in the undecidability of the distinction between them — that drawing gathers its speculative force.

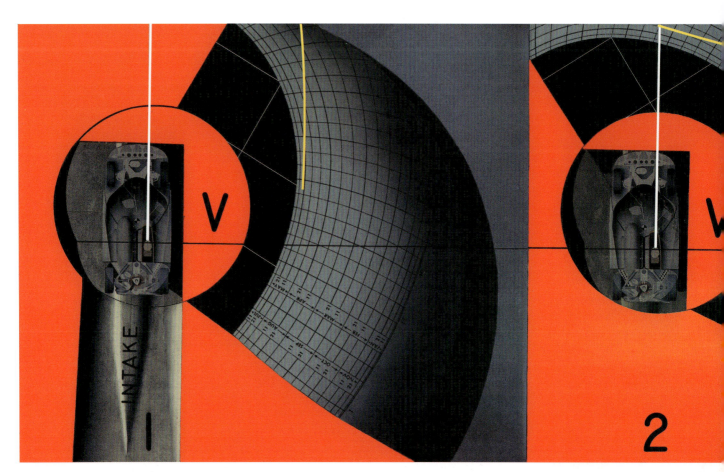

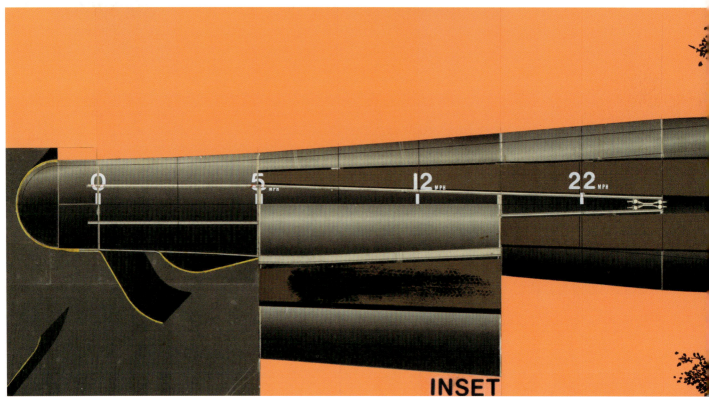

MICHAEL WEBB

Top: *Drive-in House* three-phase plan projection, 1993
Airbrush and Color-aid overlays on board, digitally enhanced, 20 × 70 cm (8 × 28 in)

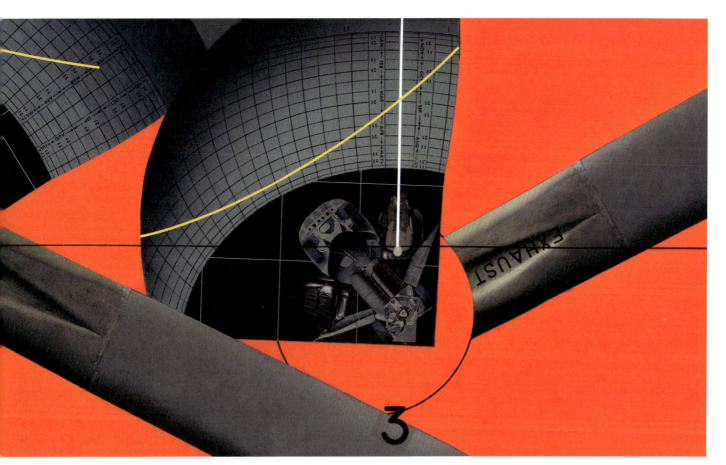

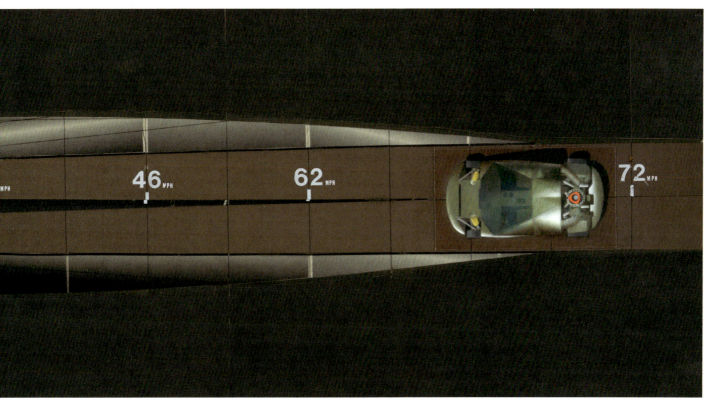

Bottom: *Drive-in House* entry tube, 1995
Collage of dot-matrix overlay and oil painting of car, 32 × 80 cm (12½ × 31½ in)

Michael Webb
The Impossible Journey

MICHAEL WEBB

I was doing a hand drawing of an air intake for a certain car.
And I realised doing that,
having to set it up by hand, and draw all the lines with French curves and so on,
that I became much more sensitive to the shape and the smooth flow of the contours than I would be if it were a computer drawing.
And I just put that before you as a possibility of some value to still doing hand drawing.

I'd like to read you a quotation from *The Great Gatsby* by F. Scott Fitzgerald. The narrator has rented for the summer a small cottage on Long Island's Gold Coast – Long Island Sound, that is. Adjacent to it is a grand mansion occupied by Gatsby. It is dusk. Stepping outside for a moment, the narrator realises that his neighbour has had the same idea:

> [Gatsby] stretched out his arms towards the dark water in a curious way and, far as I was from him, I could have sworn he was trembling. Involuntarily I glanced seaward – and distinguished nothing except a single green light, minute and far away, that might have been [at] the end of [someone's] dock.[1]

The small green light is the point in space on the x-axis at which the lines representing Gatsby's and the narrator's centres of vision intersect.
We learn that Gatsby, though, is more interested in the fact that the light must be at the end of the dock serving the house in which Daisy, his lost love, lives.
The light, consequently, symbolises his yearning for her.

I too have that yearning, although my yearning is perspectival rather than amatory: I want to journey to the vanishing point. But where does logic suggest I begin the journey? Why, at the location of the observer, of course!
For there is a strange symmetry between the two points; not a symmetry of objects that are alike, but one of opposites. To explain what I mean, please look at the diagram.

In it I have displayed a plan projection of a regatta course showing the 2112-metre-long course divided into 23 sectors of equal length, so that the lines between the sectors number 24. I have then juxtaposed alongside the plan a perspective projection of the course so that line 1 in the perspective is co-linear with line 1 in the plan. I have then drawn the perspective so that line 2 in the perspective is co-linear with line 13 in the plan. Using diagonals, I now have enough information to complete the perspective, and find to my delight and relief that line 23 in the perspective is colinear with line 23 in the plan!
There is a terrible joy in all this.

I can also extend forward the diagonals to locate the position of the observer, but here there is a real problem – the most forward diagonals are parallel to the sides of the course and they will therefore never meet. Hence the observer must be at infinity or nowhere!

That which is being observed is infinitely far from the entity observing it.

As for the journey to the vanishing point ... Imagine a red dot moving along the right-hand edge of the plan projection at a constant speed, and that we think of this construction as a time diagram. The red dot will take the same amount of time to traverse each sector in the plan projection but successively less time to traverse each sector in the perspective.
Using the simple formula speed=distance/time, the average speed can be ascertained for each of the sectors.

Via drawing I can imagine the journey to the vanishing point. But I need to define the landscape through which I will travel – halfway between two horizontally placed

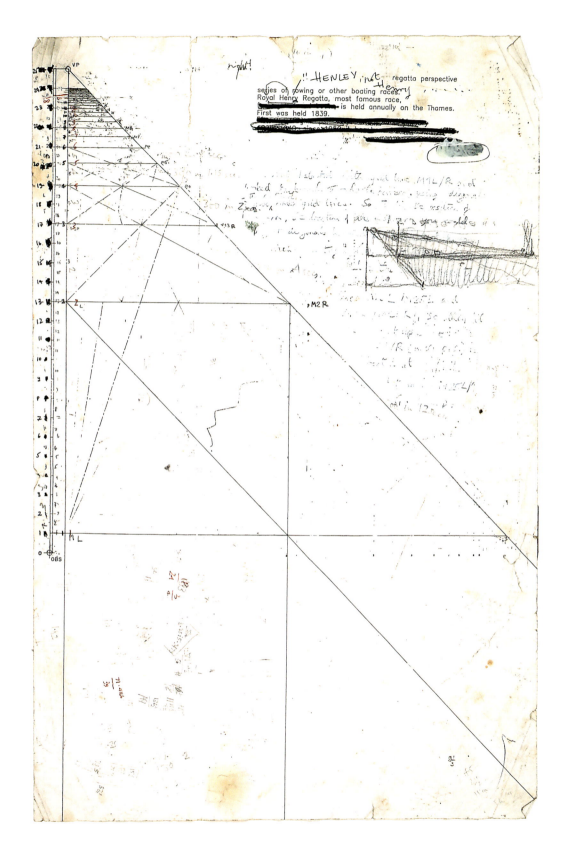

MICHAEL WEBB

Sketch of regatta course with horizontal lines fixed by the use of diagonals, 1982
Ink line on scrap paper, 38 × 25 cm (15 × 10 in)

Following page: *Temple Island*, depiction of landscape from moving viewpoint, 2002
Oil on prepared board, 155 × 53 cm (61 × 21 in)

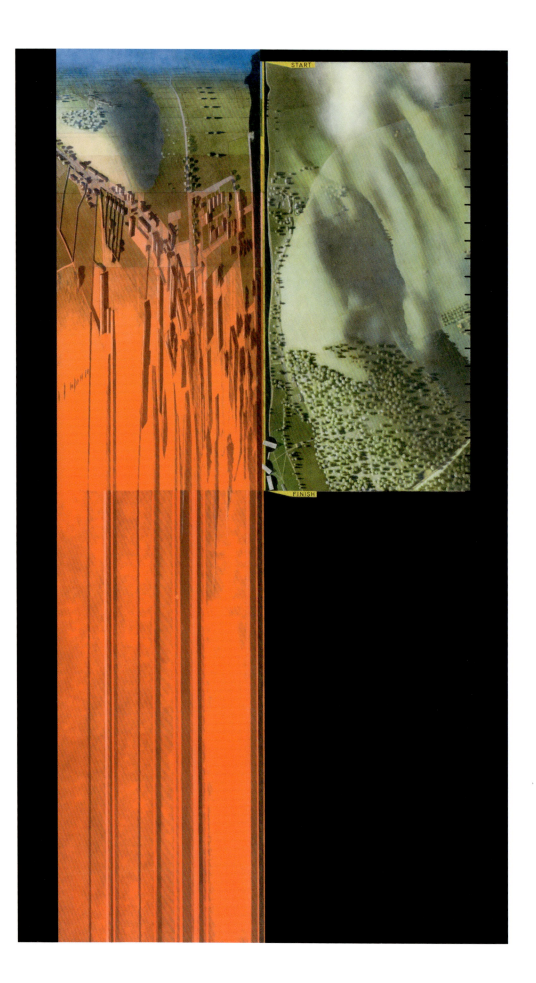

gridded planes presented in perspective projection.
Now, this is similar.
This is the oil painting ... I love laying on thin veneers of paint.
On the right hand of the river, which runs up and down the middle, it is a conventional view.
You have the regatta course, and a cloud.
Then a wood, where you get bluebells every spring.

A strange symmetry becomes apparent, more a symmetry of opposites, where the one component is the formal opposite of the other.
In the plan projection of the regatta course, the location of the observer can be shown, but not that of the vanishing point.
In the perspective projection of the regatta course, the location of the vanishing point can be shown, but not that of the observer.

In the perspective projection, space is compressed at the vanishing point to a singularity. Is it entirely specious to suggest a connection with a black hole?
And around the point defining the location of the observer, space is expanded exponentially.

Now, the rate of acceleration away from the observer's point can be ascertained from the following ...
the point moves at a constant rate up the plan projection and, looking at the plan projection in red again, I decided it would take two minutes to travel the length of one sector — that's about 300 feet.
But when measured up in the perspective projection, because the sectors are increasingly foreshortened, it takes less
than the two minutes for each sector to be traversed.
As the point nears the horizon, the time taken to cross a 300-foot-long sector will be a tiny fraction of what it was at the beginning of the point's journey.
Therefore, the velocity of the point must show a common increase and the space of the surrounding landscape must be stretched, extending forever.
Hence, the landscape will appear reddened in the oil painting because it is stretched —
it's gone towards the red end of the spectrum.

And as the point goes faster and faster, the colours will change until, when it's at infinity, it's totally blue because of the wavelength of light ... red at the bottom and blue at the top.

What I did with the book *Two Journeys*[2] was to have the painting printed slightly on the tilt, not horizontal, so that this red line would continue on, page after page, getting longer and longer, and gradually would, as you turn back through the pages, and even onto a different topic, get closer to the edge and get thinner and thinner.
So, 50 to 60 pages back, it would be a thin sliver of red.
When you were reading the book for the first time, you would think:
'Hmm, what's that red strip there? Is that some sort of mistake?'
But as you turned the pages, the red strip would get fuller, and thicker, until it finally met the painting.
Then you would realise what it was all about.

This is another much earlier painting of the regatta course.
In this one, the rule is that you're not allowed to show something that the observer at the apex can't see.
So, if they can't see behind the tree, you don't show what's behind the tree.
And it's imagined that the air is thick, the atmosphere very heavy ...
the air itself becomes translucent, but not transparent.
And here's the shadow of the tree bursting through the top surface of the landscape.

Now what I've realised is that because of a strange symmetry existing between the observer and the vanishing point, the journey would actually take forever to get from the observer's point to the first sector, and forever to get from the last sector to the vanishing point.
A similar journey was undertaken by Alice at the instigation of the Red Queen in *Through the Looking Glass*. Alice is running hand in hand across a checkerboard landscape with the queen, who keeps saying, 'Faster! Faster!'
Out of breath, Alice responds, 'Are we nearly there?'.

MICHAEL WEBB

Previous page: *Temple Island*, montage of components from the book *Two Journeys*, 2018

Above: *The Apex of the Cone is the Vanishing Point*, 2010
Color-aid papers and ink line on MDF board, 48 × 48 cm (19 × 19 in)

The most curious part of the thing was, that the trees and other things round them never changed their places at all [...] 'I wonder if all the things move along with us?' thought poor puzzled Alice.[3]

No matter how fast they went, where they ended up looked exactly the same as where they had started.

I'm very fascinated by that notion of the impossible journey.
That in fact, it may not be possible to get from the observer's point to the vanishing point.
But it does satisfy the strange yearning I have for that.

Peter Cook very kindly published my furniture building from 1958, 63 years ago.
At first it surprised me actually – Peter had written words all over my drawing, words like 'move', 'skin' and 'movement'.
At first, I didn't understand a reason for doing that.
But then I realised (and maybe this wasn't his intention at all) that he's asking that those tubes upon which he has written the words, and the lecture theatre of this strange building become more dynamic – so that perhaps when people walk through it, it starts to glow orange, or maybe the diameter of the tube expands and increases, so that you get a real response to their presence.
Rather like Paolo Soleri suggested with his Mesa City, in which you had liquids pumping through the building.
So, when it was being cold the liquids would be blue.
And when it was being warm the liquids would be red.
Which takes one back to the previous images of the red and the blue landscapes.

One thing we did in Archigram was always to borrow from each other,
and to take very seriously the critique offered, and let it feed into the project and see what happened.
And I think that's what's happened here.
So, when I did an oil painting of the building, I wrote the word 'BOWELLISM' on the tower.
But whereas Peter scrawled it on with a felt-tip pen, I set it up very carefully.
With the letters even dimensioned so that they appear to be curving round the shape.
So, there's 'MOVE', which he wrote, one of his words, and there is 'BOWELLISM'.

RIET EECKHOUT
Michael, the drawings and paintings you make are different in nature.
There's a mathematical drawing where you are calculating and working things out with line drawings, figuring out conceptually how something might work, drawing out if and how something is possible or impossible to attain.
Does all this thinking through the line drawings come together in the oil paintings you make?
Is that where you are heading always, from the drawing to the painting?
What the mathematical drawing brings might be more evident, but what does the painting bring for you, on your own terms?

MICHAEL WEBB
One drawing leads to another drawing, doesn't it? That's the trouble.
The purpose of a drawing is really to make evident to you how shitty your ideas are, but how you can, by revising the drawing, gradually come to enlightenment and truth.
Somehow you have to feel, when you begin a drawing or a painting or whatever, that there will be surprises arising out of the doing of it, that something you hadn't considered will come to light and which will then occupy and absorb you.

I think the maths comes first really.
The mathematics is not revealed through the paint.

I luxuriate in the painting – in learning how to paint a tree seen from about 500 feet up and in putting on colours.
I use the raising technique where you put one colour on, very thin, tapped on with a sponge – a little bit of a special type of sponge attached to an X-Acto-blade handle.

You tap with it, and it spreads it out very thinly.
And then after about four days, you can recoat it with a totally different colour, and you get a transparency of colour.
You have this remarkable quality that some people talk about oil paintings as possessing. They have an inner light.
The light comes down, hits the surface of the painting and is reflected off the white background into the eye, giving the painting a luminosity.
It's beginning to happen here in the bowellism painting – the white, the light reflecting off the lecture theatre is starting to look luminous.
And if I were to make this darker, that would almost appear like a source of light itself.
And that's one thing that Lebbeus Woods was always after too, that magical sense of light reflecting off a drawing.
And what I would do now to enhance that would be to add a very thin wash of oil paint diluted in Winsor & Newton's painting medium and apply it to the whole surface except for that one area ...
And you would be amazed at how luminous it would look compared to how it does now.

MARK DORRIAN

Something that I always feel about the work when you talk of the vanishing point, Michael, is that a lot of it seems to be about not getting there.
It seems to be about delaying getting to the vanishing point, if it even makes sense to put it that way.
And that's something to do with the kind of pleasure and with the slowness of the work, the fact that nothing is ever definitively completed and that everything is always somehow in motion in it.
Maybe that also has a relation to your appreciation of pentimento paintings, in which one painting has been painted over with another.
Because of the ageing of the chemicals of the paint, one starts to see the older image appearing from behind, so that the painting is in motion and transforming even when it's not physically being drawn on or painted by the architect or the artist.

It feels to me that you inhabit a world that is constantly in motion,
and that the pleasure is to do with constantly holding off arrival or negating the possibility of some finishing point or end point or condition of closure.

MICHAEL WEBB

Yes, I think that's why I'm interested in this extraordinary Lewis Carroll quotation about the journey that Alice and the Queen make across the checkerboard landscape.
They're running as fast as they can, but when they look around themselves, the landscape has not changed at all, the same trees still there.
In fact, they haven't moved.
And I realised that that is an impossible journey.
But so is the journey I'm describing here.
You would never get to the vanishing point because it doesn't exist.
This drawing here shows two grids disappearing to two vanishing points.
If you imagine crossing that landscape, the lines forming the grid would be coming towards you, faster and faster.
And you would never actually arrive at the vanishing point, even though you were speeding up over time.
Because there's no vanishing point there, basically.
And so that journey is impossible, just like the one of Alice through the looking-glass.
It's doubly impossible in my drawing, because there's no real way of starting the journey.
And there's no real way of concluding it.
I love that notion.

1 F. Scott Fitzgerald, *The Great Gatsby* (Ware: Wordsworth Editions, 1993), p.16.
2 Ashley Simone (ed.), *Michael Webb: Two Journeys* (Zürich: Lars Müller Publishers, 2018).
3 Lewis Carroll, *Alice's Adventures in Wonderland* and *Through the Looking-Glass and What Alice Found There* (Oxford: Oxford University Press, 2009), p.145.

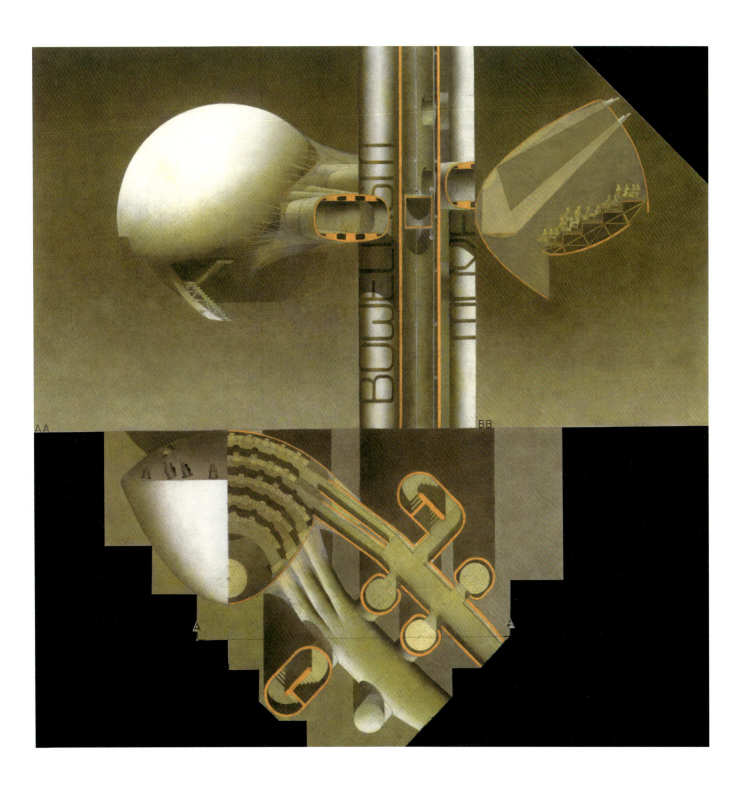

MICHAEL WEBB
Elevation and section, Furniture Manufacturers Building, 2010
Oil on prepared board, 50 × 50 cm (20 × 20 in)

Peter Cook
Knitting It

PETER COOK

So, when I was getting the drawings together for this conversation, I was thinking of the other people who are taking part in this drawing symposium, and from what I know and what I remember, nearly all of you are much more theoretical than I am.
I'm not only nervous of theory, I'm suspicious of it.
I'm somebody who really can't do very much unless it's vaguely related to something I know.

When I was trying to think and define what it is that I do, I thought, most of my stuff could be taken as sort of illustration in a funny way.
So, I asked myself the questions –
'Am I illustrating an imagined future place?', which I think I often am.
Or 'Am I using the aspects of familiarity to try and sort of lubricate the process of invention?' And as I'm asking that question, I don't think I have the answer to it,
but it does occur to me that it might be relevant to what I do.

On the other hand, I'm very self-aware of the fact that there are certain drawings that I realise afterwards were a kind of trigger for a whole train of thought.
The pieces of them do not necessarily reappear, but certainly the conversation behind them reappears.
Drawings with a lot of ammunition in them – a lot of ammunition that I've drawn from.

I think this is one such drawing.
It's a drawing done at the time when we were working in Islington and it reflects upon a piece of Islington, Highbury Corner. And it uses certain references to reality – references to, for example, the red brick
of Highbury Corner, things like the Gothic chapel ...
But most of all, this drawing is referencing work that was going on at the same time in certain schools of architecture – principally the Bartlett, the AA, and so on, where people were doing amazing work, weaving things. They're making an architecture, a sort of spun, woven architecture, potentially mobile, pulsating, moving, twisting ...
And of course, simultaneously referring an old theme, that of natural vegetation.

The Highbury Tower drawing marked a point of departure and it triggered then a couple of drawings of a hypothetical building, where there are some kinds of artificial, pulsating woven *things*.
Whatever they are ... drapes, surfaces that would actually of course be related in the section – it's really rather an old-fashioned section.
It has a lot of standard parts, but some of the edges suggest that there is a kind of quasi-mechanical, quasi-moving, fluid, digitally figured condition, but quite crude. I think the technical implication of the left-hand drawing should probably be further advanced, when looking at the jerky, tentative quality of the right-hand drawing.
This is my own critique of myself, if you like. Being a part-time academic, I'm trained to criticise things, also my own work. But instead of just criticising my own drawings and saying, 'Oh my God, I'm hopeless', you know, and the end is nigh, I say, 'Well, fuck that. So, it's got warts, but let's keep moving.' That's always been my attitude.
I'm trained to look for weaknesses, strengths, directions, potentials, blind alleys, and so on, just by the training of 60 years of teaching that runs through my head.
But doesn't stop me drawing.
I say, 'Fuck that, yeah, it's a bit crappy, but let's keep going'. And then sometimes I take that piece out, change it and move on.

Some parts of the drawing look at 'controlled vegetation'.
In lockdown, we have actually completely reconstituted our garden. We had people digging up the ground and laying things in. And it's interesting to watch it at a practical level.
The question of vegetation and control.
My Israeli wife always says that in London, you have an 'automatic' garden. In fact, in

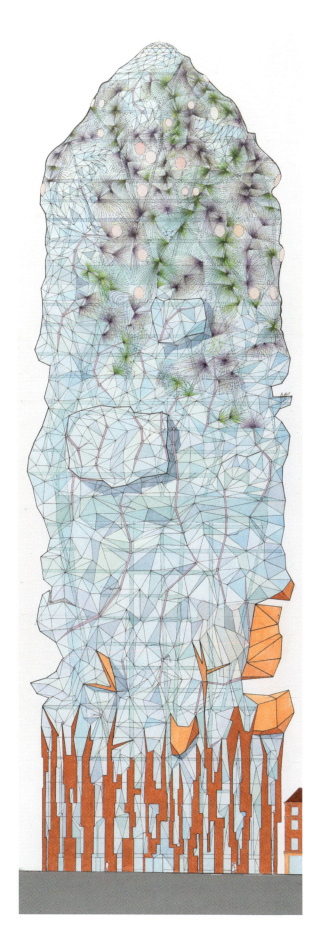

PETER COOK
Elevation, Highbury Tower, 2016
Ink, watercolour and crayon,
151 × 49 cm (59½ × 19 in)

PETER COOK
Elevation, Student Centre exterior, 2019
Ink, watercolour and crayon, 70 × 50 cm (27 × 20 in)

PETER COOK
Section, Student Centre interior, 2019
Ink, watercolour and crayon, 70 × 50 cm (27 × 20 in)

order to achieve certain ends, it's by no means automatic. It is bugged with irrigation tubes and gravel and God-knows-what to try and make certain apparently natural things happen.

It has now become fashionable territory, covering buildings with vegetation, but I think, drawing-wise, I and many of my friends were in there early on. It's just that other people got to build them. But you start to see that already. It is a kind of artifice. It's no longer an alternative to the discipline of bricks and stones and concrete and so on. In fact, it often follows the same parallel disciplines.

There is the real question of things popping out of the ground, which I find interesting. One of my favourite photographs of the little building I did some years back now, in Bournemouth, the drawing studio, shows it appearing to pop out of a hump in the ground.
Even way back, in early drawings, these little bubbles are popping out of the landscapes — contrived objects popping out of the ground and having a conversation with it is a very recurrent topic.
I keep coming back to it.
I can't escape it.

I want to talk to you about this extraordinary hill that I drew.
It is part of this Tuscan hilltop town I've been drawing, juxtaposing the natural and man-made, the ordinary and extraordinary.
'How about doing an Italian Tuscan hilltop town?' I thought, 'P. Cook style?' So here we have it.
Very early on in this conversation with myself, I drew the Tuscan hill town. It's a small town and it's on the top of the hill.
And of course, there's a watercourse very conveniently, which has its spring in the middle of the town. It trickles down the central pile, and trickles down through the wall — down the valley there are some vineyards, etc.
There's the odd little pocket of garden, curling into the wall of the old farmhouse, nearby. And then we come into the town, and you'll see that there are some rather more formalised figures — buildings. The most central building is the most preposterous building — it's in fact a sort of hill.
Is it a hill? Is it a building?
Is there something mysterious contained within it?
Or is it just a vehicle? ... Is it just that kind of hill condition which I found in Phoenix when I once went there? The only interesting thing was the fact that they have these mountains popping up. And I'm fascinated by little things that suddenly pop up, but on the other hand, I could not resist inhabiting it and suggesting that maybe it wasn't a natural hill and that this was actually something urban. I've put in some public open spaces with very ordinary kiosks, and so on. So, there's ordinary — and then at the back of this ordinary sprouts this deliberately extraordinary hill, out of which there are these things popping.
And the popping elements became more and more important … it became more and more important as I worked on the drawing to make things that were cutting into it.
Things were popping out of it, things were delving into it and suggesting fairly overtly that, sure as hell, there's something going on underneath there otherwise why do you have all these skylights and domes coming out of it?
The implication of the dome is that it is lighting a particular kind of space within, the idea of a light well, cutting — clearly there's something going on in there.

I'm interested in the idea of orifices appearing and disappearing, just as I'm interested in the idea of veils.

I started this series which is to do with veils. It started off to do with drapes, or leaves, interleaving. This is a sort of vaguely elevational drawing.
I spent a lot of time on the lower part, the base part — I'm not quite sure why …
I'm always trying to stretch the vocabulary in the drawing.
That's very hard when you try and build any piece of the 'stretched vocabulary'.
Although I would suggest not always — I have

PETER COOK
Perspective, Hilltop Town, 2019–20
Ink, watercolour and crayon, 50 × 70 cm (20 × 27 in)

PETER COOK

Top and bottom: *Elevation and interior, Filter City*, 2021
Ink, watercolour and crayon,
50 × 50 cm (20 × 20 in)

even been lucky enough to actually build little bits of what, at one time, I would have thought of as stretched vocabulary – but this drape stuff would be tricky.

The base of Filter City is saying it could be a sort of drape, which is not a veil but is a scalar drape, and then there could be another category of drape, which is very much to do with the apertures between it.
So then, higher up on the drawing, out come the capsules, the tray and the usual parts.
At the edges, the capsule and the drapes turn into one thing, there is a kind of – I don't know, a sort of orange vegetable, which is a tight enclosure but also has degrees of translucency although not to the extent of the green translucency.
It is a recurrent theme, investigating the condition of the surface through the drawing, between the transparent and the soft and the solid.

The second drawing of Filter City is where I entered.
I'm on the inside.
I have the same veils, and slightly different capsules. You can see the drifting, weaving, possibly digitally encouraged vegetation, and normal things, platforms and a slightly nonchalant kind of capsule here on the right in the foreground – it actually almost looks as if it might be made of cardboard.
I rather like their nonchalance.
And then I can't resist just a bit of cartooning, two mundane guys playing some sort of ball game.
My message is always 'it's all right guys, you know, it's quite lovely', with also a dog in the corner here.
Is that a prop or is it a kind of comment?

Sometimes I can't help putting the normal, even the mundane, even the nasty in among things to say 'this is actually a proposition you could build'.
I'm interested in stretching architecture.

Not only the colour of different objects, but also the nature of the surface is what preoccupies me in the drawings.
Some of it with growths, some of it may be affected by wear, some of it may be affected by change of material, some of it affected by acts of 'riddling'. The word 'riddled' fascinates me ...

MICHAEL YOUNG
There's a texture that comes with a lot of your work and I was trying to figure out how to describe the texture.
I was writing down things like marbling grain contours, striations, coral patterns, veiled drapes, geological flows, until finally you said it now.
You said 'riddled' and that's it. That's the word, 'riddled' surface. That's an awesome word.

PETER COOK
Yes ... the riddled surface.
But first the drawing is a line drawing, black and white, no colour, quite a different sight.

There was a process called 'true-to-scale printing', which we used in the 1970s.
Ron Herron and Zaha Hadid and I in particular were fond of it and then they stopped doing it. It would enable you to make a black line drawing and say print it red, print it green, print it dark blue, whatever, and that acted as the base of the drawing and often had a very strong effect.

But other things like that depend I think on finding density and so on. In lockdown for a while I stopped making the tracing paper drawings. A lot of these are done as one-offs – in other words, if I screw up the colour, I've screwed up the drawing.
Whereas with the tracing you just make two or three copies of the tracing and if the first one fails you stop and do another one.

Forgive the fact that I like bright colours. That's it, I like bright colours.

Going back to Buckminster Fuller, going back to Instant City, Living City, slightly growy things in among a triangulated structure.

I am an eclecticist!
I say: 'You can use that here, and you might use something else growing into it there and

PETER COOK

Elevation, Inhabiting a Tough Landscape, 2021
Ink, watercolour and crayon, 30 × 78 cm (12 × 31 in)

it might be something else coming up from there.'
It has this wallowing thing.
Like someone who likes knitting … you find yourself knitting it.
And I do the minimum amount of preliminary drawing.
I might sort of say it is going up there, this is going down there, and a bit of a pencil scribble, which I almost always ignore as I go along.
This is a collage, not a drawing.
To what extent is this not a scheme, but a collection of elements?
In the same way as the landscape drift, it is in a sense a collection.
It is bits talking to each other.
Some of them are still in one's head, some are deliberately posing, drifting with rather formalised things, with rather stupid things, with rather straight-up-and-down things.
It is a collection.

And then one comes to this, which is back to straight pictorialising.
I've always been very interested in vocabulary.
What vocabulary do you need and what do you take out of the back pocket?
And what is the effect when you peel things away, what do you reveal and what do you peel?

MARK WEST
What is most moving to me is the happiness in the work.
It might be to do with the colours I think, the large colour surfaces, the colour-textured surface.

LAURA ALLEN
Yes, happiness, but you take it deadly seriously …

RIET EECKHOUT
Do you actually plan the colours?

PETER COOK
You know, not really, the drawings often look better when they're about half-coloured, then I introduce some more colour gradually.
And sometimes I go too far, and my wife Yael comes in and says, 'Oh, you lost it! You lost it …'
So, I think I turn to the tracing paper method again — it's safer.

LAURA ALLEN
Peter, that's what's interesting about what you do as opposed to people dealing with digital drawings and drawing illustrations with Live Paint in Adobe Illustrator — they can obviously go *ad infinitum* and go backwards. But you don't have that luxury and you have to really be thinking about what you're doing consciously.

PETER COOK
Sometimes you fuck it up.
I mean, I remember — and this goes back to the days when I was teaching at the AA, so it's really a long time — giving a lecture at AA on how to deal with fuck-ups on drawings and I brought in a suitcase full of brushes and mops, all sorts of stuff, and also a particular kind of blade.
You cut a piece of the drawing out and put in something else from behind.
In fact, even on this drawing there are one or two of those little sort of coloured building things that are actually glued on top.
We were looking at it and then somebody said, 'You need a few more!' I said, 'I'll do a few more.' And I did them and glued them on.
It immediately makes it a sort of naff artwork, but ethically moral if you like …

LAURA ALLEN
There is nothing naff about that, at all.
Because that's what people working with digital drawings can do, copy and paste as many things as they like …

MICHAEL YOUNG
Yesterday, we ended up with a conversation about the marker drawings, important drawings, not only your own, also the ones authored by others.

PETER COOK
There are certain marker drawings that you're aware of yourself, certain drawings that I flag up and would mention as important.
But I'm really interested in other people's marker drawings.

I mean, certainly one is very conscious of certain drawings, like Lebbeus Woods' drawings for example. We can't ignore the importance of Lebbeus; it can never be overestimated.

He would do some sort of preposterous thing that was flying in the sky, but actually, the metal, the metal sheeting, of it, or whatever it might be, really looked as if it was weather-beaten, you know, like an old biplane.

I'm interested that when something can allude to things that are real, through its material qualities, the more the proposition might be considered likely.

You see, that really interests me.

And therefore, I always allude to the fact that a lot of Archigram projects had handrails. And the escalators were at the right pitch and they had toilets in them. Whereas a lot of the projects done by our contemporaries, say in France or Italy, they were much more gestural. 'It is a thing in the sky!' You know. 'It is there!' No.

Mine had to have handrails because I wanted it to be built.

And then I always say: look, we built the Kunsthaus in Graz, so you could build it, right? Half that stuff that people said you couldn't build is buildable, just somebody needs to get around to doing it.

So, most of what I draw, I would like to build. Now that sounds arrogant, I suppose …

But it means that always, when I'm drawing, half of me is saying, 'Yeah, you could probably make this. How would you do it, dude?'

Neil Spiller
Prerequisites for Discovery

NEIL SPILLER
You see these marks here,
they come from other drawings.
The marks here are bits of my actual drawing board that I draw on and have drawn on ever since I was a first-year student. There are marks, and the palimpsest of scratches, old masking tape, model making, drawing, sticking, gluing provides this kind of chaotic background. I like aged Sellotape and masking tape. I've always been a grubby drawer; I need that patina and noise.

MARK WEST
The noise is a kind of weathering,
and the weathering is a kind of noise
— which puts it in the world with us, I think.
Would you agree that the noise is almost like a prerequisite for discovery?

NEIL SPILLER
Yes, I don't like the white, clean and neat.
I like to choreograph chance.
I try to use any raw material around me, whether that's an old negative, a piece of masking tape, my old drawing board, as well as my own drawings, and mess them about until something comes out.
Sometimes I can mess about all day and nothing happens.

I don't set out to draw something, I set out to discover something,
enjoying the choreography of random elements.
So, the scratches, for example,
— I wish I could say I took a Stanley knife to the drawing but they are actually the lines on a piece of black lino that students at Greenwich had been using as a cutting board. I had it photographed and that is where these specific scratch lines come from.
Sometimes the scratches come from my old drawing board, sometimes they come from other things.
I just love — what you call weather — I call interference.

I discover my language through experiment — it is a reflexive thing, but also a kind of spatial embroidery.

I had been superimposing drawings back in the day by putting two slides in the same slide holder. So, for some of the drawings, I was doing that for lectures before I knew how to do it in Photoshop.
And then I made the drawing after the juxtaposition of the slides. Just to see the possibilities.

MICHAEL YOUNG
Neil, can I ask you to talk about shadows in your drawings?

NEIL SPILLER
Yes. The Jesuits taught me that all shadows come over the left shoulder at 45 degrees, and that is what they still do.

MICHAEL YOUNG
There is a strange Aldo Rossi shadow going on in some of the drawings. Do they happen simultaneously with layering and the collaging of forms, or do they happen afterwards?

NEIL SPILLER
These drawings were mapped out in pencil first, as the actual elements, and then the shadows are busked with the inking.

MICHAEL YOUNG
Busked?

NEIL SPILLER
Like playing guitar in the streets.
I don't set out the shadow, I just know that it comes over at 45 degrees.
The shadow makes the drawing in a way.
There are a lot of paradoxes in the relationships between the objects and the shadows — a lack of rigour on my part.

MICHAEL YOUNG
No, it is cool, it does a lot of work in an interesting way.

NEIL SPILLER
I always had the shadows from the first

NEIL SPILLER

Filament Mattamatics (2015), part of *Communicating Vessels*, 1998–2022
Digital print, 57 × 88 cm (22½ × 34½ in)

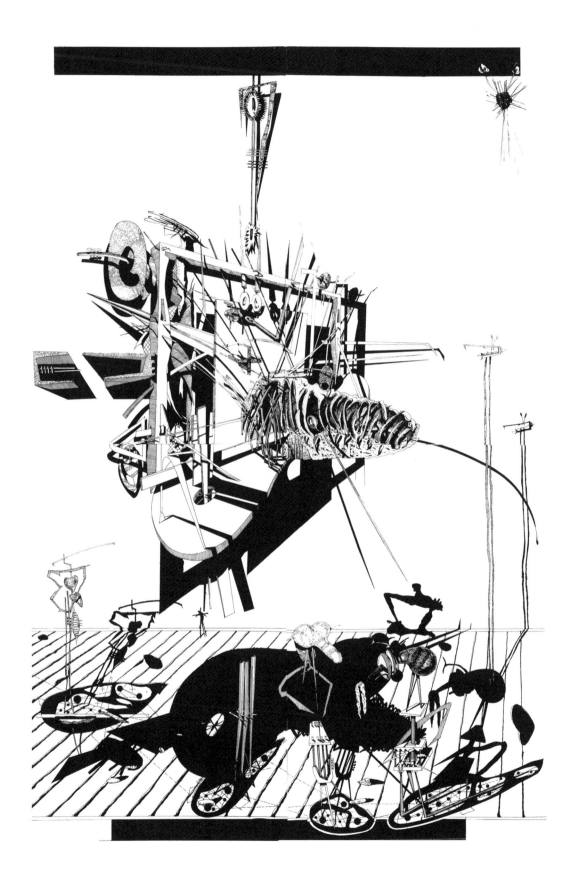

NEIL SPILLER
Genesis to Genocide: right-hand panel of tripych, *Nativity in Black*, 1995
Black ink on CS10 mounting board, 150 × 100 cm (59 × 39½ in)

drawings that I did as a postgrad student. I realised that the shadow had an amazing power in helping me get my ideas across. That is why I often play with light and dark in drawings, and with implied shadow.

MICHAEL YOUNG
Do you think the shadow perhaps talks about your relationship to the surface?
I always thought it is something about wanting to share the work more, so we can fall into it, you can have the feeling you can walk around it.
Your drawings are like gardens.
I know some of them are supposed to be gardens, but I wonder if those shadows are there to lure us in.

NEIL SPILLER
To make it slightly more real than just a graphic, to imply the formal qualities of it more. Shaun (Murray) talks about bringing things out of the surface. The shadow does that work for me.

PERRY KULPER
I like reading the shadows as a notational thing. They might have other systems of information in them rather than just foregrounding and backgrounding objects. They seem as intelligible an element as all the other things that comprise the gardens that you are building.

MARK DORRIAN
I feel the shadows escape — I mean, in a way they reinforce the objects but I have a sense that they are escaping them at the same time, as opposed to grounding them or articulating their volumetric qualities.

One thing that is interesting to me is that this kind of drawing of the shadow is usually the kind that we associate with very precise geometrical objects. It reminds me of the story of Thales' measurement of the height of the pyramids, and the way that Michel Serres tells it. Thales waits until the time of day when the length of a man's shadow is equal to his height, and at that moment measures the pyramid's.
His argument is about the way geometry's origin is about arresting time, stopping the sun in the sky.

MICHAEL YOUNG
Or you have to run really fast.

MARK DORRIAN
Either way, time has to collapse. I feel that the drawings are in touch with that kind of history of the relationship between shadows and geometrical objects, but at the same time they become detached and achieve a kind of uncanny independence from the things they're supposed to be secondary to.
The shadows depart; there is that tension.

JOHNNY LEYA
Related to the idea of the garden, the idea of the enclosure as the modernist ideal, on the other hand you have these strong symbolic elements in your drawings. What are you trained to escape from?

NEIL SPILLER
The way I was taught by the Jesuit modernists, there were very few allusions to symbolism and semiotics. And of course, I like to think my work is drenched in it.
It started originally as a naughty thing to do. When I came out of college after graduating, the first thing was try to make an architecture from bits, element by element. So, one of the first things was to try a column, which had a bit of Mackintosh in it, a bit of heavy metal … a very beautiful drawing that was inspired by an essay by Charles Jencks on the representation of columns.
Which was just outrageous behaviour for the Jesuits, whose columns were just *pilotis* … if you were lucky.

And so, that was an important thing.
And why Surrealism is important to me, that weird system of signs, is that I can deploy and develop it in my own way. It was always a fight about pushing away from modernism and the economics of practice … I spent ten years in classical architectural practice, terribly bored most of the time.

PERRY KULPER
You talk about the work in really visceral

NEIL SPILLER

Ballad of Crafty Jack, Virtual Objects and their Virtual Shadows – Garden Removed: Walled Garden for Lebbeus, 2013
Photoshop collage, 17 × 25 cm (7 × 10 in)

terms, even the drawings, which are evaporative and scratchy and levitating. The drawings have a commitment to material conditions and embodied immediacies and so on.
Now, your more recent work is very much digital. What is the material condition in this digital environment? What kind of material practice is involved when not using pencil and pen?

NEIL SPILLER

Central for me is the issue of 'choreographing chance'. It is very much about the dislocation of the architectural self as I always call it, to try and find things that I would never preconceive as a designer …
I'm very pleased when that happens.
And it's been happening, you know, for over a decade. But now the technology does allow me to do things that I couldn't graphically do with a pencil, an ink pen and some nice mounting board.
I seem to have lost all sense of architectural guilt that was inculcated into me during a long and arduous architectural education.
I started taking stuff into Photoshop, whether they were some of Vaughan Oliver's record covers or my own previous work, and just had a ball producing these initial sets of digital drawings …
These works are hybrids, they cross between handmade drawings, scans, photographs, PMTs, all sorts of stuff.
I scan it all in with my A4 scanner. The composite drawings are produced by juxtaposing scanned images and pieces of old drawings in Photoshop. So, working with this material, there's this constant kind of search, that 'fast visioning'.
I like to work quite fast in this digital mode.

PERRY KULPER

Neil, it is interesting to hear you talk about two different techniques and the degrees to which they have produced radically different, but at the same time similar, results. The Photoshop world seems to have opened up thinking – combinatory logics, inflections, speciations …
I am interested in the degree to which techniques elevate your practice?

NEIL SPILLER

What Photoshop introduced is speed!
I can try an idea and if it doesn't work, I can delete it.
Some of the analogue drawings take months to draw. Now I use digital techniques in the way I layer and bring images, drawings and other fragments together …
And then I throw it around, juxtapose it, superimpose the plan on the perspective form, archaeologically drag up bits and pieces from previous projects that I haven't used yet, or not widely known drawings or unfinished drawings, drawings that I didn't enter for that competition. And I put them together as a series of layers, compacting them.
I also got into 'content aware', this Photoshop command that removes unwanted objects and replaces them with image detail from surrounding areas. I would take a drawing, delete certain things and, based on the drawing, the software decides how to fill the space I've deleted.
And I love that, because it obviously chimes with the choreography of chance.
But it also allows me to kind of speculate and reread the drawing.
I like the way it gives you these kinds of annotations or these dribbles,
they could be scratches, blobs of ink.
These juxtapositions come sometimes in a very fortuitous way.
And when I do something that I like and I don't know what it is,
I call it a 'sector of the Surrealist city'.

NATALIJA SUBOTINCIC

I find it interesting that the work you produce also speaks about the place of a drawing.
For me, especially this most recent work, it's all about the placing of a drawing or how a drawing can exist in some larger context.

NEIL SPILLER

Yes.

NATALIJA SUBOTINCIC

And in your case, it's always within a drawing, within another drawing, within other things, but I think that's a really important part of what's actually happening now in your work.

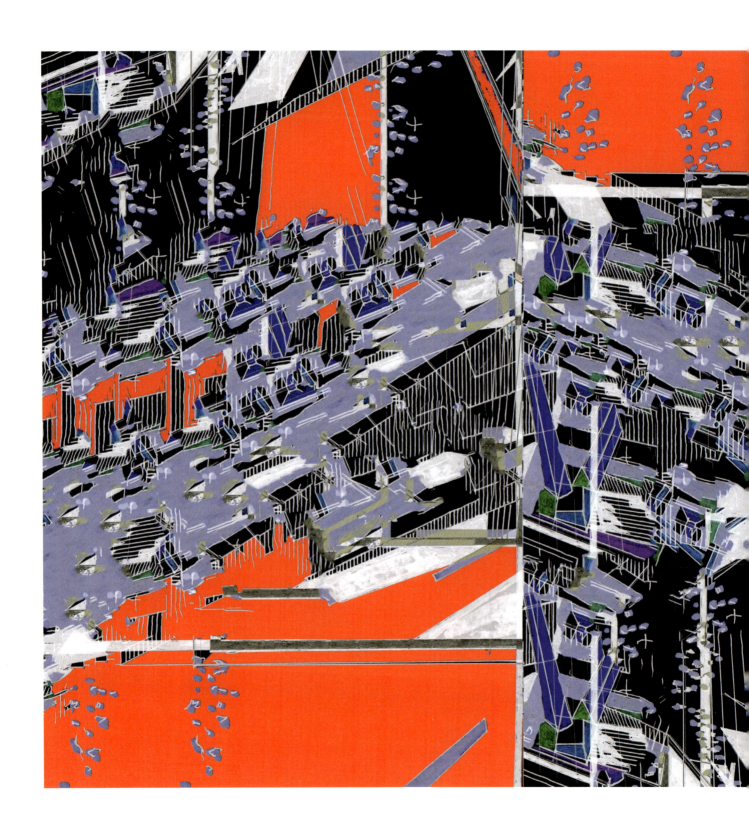

NEIL SPILLER

On the Waterfront, 2021
Digital print / Photoshop, 30 × 59 cm (12 × 23 in)

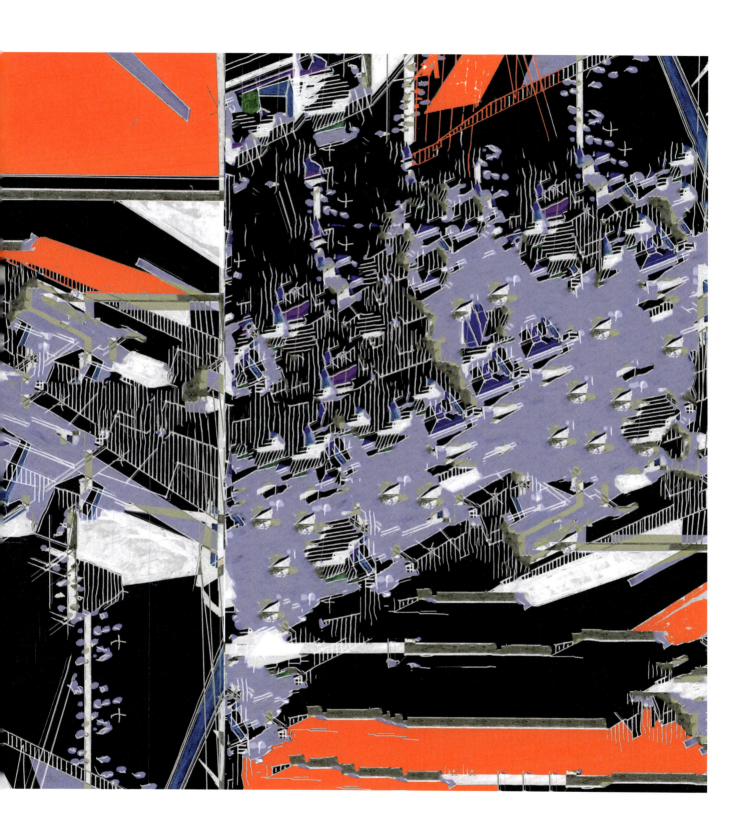

NEIL SPILLER

Yes, yes, definitely … this process allows me to fold paths into the new work.
The project *Communicating Vessels* was always predicated on that folding. So, it's like all my work is kind of 'dough', and I am constantly kneading it to make new work. I mean, I'm taking stuff from the web, I'm taking iPhone photos of stuff, to use in the drawings. If I look for example at the layers of very recent drawing, my last piece … the layers in that are extraordinary.
There's some of the Quay brothers' photographs of their studio decors, the wires of my headphones scanned, shopping lists, a photo I took of a little substation with graffiti on it, the long house plan, my old drawing board.
There is all sorts of stuff in there. It's like a real compaction of … I want to use the word 'grist', my Spiller-grist in a way.
So, it goes back over time – the drawing board I worked with since I was 18 and bought as a first-year student. So, it has this kind of variety.

There are the nuances that this drawing in particular has that I'm still in love with – as I am, every now and again, when something appears in the Photoshop mix – that really gets me. But also, as I said earlier, there are enough architectural clues in it to realise that it's not an abstraction but a postulate about architectural space. I mean, as we go forward, I feel a lot of architects are narrowing down their perception of what the art of architecture and the art of space-making is. But at the end it comes down to what I've developed as my kind of individual, personal aesthetic sense, about composition, and what's a 'Spiller' and what isn't. And that's that, I can't describe that in words. It's about the alignment of things on drawings in a way.

MARK WEST

Neil, we're seeing these things on the screen now, and you make them on the screen. But what happens when you print them?
Do you think of them in the print version? Or do you think of them in the screen version?

NEIL SPILLER

I think of them in the screen version. Often the print can be slightly disappointing. Or it can be really great … if you zero in 100 per cent on one of these, there's a lot going on, and it shows that it's of its time. Different resolutions have all been composited together in a way.
So, it shows that it's a thing made by the computer and I kind of like that, you know, that when you step away from it, its resolution improves.
And sometimes that scares me.

MARK WEST

You're talking about a printed physical thing, and that the resolution changes as you go forward and back from it?

NEIL SPILLER

Yeah, as you get closer, you can start to see much more patina. That it's sometimes not as resolved. Do you know what I mean?

MARK WEST

Like, flaws or something?

NEIL SPILLER

Yeah. So, I'm thinking about Monet's water lilies …
As you step back, you see the water lilies, as you get closer to it, it reverts into an abstraction in a way.

MARK WEST

Right, Rembrandt's paintings would do that.

NEIL SPILLER

Yes … I like that. Very much opposing the idea we've been brought up and educated with – that an architect's drawing needs to be very, very specific all the time.

MARK WEST

Because the thing about working with Photoshop is that the drawing is born and lives in Photoshop. And printing it, is like this, I don't know what it is, it's something terrible, and I don't mean terrible, as in awful, I mean, terrible, like terrifying, like, it is a terror in the difficulty …
It's always difficult to get the thing out of

the machine ... always difficult.
And that's because these worlds are not
the same world.

NEIL SPILLER
Absolutely – I agree totally.

MARK WEST
I know for me, I've escaped the terror of the print in my practice by treating the print as just another piece of paper that I'm going to work further with after it comes out of the printer.

RIET EECKHOUT
Neil, notwithstanding the dichotomy between the analogue and the digital modes of working, can I ask about how you consider the nature of the older drawings, those singular crafted drawings, the old-school pencil-and-ink drawings that take months to produce in relation to the series of intuitively fast produced digital drawings?
In the latest digital set you brought here, the drawings seem sequential, developing in the next drawing with further resolution, reading into the drawing, combining new things.

NEIL SPILLER
Yeah.

RIET EECKHOUT
Maybe quite similarly, we can look at Perry's crafted *David's Island* drawing in comparison with the *Fast Twitch* drawings that he has been producing lots of and that also seem
to be done intuitively, digitally and at a certain speed.
Are they in essence a different type of drawing – a drawing with a different agency and a different return from the drawing to the maker? Also, are they each separate drawings, saying something particular as separate drawings, building up to something else?

NEIL SPILLER
I think they're building up towards other things. The *Communicating Vessels* project, which I've been working on for 23 years really – they're all parts of it.
Apart from the early black-and-white ones, they are a much more expansive intellectual exercise that I've been involved with since 1998. And it is, you know, a memory palace – it's all sorts of things, it shows me where I've been and what I've been interested in. So, it's really kind of a conversation with myself, with art history, particularly with Surrealism, but not just defined by that, and ways of thinking and operating in the world. To me, all the work is leading up to something.
The drawings are conversations, sentences in my book, in a way, and I don't mean a physical book, but a series of episodic eventualities ... so, that's why I keep folding the dough.

PERRY KULPER
Neil, today, while looking at the recent drawings you brought to discuss, I granted myself the possibility of trying to access the drawings through different lenses:
so I would follow a handful and say I'm seeing these as 'diagrams'.
I would then follow the next couple, and say these are 'atmospheric', these are 'material phenomenal things', and then I would follow a few and I would say that these are just 'relational'.
And I wonder if that is just me maybe having enough small knowledge about representation, allowing myself to encounter this as a diagram, not as shadows, not as a figurative garden, and so on ...
Is that ever in your mind, that these can be accessed through different lenses?

NEIL SPILLER
Yes, and that's all part of the process of when I reread them, and they start to tell me what I'm doing, if I'm lucky. I reread them in certain ways through different lenses to try and find meaning for them.
And some of that is artistic, some of that's kind of semiotic.
And some of that is architectural, really ...

PERRY KULPER
That's quite a nice way to set up the work, maybe ... the weights between those different families of communication, semiotic and architectural. It would be nice to develop the categories that are being leveraged like the ones you just mentioned to produce a piece of work and writing about that.

NEIL SPILLER
Communicating Vessels: Longhouse Roof Garden
augmented reality plan, 1998–2021
Digital print/Photoshop 'content aware', 30 × 20 cm (12 × 8 in)

NEIL SPILLER
Communicating Vessels: Longhouse Roof Garden
augmented reality looking up tower, 1998–2021
Digital print, Photoshop and coloured pencils, ink on mounting board,
73 × 50 cm (29 × 20 in)

NEIL SPILLER
Communicating Vessels: Longhouse Roof Garden augmented reality plan, 1998–2021
First pass Photoshop collage, 30 × 20 cm (12 × 8 in)

RIET EECKHOUT
As you're articulating these three categories, artistic, semiotic and architectural, it implies that there's a part of the drawing that is sitting in the realm of the architectural, but there is a part of it which doesn't?

NEIL SPILLER
Yeah.

RIET EECKHOUT
Is that a decision or is that a question? I mean, there might be something as simple as 'I'm an architect, so, everything I do …'

NEIL SPILLER
Well, I never ask myself that question, but there is that kind of mindset, deep down. If you said, 'What do you do, Neil? What have you been doing for the last 35 years?' I would say immediately: I do architectural drawings.

RIET EECKHOUT
Yes, definitely.
I have heard Bryan [Cantley] also question 'how the work fits within the discipline of architecture'. Is it sensible to be preoccupied with or evaluating this question in the work?

NEIL SPILLER
What constitutes architecture two decades into the 21st century is definitely what I am preoccupied with. That's what I'm trying to do. We're all trying to do it in different ways. And it's good that there's this kind of wonderful variation of like-minded people that are looking to the periphery of architecture in a way and pulling things back into the centre.
To use Archigram's expression, 'To inject noise into the system'.

Smout Allen
Dynamic Drawings

MARK SMOUT

When you look at a standard sketchbook of ours, you see certain motifs and bits of language like chevrons or almost-a-circle, or the offset jaunty line, or other quarter cuts, the sack, or the soft worm – which is a particular favourite – and things like that.

These sorts of motifs recur like a kind of language throughout the work that we do and have been with us all this time.
I guess one of the places it started with was our project *Retreating Village*, the clifftop village of Happisburgh in Norfolk falling into the sea, where we started noting these drawings and sketches down in sketchbooks that then became larger drawings that described a village that was retreating away from the sea, into a different social condition.

LAURA ALLEN

'Dynamic drawings' is what they are called. These drawings are an attempt to show the dynamics of something. The drawing of the *Retreating Village* was drawn flat but then folded, and when you fold it in, the drawing suggests the retreat of the cliff over five years.

We're interested in technology and nature and how the two interface, how architecture can perhaps illuminate some parts of nature through, not necessarily a direct technical link, but some form of technical conversation. We produce devices that look at the relation between drawings and landscape. All of these devices derive from kind of a technical performance, but at the same time try to make a physical manifestation something as quirky as the sketch.
The majority of the instruments allude to a function, rather than actually function – they might function in a different way than we expect.
But they're sort of 'sited' rather than functional.
In our projects, drawings turn into models, and then turn again into drawings.

Some drawings that turn into models are used to test ideas rather than being a model of the thing itself.

We've always enjoyed playable drawings and playable models.
Drawings shouldn't be stuck behind sheets of glass, they should be things that are on tables, allowing people to play with them and look at them and add things to them if they want.

MARK SMOUT

Rescue Lines, our latest project at the Venice Biennale, is about ecological forms of escape. As the south of Britain heats up, and becomes hotter and hotter, and becomes Mediterranean, all the flora and fauna need some routes to escape out of the south of England.

The idea is to create natural forests that go from the south of England to the north, vertical lines that would go through the UK, and we call them 'rescue lines'.
So, we looked at lots of instruments, proving grounds, experimental forests, heating chambers, soil heating chambers, experimental wetlands, areas where they bombard a plot of land with carbon dioxide rather than with oxygen and see what the effects will be.

We also were very interested in the idea that hedges may be the forerunners for these rescue lines, seeing the amount of life that that a hedge can support.

LAURA ALLEN

The approach is to think about a forest as a cultured environment and the hedge as a precursor of woodland. So, you can either keep forests friendly by turning them into hedges, or you can allow those hedges to run amok and become forests.

MARK SMOUT

We would like to propose this new situation, where we have these new hedgerow forests, and they link up the old ones.
We started with a sketch like this for the actual baseboard for this model and then rapidly turned it into a large drawing with

different green areas.
The light green is the new forest that we're suggesting, the hatched white bits are ancient forests that we're trying to connect together, the parched minty colours would be proving grounds along the way to have some accommodation where people would interface with the forests.
And the darker green areas are nurseries — what we call 'landscape zoos' — where we propagate new plants that will then go out into the forests.

In the drawing we tested out ways of representing different forms of forest and growth and architecture. Some bits, some of the more raggedy bits, we painted by hand. Other bits we printed on a massive flatbed printer.

Then alongside that we had to submit another model for something called the 'Future Assembly'. We didn't want to do it, but it kind of slowly came together.
It was partly because we couldn't be bothered to tidy up the house either — the house was turned into a workshop and there were just all these bits lying around. I know it sounds silly, but I think that there are certain conditions that conspire to make things happen sometimes. This model took us a long time actually compared to the rest of it.

NEIL SPILLER
The time-consuming bits are obviously the creases in the operative's trousers. They are very well dressed for operatives, aren't they? Maybe they're Italian.

LAURA ALLEN
They are Italian.

MARK SMOUT
It's weird when you do a huge project and someone says, 'Well, could you just distil that into an A3-sized model?' It's very weird.

LAURA ALLEN
We chose the hedgerow for this small model. A lot of the ideas were revolving around the landscape being cultured and tailored but also seemingly natural — that there are people playing in the trees behind the woods; that the zone would be demarcated and you wouldn't necessarily be aware of that; that there would be a sort of register set up for all of the flora and fauna on that site to allow it to escape.
So, it's really about the goings-on around a hedgerow.

They're completely tailored and looked-after, seemingly natural but not quite, and the model here was about combining some of our drawings and the ideas about the attention that it would require really.

We're looking at the houses because the house and the hedge become the same thing, a 'house-hedge' — green infrastructure is a really important way of spreading the forest. We're looking at the Landscape Zoo, suggesting certain things like extracted peat and boglands held in a kind of laboratory microcosm until ready to be put somewhere else.
So that is all part of what we're looking at with the science of it ... and the kind of weird fiction of the landscape forest.

RIET EECKHOUT
The project is installed now at the Venice Biennale, but you are working on new drawings of the project. Are you in the habit of producing drawings after the project has finished?

LAURA ALLEN
I think the problem is that there are a million really interesting things about all of the history and future of cultivating the hedge in relation to the forest.
So, at the moment we're doing some drawings further exploring some of the bits of architecture and test grounds on that site. Some of the drawings we are working on now were small tiny sketches we made during the project.

There are brilliant test sites ...
For example, pine forests with huge amounts of plastic sheeting on the ground, where they're trying not to let the tree have any water.

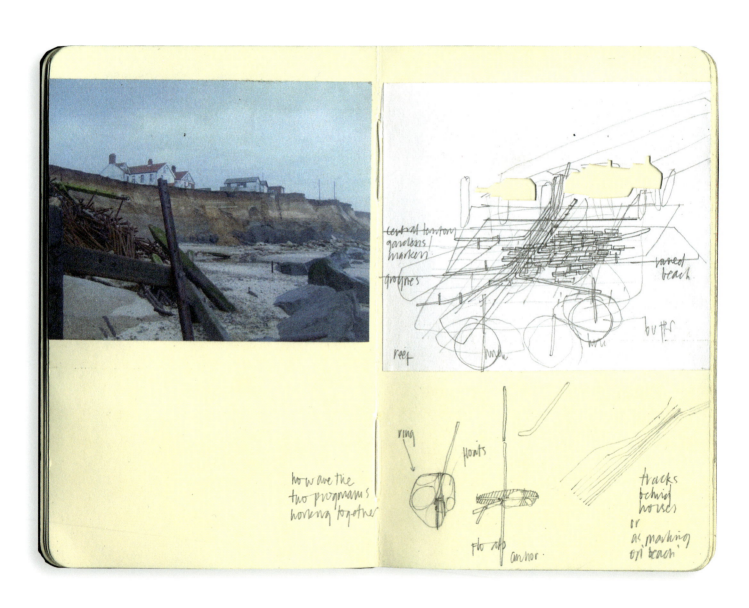

SMOUT ALLEN
Retreating Village sketchbooks, 2004
Moleskine sketchbook, 9 × 14 cm (3½ × 5½ in)

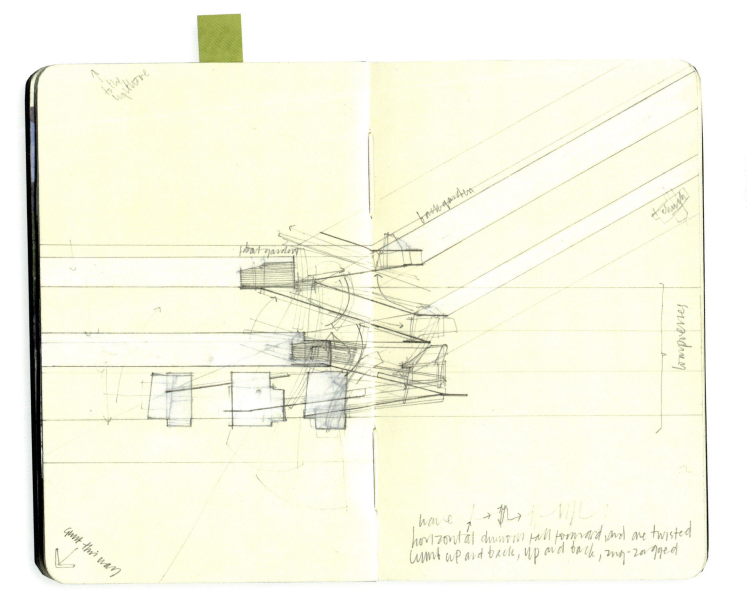

horizontal division fall forward, and are twisted
climb up and back, up and back, zig-zagged

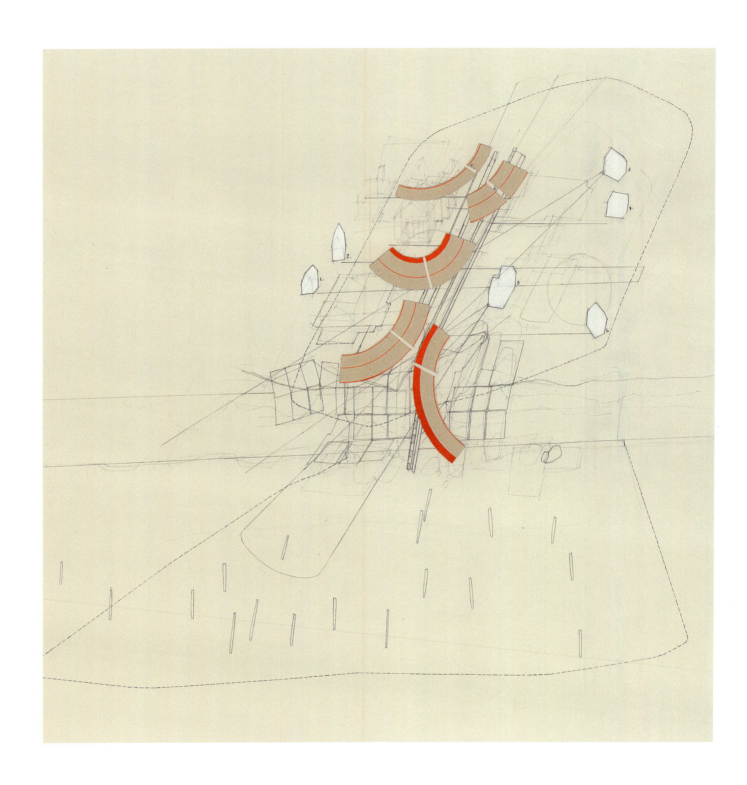

SMOUT ALLEN

Retreating Village: Beams, Arcs and Mattresses, 2004
Graphite and coloured pencil with card collage on Redeem paper,
70 × 50cm (27½ × 19 in)

A huge forest with all of these suffering pieces of plant life, as we try and predict what's going to happen in the future. And they look mad, really mad, but are producing a really amazing science.
So, in the project those experimental sites are the 'picnic sites'.
They become the houses,
they become the places where you live,
and you are a steward of the experiment of the forest.
Well, that's what we're trying to draw out at the moment.

MARK SMOUT

During the project, we did quick sketches and drawings that we would take to the workshop for model-making purposes and to use them as a starting point. It's like putting something underneath your sheet of trace before you start.
And we take those down, then they turn into something else.
And then we really draw them and then sketch them again, and then they turn into something else again.
It's very much an iterative process.

LAURA ALLEN

I think what was particularly interesting is the thinking time allowed by that process.
Because if we made this on the computer you have to make brutal decisions,
there is no construction line,
there's no potential line,
you just eventually get really quickly a solid of your concept.
In this project we purposefully slowed it right down with handmade models and handmade drawings so that there was an in-between, between the finished object and the process.
The last couple of projects we've worked on we've done entirely digitally and although that computer model itself might contain 400 hours' worth of modelling, it's all compressed into a finished thing.
With this project, we were quite interested in the time of the project, because there's time within the whole concept of this piece of architecture as well.
It was also really nice to make models out of the pear wood.

The pear wood would limit what you could do, how fine you could be because of the grain in the wood.

In previous models we've made with a 3-D printer, you model the design to the detail of your 3-D print and out it comes. You dye it, you colour it, you put the pieces together, but there's nothing you can change along the way. Whereas when making this model, by hand, it was full of interesting bits of discerning whether the mound was 'moundy' enough, the ridges deep enough – all sorts of things happening along the process of making it by hand, which develops and questions the design.

MICHAEL YOUNG

I have a nerdy question about the 'soft worms'. It's about curvature.
How do you guys regulate or draw curvature? Does it start with a freehand sketch? Does it start with arcs? There's a lot of use of compound curvatures of arcs. I don't see many drawing compasses …

LAURA ALLEN

We use a circle template if we want to draw a complete circle.
But I have got a drawer full of a thousand-and-one curves. My dad was an engineer and all his family were engineers. So I've got them in my drawer but I don't need any of them.
I just draw it.
What I find very frustrating is when a curve joins another curve over again, and it doesn't work very well, because you've not drawn it freehand.

MARK SMOUT

That's also our frustration with the interface with a computer perhaps – for us it's not quite there yet.
There are tiny little inflections that happened in curves and things like that, and we don't quite know how to get that to work on a computer just yet.
That's why we always start with a little sketch, whole loads of sketches, and you just sort of filter your way through them.
Some of them just have a little nick,
or a little turn in them that you really enjoy,

or that just throws the balance out of the drawing.
And you want to try and capture that spirit. The problem is if you start trying to draw it too carefully, or too hard, you lose that spirit somehow.
Is it spirit or language?
I don't know…
The tiny starting sketch might be about the sort of arrangement of some pieces on a drawing perhaps. We'd start at that size, then kind of religiously copy some of those moments and some of the aesthetics of that into the next drawing.

When we did the Egypt project, at some point we were struggling to try and work out the arrangement of the planters on the top.
In the end, we just threw a bag of lentils on the top of the drawing, and drew round each lentil by hand which was quite exciting and effective.

LAURA ALLEN
It's an aesthetic as much as anything, isn't it? I think one of the things is that, if you've been educated and have grown up with drawing things, and the drawing you do is the end-representation of your idea
— which is for us what it always is —
if it is easier to do by hand and more complicated to do by another method and time is against you,
we end up keeping it by hand…

PERRY KULPER
Among many things in your work,
I often think that you trigger, respond, send things into motion, backload things, a whole set of temporal dimensions…
and I wonder, for example, in the *Rescue Lines* project, do you think about levels of fitness or optimum states, or how do you think about the longevity or the duration?
I think that your things are phased and they initiate other responses, and they drive other things and I just wonder, do you sort of mentally diagram those behaviours of the performances or the comings and goings?

MARK SMOUT
We do think about fitness…

The longevity of the projects we always feel is to do with the human relations them.
So, with *Rescue Lines* particularly, the longevity is of interest in the way that we can allow people to take ownership of the scheme once it's out there.
I know it's a hypothetical project, but to us it's hypothetically real.
We are crafting ways that anyone can come along and feel like they are part of this process.
They can live there,
they can work there,
they can pass through there,
they can enjoy and can play there.
But most of all, can they take ownership of it? And can they read the situation?

So, a lot of our work is about giving it a timeline in relation to that.
But, yeah, we kind of draw the dynamics of the project.
You know, going right back to Happisburgh, the *Restless Landscape* project,
you've got a drawing that you can unfold, and see all the time lapse happening before you. But the reality is, we don't know which way the cliff will fall down and at which point, but we do know that this is one way that it might happen and this is one way it might retreat.

But the idea for that project, the same as for *Rescue Lines*, is about how to get people to own it.
So, you put them in a village and allow them to pull the ropes, allow them to decide where their gardens will be, allow them to decide the new orientation of their houses.
So, *Rescue Lines* is pretty similar to that, I think.

PERRY KULPER
There's a kind of real liberalness now to the ways in which you ideate and generate things.

MARK SMOUT
Yes, a number of years ago we would be wondering about how we might do something and how it might be different or worrying that somebody else might have done that before or where we were in the world.

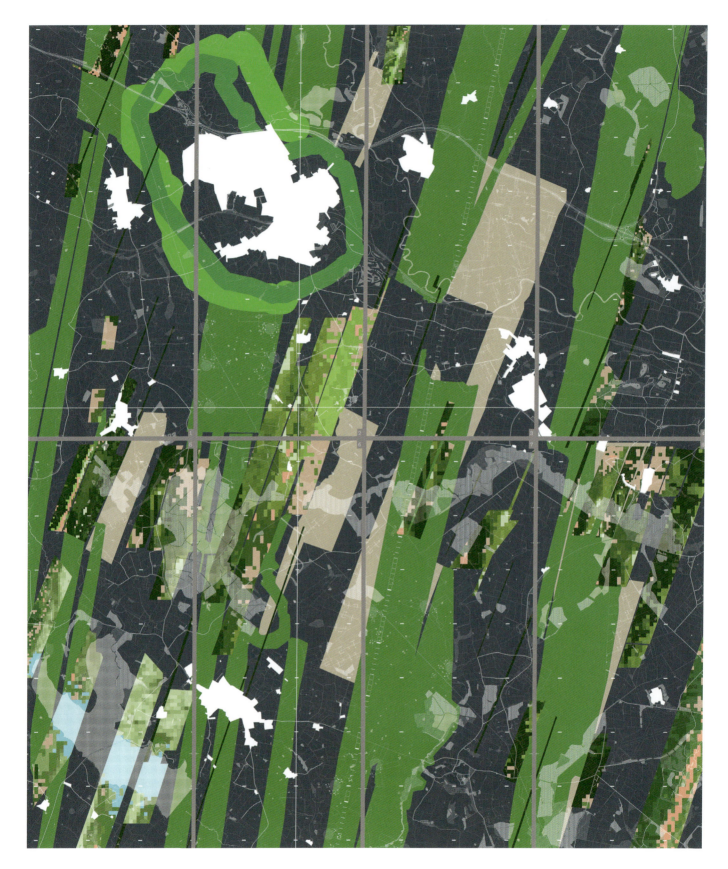

SMOUT ALLEN

Previous page: *Retreating Village: Chronographic Architecture*, 2004
Graphite and coloured pencil on Redeem paper,
folded size 100 × 50 cm (39 × 19 in)

This page: *Rescue Lines*, 2021
Digital print on acrylic sheet with back-painted forest plan,
310 × 260 cm (122 × 102 in)

But now, I think that that has certainly shifted for us over the years.

We have to mean something when we do it. So, there's much less deliberation at the front end, I think, and more deliberation about 'What are we trying to say?' and 'Do we mean it?'

SHAUN MURRAY

You mentioned the relationship between what is and what isn't managed by you … the drawings, on the one hand, would you say are undisturbed, they are kind of always constructed by you both?
But these models are inhabited by people roaming around, people can touch it, people can kind of mess with things and crawl through things –
it's a more complex opportunity. I would say that they can weave into this three-dimensional playground to understand things differently. You manage this scenario but then it's unmanaged how and what people do with it.

MARK SMOUT

Yes, the drawings are just like a bit of frozen imagination,
you know, how this envisioned situation could be.
Because you're free of everything in the drawing, there's nothing to worry about at all. The drawing doesn't need to finish in any particular way and it can just tail off into nothingness,
or you can just decide to occlude lots of bits of context.
Models are a bit more difficult, because we do genuinely want people to play and touch and feel these things. Maybe models are things that draw people together, around an idea. And also, the meta layer to this in the project is that it's describing a situation where it can be played with.
So yes, we are happy that the models are situations that are messed with,
the drawings much less so I think.

I think the very fact that you can move your head around a model and you can put your hand in there and you can look underneath it and twist it around in your hand, affords you that opportunity, which you don't necessarily get with drawings.
It's a different situation, isn't it?
Occasionally you'll do the drawing, and you'll leave it on the board or you put it somewhere and then the next day you walk towards it and it will be upside down or something, and you'll suddenly see it in a whole different way, you'll understand it in a different way, which is quite interesting.
I feel with the model you're doing that all the time.

But, I think the message to get from what Laura and I do, perhaps, is that we feel the relationship between drawings and models is very profound.

SHAUN MURRAY

Is it instructional would you say?
Are the drawings instructing how the model might be used, or are the drawings an extension of the model?
The model is something to explore, but the drawing is something to understand the project content on a wider set of paths?

MARK SMOUT

Yes, both drawings and models say quite different things.
Maybe one's talking more to architects and the other is talking more to the general public?
For instance, when you look at at Enric Miralles' drawings, they really do talk to architects, don't they, those drawings,
and you really appreciate the way that they describe things?
But if you show it to someone who is not an architect,
I doubt they'll have the same emotion.

MICHAEL YOUNG

There's also another interesting take on the model.
You showed us the famous model of the Mississippi River basin, which is one of those kind of insane things in the world …
I'm happy that it exists.
But there's a connection somehow between that as a model, but then also the test site as

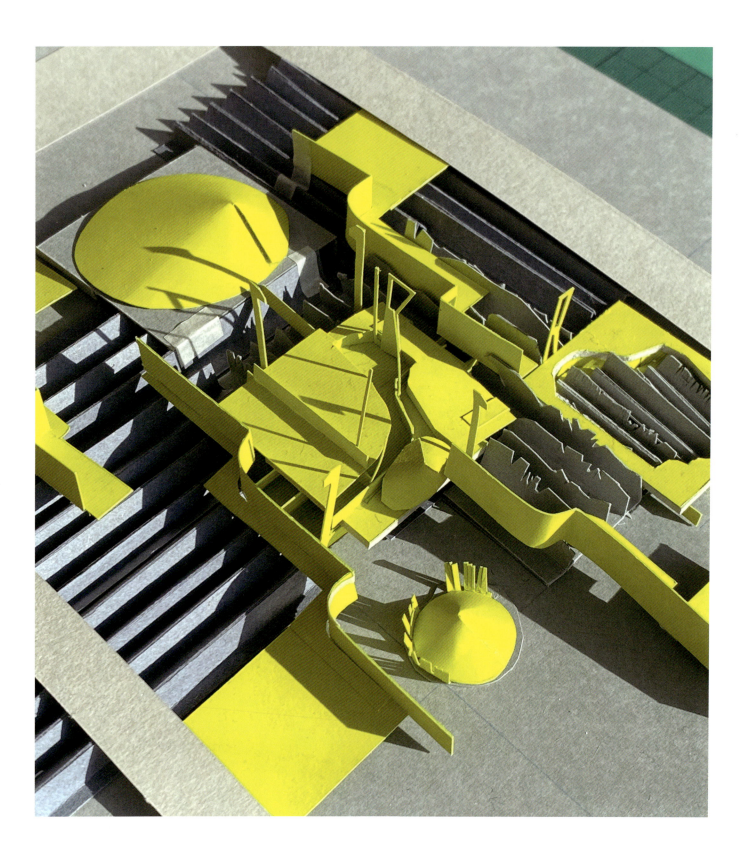

SMOUT ALLEN
Rescue Lines, 2021, Landscape Zoo sketch model, 1:500

SMOUT ALLEN
Rescue Lines, 2021, Landscape Zoo sketch design, 1:100
Graphite and coloured pencil on Redeem paper, folded size 100 × 50 cm (39 × 19 in)

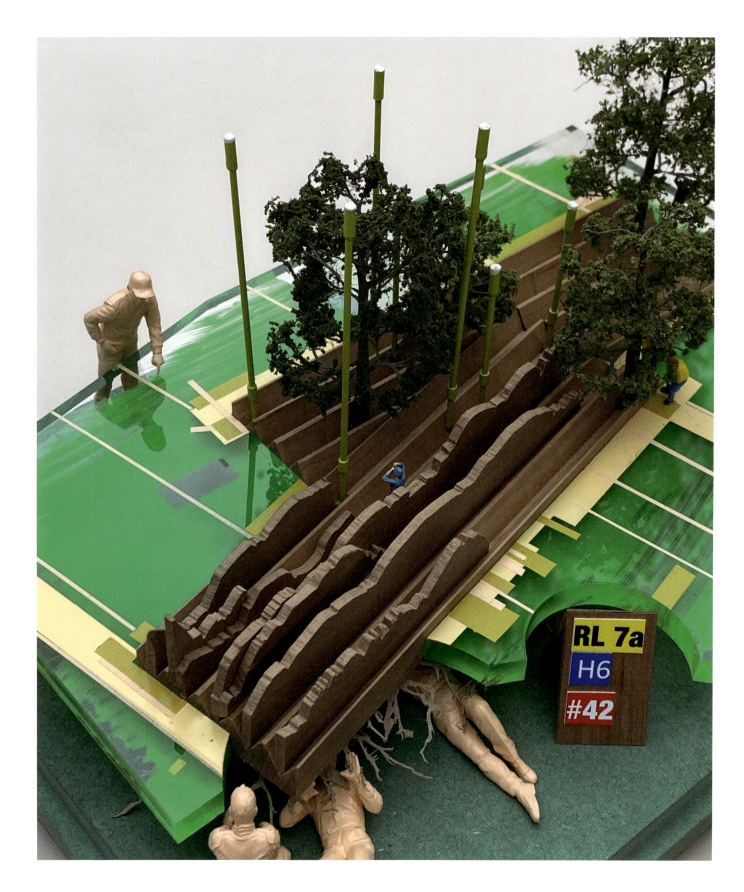

SMOUT ALLEN
Rescue Lines, 'Hedgerow' detail model for Future Assembly exhibition, 2021
Wood, painted acrylic with scale figures, 30 × 20 cm (12 × 8 in)

a model, meaning that it's full-scale now. It is testing real phenomena, real natural environments, real carbon dioxide, real heat, but it's still modelled in a way, because it's a controlled situation that is testing out variables upon uncontrollable results.
So, I think there's something really interesting about scaling up the models that you're working on, because they're coming closer to this sort of in-between world.
They're no longer just the representations of the drawings in physical form, but they're now interactive and performative — they're like test sites in a way that kind of slips through other scales.
And I think there's something kind of wonderful about shifting that sort of understanding of the relationship between drawing and models.

LAURA ALLEN

Yeah, the idea that you might design something that is both a model of something, and a model for the analysis of something else, is interesting.

BRYAN CANTLEY

When I look at your work, the drawings seem to talk about a kind of implied dimensionality and spatiality. And the models have a real — and I mean this as a compliment — graphic flatness to them.
The models and the drawings occupy the same territory —
they are neither over-categorically models or over-categorically drawings.
They have an ability to explore this autonomy and of not having to subscribe to either one of the camps.
I see them talking back and forth to each other.

LAURA ALLEN

You must all know the Cinder Lakes field — NASA used this site as a practice ground for the Moon landing.
They drew out the craters of the Moon and exploded them to make practice craters.
That kind of one-to-one model of an environment made for a particular purpose is our kind of thing.

Keyword Phrases

MICHAEL WEBB

A STRANGE SYMMETRY

At the risk of being dismissed as a clueless amateur mathematician proposing as breathtakingly original that which is old hat to those in the field, I shall nevertheless risk all by presenting to you these ruminations on the theme of perspective projection.

The following is a recipe for constructing a perspective drawing off an orthographic plan, the subject being the 6930-foot-long regatta course at Henley-on-Thames in England.

a. First divide the overall plan of the course into 23 identical sectors.
b. Draw lines between the sectors and at either end of them that will number 24 (don't ask me why 24 – divisible by 1, 2, 3, 4, 6, 8 and 12?).
c. Make line 1 in the perspective align with line 1 in the plan (the course finish line).
d. Make line 2 in the perspective align with line 13 in the plan; line 3 in the perspective with line 17 in the plan; and line 4 in the perspective with line 19 in the plan.
e. Using diagonals there is now enough information to complete the perspective, and find to my surprise, delight and relief that line 24 in the perspective aligns with line 24 in the plan (the course start line).

The course is viewed from a distance of 300 feet from the finish line, safe within the exigency of avoiding image distortion. Students in a drawing class were always warned of the dangers of getting too close to the object they were drawing, for distortion would result. It is, however, just this sort of area I am interested in graphically exploring.

So I will now extend the lines forward, hoping to find the location of the Cyclopean observer. The diagonals, which had been useful in establishing the lines between the sectors, have become parallel to the sides of the course and thus are useless. As I project the drawing forward, it starts to suffer from an ever-expanding elephantiasis ... it takes up a vast amount of room, a large sheet of paper with one line on it.

The observer cannot be located on the drawing. He, she or it is at infinity, but then so is the vanishing point. Indeed, a strange symmetry exists between the two points ... a symmetry of seeming opposites. When the observer observes the vanishing point, what is seen is the point surrounded by a veritable black hole of lines. If we could imbue the vanishing point with the ability to observe, he, she or it would see the observer surrounded by the self-same black hole of lines.

TERRIBLE JOY

In the above title the adjective seems to contradict as well as modify the noun, unless of course one is a masochist. I wonder in fact whether the phrase was a misprint. Maybe I had intended to write 'terrible job'. But let us accept fortune's contradictions and flavour the description of the following drawing with terror and with joy. For when constructing even the simplest of perspective projections one is creating a domain the size of the universe; or, differently put, one is simply drawing the universe. You see, when we establish the location of the vanishing point in our drawing and plan a journey there based on a constantly accelerating speed, the journey will be everlasting. World without end. Amen.

First-year drawing classes used, it has to be said, to offer instruction in how to draw an object in perspective, most often the perspectival image being constructed off the orthographic plan and elevation. However, because of my interest in the mathematics of foreshortening, I decided to have a go at mooring the nascent perspective projection *alongside* the plan, being in this case the 6930-foot-long regatta course at Henley-on-Thames. It gets unavoidably technical now, so let us reprise the aforementioned recipe:

a. First divide the overall plan of the course into 23 identical sectors.
b. Draw lines between the sectors and at either end of them that will number 24 (don't ask me why 24 – divisible by 1, 2, 3, 4, 6, 8 and 12?).
c. Make line 1 in the perspective align with line 1 in the plan (the course finish line).
d. Make line 2 in the perspective align with line 13 in the plan; line 3 in the perspective with line 17 in the plan; and line 4 in the perspective with line 19 in the plan.
e. Using diagonals there is now enough information to complete the perspective, and find to my surprise, delight and relief that line 24 in the perspective aligns with line 24 in the plan (the course start line).

What happens now leads to something exquisite. Choose a unit length (the length is immaterial): I happen to have chosen the width of the course in the plan projection as a unit. Place it on line 1 in the perspective projection. Now place on line 2 in the perspective projection a similar unit 2 times as long; on line 3 a unit 3 times as long; and on line 4 a unit 4 times as long. When the lines are connected up, there emerges this elegant hyperbola that is symmetrical around the right-hand edge of the course. And might the plane of the hyperbola be a vertical section cut through a right cone whose apex happens to coincide with the vanishing point? The answer is yes.

PETER COOK

STRETCHED VOCABULARY

Almost all my work – the drawn, the modelled, the built – is intrinsically involved in the extension of the formal and physically manipulated vocabulary. Maybe this was helped by:

a. wanting from early age to be an architect and therefore constantly looking at the stuff;
b. starting in an architecture school at 16 after two to three years of raiding the local library shelves on the subject;
c. never being a car driver, but always looking out of the window.

A convinced modernist at 15, but having to measure and draw all five classical orders by 17; already irritated by neo-Georgian at 17; amused by Jugendstil by 20; irritated by Po-Mo at 30; and intrigued by the fact that 'not quite so good' architects are more interesting than the heroes, because you watch them struggling and *nearly* getting it 'right'. Then allowing yourself to do elaborate versions of 'doodles' – otherwise known as 'projects' – with invented sites, invented briefs, no site, no brief, etc. Just naturally having a low threshold of boredom, so naturally lashing out against 'boring' architecture. Admitting that the dangerous edge of this position/taste verges on the English tendency towards the picturesque.

WALLOWING

Bach is intense, calculating, often pure. So is extreme minimalism in architecture. Wagner is indulgent, meandering, sometimes bombastic. So is Expressionism and much inventive architecture. The Gothic builders were much more adventurous than most classicists, the former pushing the limits of fabric, structure and strange mannerism all at once, seeming, even, to 'play it by ear'. Neoclassicists yearned to show how strict or 'clever' they could be in playing against a series of inherited mannerisms and rules.

I like to let the drawing start to take me by the scruff of the neck and almost dare me to go further. Then, along such a path, I might start to indulge with delight – the rocks getting 'rockier', the skins getting 'skinnier', the big patches of red getting 'redder' ... always, of course, with the danger of the meretricious at hand.

You may note that in both these responses I am tending to refer to architecture itself, rather than to drawing as a separate phenomenon. This underlies my intentions. I see building and modelling as totally inseparable from 'drawing', and vice versa.

NEIL SPILLER

CHOREOGRAPHING CHANCE

'Let us not mince words: the marvellous is always beautiful, anything marvellous is beautiful, in fact only the marvellous is beautiful.'
André Breton, *Manifesto of Surrealism* (1924)[1]

My conception of the world is one of exceptions not equivalents. So naturally I'm drawn to Surrealism and proto-Surrealists such as Alfred Jarry and Raymond Roussel. My drawn work methodology echoes the Surrealist practice of the Exquisite Corpse.

Exquisite Corpse is a Surrealist game that named itself. It is a game of folded paper, which consists in having several people compose a phrase or draw collectively, none of the participants having any idea of the nature of the preceding contribution or contributions. The classic example, which gave its name to the game, is the first phrase obtained in this manner: 'the exquisite corpse shall drink the new wine'.

My work seeks to find astounding new combinations of forms and ideas by layering and juxtaposition – in effect, by choreographing chance.

These protocols of chance, disturbed context, hybrid formal juxtapositions and variable meanings are writ large in the contemporary

[1] In André Breton, *Manifestoes of Surrealism*, trans. Richard Seaver and Helen R. Lane (Ann Arbor, MI: University of Michigan Press, 1972), p. 14.

city. Many hands, with many disparate aspirations, make our cities with many scales of operations, perceived and acted within by myriad consciousnesses. Some of these actors comprehend the semiotics of the city, but the majority do not.

The city is also a time machine, stretching backwards and forwards. It is like looking at the night sky, with the light of the stars, all from different times, converging simultaneously on the retina. The city bombards the eye and mind with differing times and differing philosophical understandings of humanity's place in the cosmos. Cities have alternative realities, some drawn and mapped, some not.

DISLOCATING THE CREATIVE SELF

The city can be read like a trillion parallel texts completed and composed in cahoots with the viewer. The great mother/lover, the Surrealist city is an analogue computer, churning out combination after combination of objects – humanity's passions nurtured and sustained by the flow of time, a succession of lives and capital across the city. This hallucinogenic space of reflection, poesis and desire, providing a cornucopia of new images and concepts, was complicit in the powerful Surrealist city literature composed by André Breton (the so-called 'pope' of Surrealism) and Louis Aragon. Their books are love letters to Paris. Aragon was first to recognise the surreal fertility of the city in his *Paris Peasant* (1926), the narrative of which involves a visit to the Parc des Buttes-Chaumont.[1] As the contemporary landscape architect and academic Ferdinand Magallanes has written:

> For Aragon, Parc des Buttes-Chaumont was a site filled with abstract fictive possibilities and more concrete visible objects, such as oddly placed Greek follies, engineered bridges, and reconfigured artificial landscapes containing magical and psychoanalytical meanings. The animist qualities found in the park objects, the deaths produced from numerous suicide jumps off a bridge in the park, and its tormented quarried past were magical to the writers in reconfiguring a surreal place.[2]

Breton contributed to this newfound urban oasis of possibility with his book *Nadja* (1928), which describes André's perambulations around Paris in search of intellectual, creative and emotional stimulation.

He would know when he found it. Casting himself into the vortex of the city's storm, he finds Nadja, the object of his desire and his interpreter in this unfamiliar terrain. Nadja, like the city seen through her eyes, is otherworldly. We find out she is mentally ill, an 'idiot savant', sometimes cogent, sometimes delirious. Latterly she melts away, and the narrative is sustained by her absence – the prose, maybe even more surreal, defined by her loss. The last sentence of the book was to become a Surrealist maxim: 'Beauty will be convulsive or will not be at all'.[3]

In his seminal essay 'The Soluble City', Roger Cardinal defined six Surrealist readings of the city – as a dream, as a love affair, as a palimpsest, as a poetic text, as a psychic labyrinth, and as a system of signs.[4] These are not mutually exclusive, but simultaneous and concurrent. Like quantum fields of events, everything exists at once as potential until it condenses, momentarily provoked by an observer, read and captured as a trace of another reality where the familiar rules are not obeyed.

1 Louis Aragon, *Paris Peasant*, trans. Simon Watson Taylor (Boston, MA: Exact Change, 1994).
2 Fernando Magallanes, 'Landscape Surrealism', in Thomas Mical (ed.), *Surrealism and Architecture* (London and New York: Routledge, 2005), p. 222.
3 André Breton, *Nadja*, trans. R. Howard (New York: Grove Press, 1960).
4 Roger Cardinal, 'The Soluble City: The Surrealist Perception of Paris', in Dalibor Vesely (ed.), *AD Surrealism and Architecture*, 48 (2–3), 1978, pp 143–9.
5 Ingrid Schaffner, 'Après Exquis', in Jane Philbrick (ed.), *The Return of the Cadavre Exquis* (New York: The Drawing Centre, 1993), pp 43–71.

Surrealist spatial aspirations, mnemonic sensibilities and an interest in the desiring, fractured Surrealist reading of the city have continued to underpin many of the most interesting architectural and artistic works of recent years. The contention is that the Surrealist influence isn't waning, it is actually growing stronger and, further, a Surrealist understanding of architectural space will enable architects to conceive and create architectures that were hitherto impossible within the restrictive confines of traditional modernist architectural dogma and simultaneously within the advanced technologies currently at the centre of the vertigo of the modern. As the curator Ingrid Shaffner has written: 'Working outside Breton's jurisprudence, David Lynch's ant's-eye-view, Angela Carter's violet pornography, Bob Dylan's tombstone blues, and virtual reality could also be called surrealist'.[5]

This is what I try to achieve in my drawings by doing things that are not preconceived, dislocating my creative self by using Surrealist protocols and tactics of space-making and lyricism.

LAURA ALLEN AND MARK SMOUT

THE WEIRD FICTION OF THE FOREST

Our collective imagination of forests as sites of myth and legend, as mysterious, seductive and even enchanted landscapes, can be read hand-in-hand with their peculiar reality. During research for our *Rescue Lines* project, complex and interwoven narratives of land ownership, carbon offsetting credits, biodiversity loss and clearfelling schedules were revealed. These are overlaid on our understanding of the forest, particularly in a UK context, and its interplay of temporal events, from seasonal growth to lifespans that far exceed human time.

Forests are perceived as having both physical and intangible value, much of which is now measured as 'natural capital', referring to a diverse range of material economic assets as well as ecological ones. This value or measurement of landscapes that are both cultured and natural within the same framework is interesting to us, and we started to expose the interrelationship of built worlds with human populations and natural landscapes with their non-human inhabitants.

We began to conceive of forests as living laboratories, an extrapolation of the Tomakomai Experimental Forest in Japan and the BIFoR Laboratory in Staffordshire, UK, which are settings for testing how environmental, geographical and geopolitical actions can be monitored in situ and their outcomes predicted.

The timescales and environmental narratives of the forest are difficult to comprehend. We are all familiar with images showing felled tree cross-sections marked up to correlate tree ring growth with time and to demonstrate a literal slice through history. The Natural History Museum in London displays a specimen of giant sequoia that was felled in California in 1891 when 1300 years old to prove the existence of gigantic trees 'discovered' in the American West. This artefact, called the 'Mark Twain Tree', is inscribed with diverse information such as the dates of the Viking raids in Europe and the publication of *The Origin of Species*, but it also illustrates under dendrochronological investigation the conditions in which the tree grew. Environmental impacts such as changes in climate, wildfires, droughts and atmospheric pollution, for instance, are registered in the tree's cells, held within a living organism that should not need to be destroyed to understand the evidence it holds.

DYNAMIC DRAWINGS

The production of measured drawings with fixed scales and viewpoints can be a frustratingly inert stage in the design process. Practices of architectural drawing in which their logics and protocols are revaluated, and the 'body' of the drawing manipulated beyond traditional constraints, provide alternative ways to imagine and represent architectural space. Describing complex environments in which conditions such as time and motion are also present confronts the draftsperson with the dilemma of where to fix time and freeze movement. In our work, environmental change, together with architecture that also changes over time, are key components, so we have developed ideas for folding drawings, collage and overlays to work with and to describe these dynamic conditions.

When drawing by hand, one is of course unable to zoom in and out in the way that one can with digital interfaces, which enable scrutiny of detail. This fixed view of a hand drawing is perhaps an incentive to imbue the drawing with other dimensions and to overlay rather than supersede.

Articulating the drawing with extra dimensions of time, scale and place can remove it to a distance sufficiently far from a literal interpretation to allow other conceptual ideas as well as realities to be imagined. Fixed and transitory entities can also be synthesised in the drawing. Drawing was described by John Berger as an act of discovery,[1] but there is also a temptation to see drawing in this manner as play, and the production of the drawing as a dynamic event in itself. So, there is an idea here of action – of the action of drawing while thinking and imagining – and the action of viewing and interpreting as two independent events in the life of the drawing. There is also the opportunity for misinterpretation … and that's OK too!

1 John Berger, 'Drawing is Discovery', *New Statesman*, 3–9 May 2013, p.53. Available at: https://drawingmatter.org/drawing-is-discovery-1953/ [Accessed 28 March 2020]

METHODS AND MODES OF WORKING

Mediating Drawing Practice:
Curatorial Reflections on Encounter and Dialogue

Carole Lévesque
and Thomas-Bernard
Kenniff

'Drawing Architecture' symposium, New York, April 2019. Left to right: Mark West, William Menking, Nat Chard, Shaun Murray, Riet Eeckhout, Michael Webb, Michael Young, Natalija Subotincic.

In the field of architecture, drawing is often understood as a means to an end, an idea that needs to be translated into built form. Yet drawing is also a project of its own. Beyond its communicative task and its ties to the profession, drawing can be understood as a performance taking place within a practice: a reflexive exercise, consistent and systematic, where the application, search for, or exploration of a method conditions one's engagement with the discipline. This kind of drawing practice is defined through its devotion to better understanding and to expanding the ways in which it reflects upon architecture. Situated and contingent on material, spatial and temporal conditions, drawing is both a means to, and an end of, focused investigation and knowledge production.

Whilst a given drawing might be declared complete, left temporarily, or even abandoned, it nonetheless may take part in an ongoing investigation, one that can never really be finished. As such, the practice of drawing can be understood as an open-ended conversation comprising an internal dialogue, internal to a drawing, a single person or a practice, and an external, with other drawings, people and practices. But it also operates through an engagement with the world in a much wider sense. Although it may not always be involved in the formal realisation of the built environment, it participates in its production through the ways in which it explores ideas and discourses, and affects the disciplines involved in its production. Working toward the elaboration and the experimentation of ideas, drawing investigates the means and processes of its own realisation as much as it is an inquiry within our built environment and the social practices it supports.

For these reasons, considering drawing-as-a-practice, rather than drawing-as-an-artefact, raises several challenges in terms of its mediation. How can conditions of practice and process be re-presented and received? While individual drawings may be appreciated for technique and aesthetic quality, how can their overall critical stance and underlying investigations come through? How to speak of the ways in which individual practices engage with the discipline and the profession of architecture? How are common denominators and differences traced between them so that their encounter and dialogue approach a definition of drawing practice, one that may be influenced and made sense of by a given public or audience? To answer these questions, we propose to consider drawing practice through four themes: process and time; materiality and environment; investigation; and conversation. Taken together, these give us a way of speaking of, analysing, exhibiting, and mediating drawing and its practices.

Process and time

A practice of drawing unfolds over time: over the course of a single day, over months, over years. To understand drawing as a process means to follow lines across an evolving engagement so that individual works become markers of time, dynamic chronotopes whose consequences reach well beyond those of static milestones: past projects reappear in current work, traces carry over from tools or concepts, new ideas forecast future actions. Drawings can be left untouched only to be re-engaged years later, and multiple drawings may be worked on 'at the same time'. In some work, process is made apparent intentionally, leaving traces such as construction lines, which allow the messiness of practice to be revealed. The opposite might be said of other works, where the same traces are removed or erased so as to focus on the signification of time in the image rather than the time of process or practice. In this case, practice is concealed and any notion of process must be inferred. Drawing time, then, is not only the chronological measure of practice. It qualifies a process and materialises a sequence of events, a series of actions, which in turn reveals different and/or possible temporalities. In that sense it is drawing in time – a temporal expansion of drawing practice – that is brought about, manipulated and experienced. The task of understanding thus falls back on our ability to register – draw-out, so to speak – the markers of time that are drawn-in as a series of discontinuous elements, relations that readily challenge the flattening of time in the produced image.

Materiality and environment

Drawing requires our physical presence, perhaps in a room, on a given day, on a chair, over a table, using diverse tools. When understood as a situated, site-specific practice, it becomes possible to see within drawings the inscription of their material conditions. As with time, materiality can be sought in drawings so that the material conditions of their production come to light: the materiality of drawing site/s (tools, hardware/software, screen, studios, workstation, working and worked hours, organisational and notational systems, climate, lighting, sound and music), as well as the materiality of process (drawings discarded along the way, preparatory drawings and sketches, exercises, layers and templates). All that surrounds and participates, however tangentially, composes an ecology of things, tools and spaces which collaborate in the production of drawings.

Understanding this ecology can be both intensely focused (the type of medium or tool and how they tie into production processes) and expansive (reconfigurations of environmental conditions, digital, virtual, physical). In either case, drawing moves beyond its object and its technical language so that it responds to and incorporates a series of material situations and conditions.

Investigation

Either by invention or discovery, a drawing practice is a way of making sense. It figures things out that can, over a single drawing or a series, throw light on what a practice of drawing may mean to the discipline and how it may challenge our understanding of the built environment. Some drawings are the result of ongoing investigations, outlined objectives and/or established hypotheses looking for answers. Some drawings are means of working out, probing, testing and coming up with questions. In all cases, the architectural drawing practice is reflexive, a to and fro between questions and answers, knowing and not-knowing, action and reflection. In practice, temporal, spatial and material conditions of drawing set up the space for reflection and investigation over time. Understanding drawing as a practice means understanding the particular ways in which these conditions are set up so that the produced drawings pose more questions than they answer, and invite one's attention beyond what they immediately represent or signify.

Conversation

Drawing is dialogic in its nature. Its investigations are moved forward by action and reflection, tactics and strategies that set up encounters between gestures, drawn elements, other drawings, questions, discourses and external exchanges. These repeated encounters open it up to transformation, avoiding stasis and transposing its meaning from one exchange to the next. As we have already suggested, drawing dialogues are both internal and external. Internal to the work as a conversation takes place between a practitioner, the tools used, the objectives and uncertainties of a given project. External to the work as drawing also advances in conversation with other practices, people, influences, prompts, discourses, ideas from myriad sources, and forms of mediation that act to expand its horizon. This two-fold dialogue makes the practice of drawing impossible to reduce to single voices. Seemingly focused and controlled production is inevitably polyphonic, as is any single drawing. The play between conventions and deviations, orientation and disorientation, completion and incompletion are intrinsic to a drawing practice that investigates rather than illustrates. Critical practice both generates and requires these dialogues to take place so as to find a productive tension between its modes of production and the investigation it carries.

Understanding drawing practice from the point of view of process, materiality, investigation and dialogue invites us to reconsider the way in which it may be exhibited. Rather than seeing drawing practice as an individually contained process, coherent within itself, internally organised and consistent chronologically, we propose that its mediation is best achieved in conversation, resonance or tension with other practices. Presenting a single drawing practice limits its capacity and desire for dialogue. To support this dialogue and to consider the practice of drawing as we have developed it here, it is necessary to mediate the temporal, material and investigative dimensions of individual practices collectively. New dialogues emerge from this encounter, both dissonant and harmonious, and the internal logic of practices is confronted and opened up to a wider and unforeseen audience, both in drawings and in publics. Experiencing a conversation in progress, rather than witnessing a curated monologue, invites us to engage in a communal exercise of making sense. In this exchange, a collective translation of drawing practice occurs in which the specific objectives and significations of single drawings are not subsumed, but dialogically expanded. Prolonging the dialogues of practice, both internal and external, engaging with drawing conversations over single artefacts, allows the commonalities of practices to come forward, and in so doing, leads us to a shared understanding of drawing.

With thanks to the editors and Louise Pelletier for their careful reading and suggestions.

C.J. Lim
Two-and-a-Half Dimensional Drawings

C.J. LIM

Walter Benjamin said the defining characteristic of the architectural drawing is that 'it does not take a pictorial detour'.[1]
As far as I'm concerned, I say bollocks to that — I love pictorial detours.
If architecture and space-making is about celebrating life, then those vessels should be embedded, imbued with narratives. I'm always fascinated by the ambiguity of texts, words, sentences and stories.

I'm just very keen that imagination, especially the drawn kind, has a voice — not necessarily mine — but a voice from where I come from, the East.
My project for the Venice Biennale in 2004 is very much about that. It was my turning point where I couldn't give a fuck if I actually don't do a building. I just want to do something meaningful and find a voice through drawings.
And it was incredibly exciting and liberating. The project *Virtually Venice* revolved around the story of Kublai Khan and Marco Polo. History has been written from a Western point of view. So, I was determined that this project would be one seen through the eyes of Kublai Khan instead of Marco Polo — metaphorically speaking — and in that way the project is very much a project of cultural identity.

We actually sat around a table, a few of us, *quilting* the models and drawings, crocheting away, knitting away, whatever you call it. And as we made the pieces, cut these small pieces — some of the pieces of the collage were so small, we actually had to use tweezers to make them — we made stories, we made spatial stories based on cultural influences from the East.

THOMAS-BERNARD KENNIFF

When you talk about the quilt and the quilt-making, which stands as a narrative structure for making those early drawings, I'm wondering in the most recent work, how does the quilt-making work?
Is there still that idea of collaborative effort or making sense together around the same project?

C.J. LIM

I work with many collaborators and the way we work in the digital world of 'quilt-making' is that we print the drawings out, and we will add layers to it, I would sketch over it, and then, other layers will be added to it, and so forth.
So, it's an add-and-subtract process.
And spatial ideas and metaphors are just knitted together to make a holistic narrative as we go along. And that's why I think the articulation of the almost flat-on views are most easy to handle, because it allows different hands to touch it.
The quilt here is a collaborative medium in a way that each patch has different spatial stories, but the collective of the different stories makes the whole.

MICHAEL YOUNG

Can I ask about the shallow-relief models, or the bas-relief, or the thick drawing that is just relieved with enough depth and shadow, potentially oblique, potentially flat, but never deep, and its kind of recession of perspective …
Do you think about it in these terms?
I find myself constantly flickering between desires for it to be flattened,
desires for it to be deep, but I am happiest when it's shallow.
I don't know if this makes any sense for you?

C.J. LIM

Yes, that's why I call them two-and-a-half dimensional drawings, because they are neither one nor the other.
The drawing is not a flat 2-D drawing nor a 3-D model.
And sometimes, here, it allows me to indulge, I guess, in the aesthetics.
I really very much enjoy the aesthetics as such. I really do.
It allows me to curate, to embellish, to make the layers of spatial stories I want to make through this method.

C.J. LIM

Top: *Virtually Venice: Giardini*, 2004
Watercolour paper, photocopy paper, wood glue
59 × 84 cm (22½ × 33 in)

Bottom: *Virtually Venice: Lido*, 2004
Watercolour paper, photocopy paper, wood glue
59 × 84 cm (22½ × 33 in)

C.J. LIM

Inhabitable Infrastructures:
Science Fiction or Urban Future?, 2014
Digital, 84 × 119 cm (33 × 47 in)

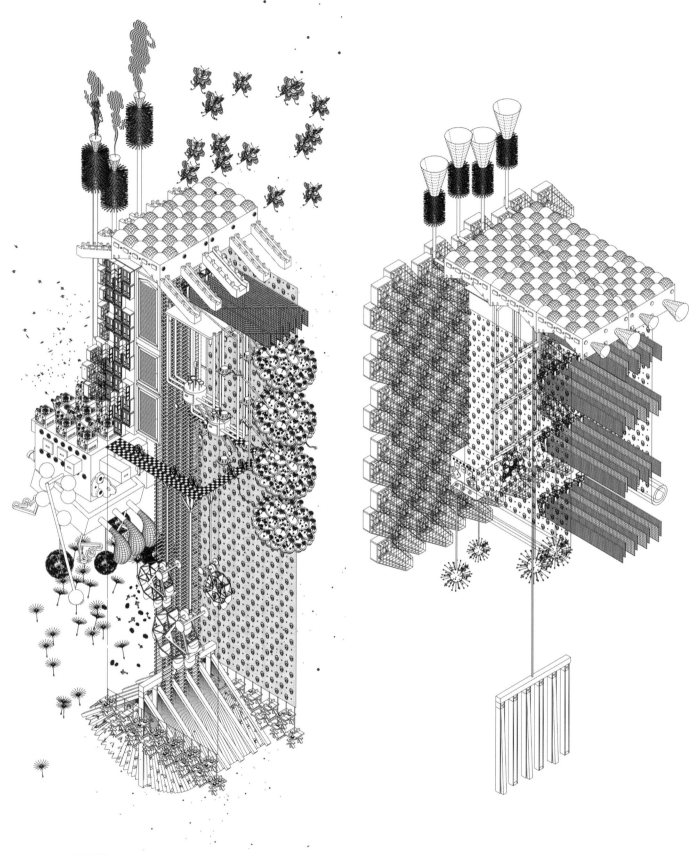

C.J. LIM
Once Upon a China: Dream of the Red Mansion 1, 2019
Digital, 59 × 84 cm (22½ × 33 in)

Even when the models and drawings are photographed, there's always ambiguity present that goes back to my interest in architecture not being finite or highly defined – the kind of ambiguity to express, ambiguity to change, to morph, and to suggest possibilities.

BRYAN CANTLEY

I think these are the collages that mine want to be when they grow up.
I'm familiar with the earlier work, and this more recent work has the same kind of relational energies … I see them as being graphic collages, as opposed to physical collages.
I think there's something quite liberating about thinking of the act of drawing, behaving in the same way as the act of physical collaging.

C.J. LIM

Absolutely. I think you're spot on, Bryan. That's how we design.
So, the collages really gave me a way in to design three-dimensional volumes and spaces. I see spaces as layers, I see spaces as fragments that you can peel away, and you can add on. Just like a collage technique, you know, you like a piece and you can add it on to the work; you don't like it, so you can slice it off. They are flat drawings.
The drawings are not rendered, the composition is not made from a virtual world on a virtual digital model. There's no digital model. These drawings are very much done in the same mode of the two-and-a-half dimensions, but done with Illustrator lines. So, it is exactly the same, it allows me an entrée into layering my spaces, I guess.
And I like very much to work in this sort of near-flat view of the world – a world that is layered and the layers are almost interchangeable.

MARK SMOUT

You say it's flat.
But I think it's a bit more like being in a planetarium, with some sort of constellation around you, or sitting over you like a hemisphere. I imagine you drawing from yourself, outwards to all these points.
And you use repetition as well as a form of dynamic notation. I always imagined you just sitting there thinking about a kind of sphere over your head where you're placing these objects.
So, it is two-and-a-half-D, isn't it? It's a 2-D drawing, but placed on a kind of hemispherical surface almost.
It probably touches on Nat Chard's world …

C.J. LIM

You mean there is something of the diorama about it?

MARK SMOUT

I definitely imagine it. Because your head is always wanting to turn left or right or up or down when you look at them.
Like the ones we see here – there's clearly something going off, going off to the right and above, and to the left. It's quite interesting in that respect.

RIET EECKHOUT

C.J., all of your recent drawings are in black and white. Do you keep colour out on purpose?

C.J. LIM

I somehow have this thing for black and white.
I grew up with film noir, you know, the black-and-white movies of the Forties and early Fifties, and I absolutely love that contrast of light and shade. The way that they light each actor, you know, in the film on the stage, it's quite incredible. Films like *The Third Man* and so forth.
The lighting is so, so beautiful. So, this is what we try and create in the drawing.
I'm fascinated by the kind of ambiguity that is created by black-and-white drawings; the contrast is very stark and blurs the idea of boundaries, just like film noir.

MICHAEL YOUNG

This relationship you mention with film noir is interesting.
There is a great quote from Raymond Chandler that I always use from when he was asked to describe the difference between his black-mask, pulp-fiction, hard-boiled

C.J. LIM

Once Upon a China: Journey to the West 1, 2019
Digital, 59 × 84 cm (22½ × 33 in)

Once Upon a China: Journey to the West 3, 2019
Digital, 59 × 84 cm (22½ × 33 in)

detective stories versus a more traditional murder mystery.
His stories were released initially, not as a full collected novel, but week by week in these journals for detective stories and whatnot. He wanted to make sure that you would always be enthralled with the story, regardless of whether you ever figured out who did the deed or committed the murder.

And in order to do that, he would write the most intensely detailed and specific episodes he possibly could, of scenes next to scenes. He would then put them on his desk and, a little bit like William Burroughs, would move them around until two episodes came up against each other. And there was some sort of friction or resonance or tension between two episodes. And then he would just put them next to each other and into the book. That's why a lot of his stories in a lot of the film translations don't really make any sense as a full linear narrative – they work in these sorts of episode-to-episode frictions.

And now I'm looking at these drawings from the book that you just published and I'm seeing a lot of that, these things that kind of work in friction with each other. And each drawing is highly detailed and highly specific in its own frame, in its own sort of world.

C.J. LIM
You're quite right.
I really tried to create for each drawing its own universe in a way,
the connection between the tectonics, the connection between scenes.
I would like the reader, and the person looking at it to stitch it together.

And that's why I enjoy Nada's paintings so much, I think.
I asked Nada if they were intended to leave clues, and provide ambiguity, so that when the reader looks at it, he or she will find clues within and can make up the story.
Just like the way we experience space. We don't all have the same experience in the same space. We all have different emotions poured into the spaces that we encounter, the way we use spaces during day and night, summer to winter, if we've company or if we're alone, so even the same space would be read differently.

Drawings should have that ability to conjure up the different emotions when you are reading them. And the same goes for texts. For example, *Invisible Cities* by Italo Calvino is one of my favourite books of all time.[2] When I read it in the first year of architecture school, I probably couldn't understand the surreal abstraction of what was described in it, but I think I took a little bit away, and then years later I read it again and I think I understood a bit more.
And then when I read it again, when I did *Virtually Venice*, I probably got a lot more out of it.
I guess for me, just like my interest in social politics and cultural identity in my projects, I wouldn't have known what that was when I first started with early books such as *Sins*, or *441*, or *How Green is your Garden?*.
But now, as I get older, you know, my interest in different things in life also pours into the drawings and changes the way I conceive narratives for the projects and the research. I think current affairs plays a large part in what I do.
But when it comes to social politics and cultural identity, I'm just hoping that architecture could have a voice in the discourse of those issues, rather than just us creating without engagement.
Because otherwise I'm fearful that one day, the money man, the capitalist, the developers will have all the say, and we architects have no more voice.

MARK DORRIAN
I'm thinking about authors who sometimes speak about readers that they imagine writing for or that they imagine being in some kind of dialogue with.
And thinking about books and the way that they move, and the way that they are read in different locations.
Books are intimate things, in the sense that we carry them with us,
and we encounter them,
and they travel with us to different places.
I just want to ask you about the kinds of environments in your books and the

environments in which they're read as well. And if you think about that relationship, or how you might think about the place of reading of the books in connection to what they make or what they show.

C.J. LIM
I think of them with different layers of emotions, I guess.
I would say that this project here, for example, 'Dream of the Green Mansion' in the book *Once Upon a China*, is very melancholy.
It deals with energy consumption, it deals with domesticity, and it also deals with the fact that women in China are not treated as equals. Despite that, woman are emerging as politicians and very good architects, a whole generation of them. It really says a lot about the kind of sadness of inequality that there is still a great feudal system that exists.
Hence the roof becomes the bed and the bed symbolises the death of equality in China.

Yeah, I like your question a lot Mark…

When the projects are conjured, created and imagined, I attach emotions to them.
I think it was Lebbeus Woods who said that, and I'll paraphrase, 'Drawing is only meaningful if you embed emotions into it'.
And I think for me, emotions are really, really important because in the contemporary practice, architecture is almost conceived without emotions, with mostly only care for financial gain.
And, even when we call projects 'social projects' or 'social housing', it mostly lacks that level of empathy and humanity.
Somehow, the project here, I don't profess that it actually covers all that, but there is an attempt to address the lack of humanity.

My drawing never sets out to make political statements, but I think I feel really most comfortable when I'm dealing with cultural and social identities that might nurture imaginative and even impossible creative ideas.

1 W. Benjamin and T. Y. Levin, 'Rigorous Study of Art', *October*, 47 (1988), pp. 89–90.
2 I. Calvino, *Invisible Cities* (New York: Vintage, 1997).

SHAUN MURRAY

Sketchbook Diaries, 2021
Pencil on paper, 21 × 26 cm (8 × 10 in)
Walking through the site while constructing the sketch

Shaun Murray
Drawing for Potential

SHAUN MURRAY

The sketches are journeys, they are linear. Some of the sketches become other things, some of them reside in the sketchbook and don't go anywhere else.

I don't draw as a conclusion in a sketchpad. When I draw, I'm drawing for potential, to think of something becoming something else and letting my imagination develop through the sketchbook.

I use this type of paper because you can see through it, and I can edit a composition on the next page.
The sketch becomes iterative through the sketchbook pages and I bring things through from one page to the next.
The right-hand page is usually the starting point for something. The left-hand page can be brought through from a previous page.
So, what I draw is layered already in the way I work with drawing.

I use a system of layers.
The layers start to reach out, out of the canvas, and I am trying for the drawing to become more spatial.
Layers will start to buckle, and I get the layers of transparency and opacity as I work through them.

I usually work in small and then I make a large drawing.
The reason I work small is because it is more immediate, it is closer to me, and communicating the agency of drawing.

I can travel with these; I can do things on the move.

I make notes, register things across the canvas, things that get privileged.
I also make up words to focus on what I want that part to be about.
And by naming it, I consider unpacking it and how I could see the drawing and the respective term evolve over a longer period of time.

MARK DORRIAN

It is interesting what you say about the sketchbooks, the particular qualities of paper. There is a certain kind of transparency, but it is not extremely transparent, and that is kind of important.
They screen out as much as they transmit, and you get a sense of sedimentation.
You can see through a certain number of sheets, and in that way, what your drawing actions seem to do is reorder that sedimentation.
They bring some things that are fading into the foreground again, and retain those as you move through. That is quite unusual to find someone who works so sequentially.

I spent most of last year looking at sketchbooks in the Department of Prints and Drawings in the British Museum, dating back to the 17th century …
They are manipulated in all kinds of interesting ways, and sometimes turned back to front and restarted, and very occasionally you get interruptions of blank pages through which things show through.
There is a kind of embedded itinerary within them as well,
and the sequence becomes really important. But here I think it is about the transmission of the drawing and also the fading.
Borges wrote a story, 'Funes the Memorious', about someone who could not forget — like drawing in absolute transparency all the time. It would be a kind of madness when there is no fading at all.
Here in your case, there is this complex process of selection, projection and transmission through the sketchbook.

Could you describe these as diaries?

SHAUN MURRAY

Yes, you could do.

MICHAEL YOUNG

What is really interesting about the sedimentation of the papers is that there is enough of a translucency and screening with

SHAUN MURRAY

The Screen and the Pendulum, 2021
Airbrush ink on lineboard and four acetate layers, 30 × 50 cm (12 × 20 in)

SHAUN MURRAY
The Screen, the Spectrum and the Pendulum, 2021
Airbrush ink on lineboard and four acetate layers, 50 × 100 cm (20 × 40 in)

SHAUN MURRAY
Ineffaceable Illuminati, 2021
Airbrush ink on lineboard and four acetate layers, 50 × 20 cm (20 × 8 in)

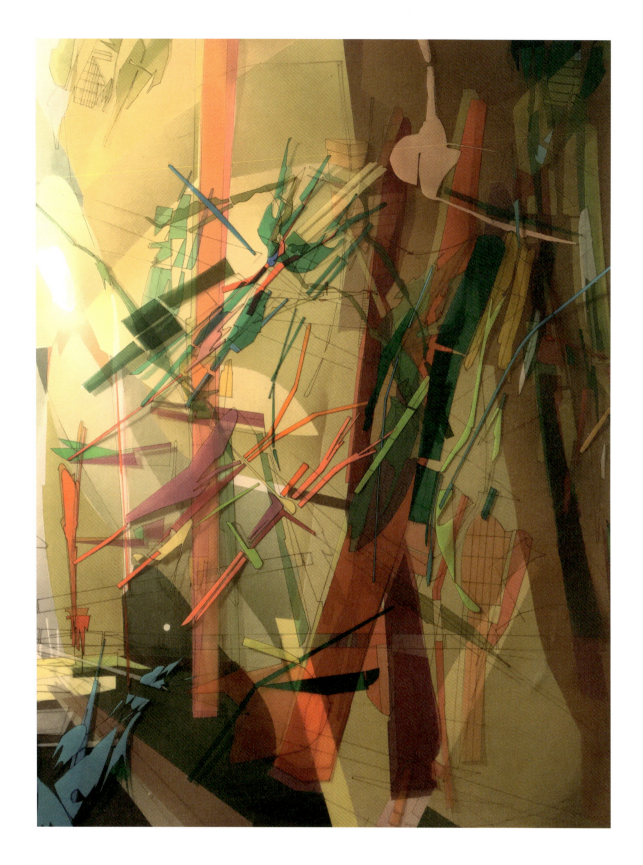

SHAUN MURRAY
Mirror Curtain, 2021
Airbrush ink on lineboard and four acetate layers, 50 × 20 cm (20 × 8 in)

SHAUN MURRAY

The preliminary 'Scaffolding Drawing' of
The Screen, the Spectrum and the Pendulum, 2021
Ink lines on acetate layers, 50 × 100 cm (20 × 40 in)

this paper that it seems that the next step is to the tracing paper. The tracing paper is a little bit more transparent, and then from there to the acetate.
The acetate is incredibly transparent, so the materiality of the surface you are working on provides a layer of screening and concealment that allows you to read, select and choose what is coming through until it hits the acetate.
And then you need colour to begin to provide a level of obscure-colour layering that allows it to then bring depth. Because without that …

SHAUN MURRAY
Yes, the black-and-white drawings don't make any sense until I apply colour to them and a layering becomes apparent.

MARK DORRIAN
Another interesting thing here is the question of agency.
The screening shifts from the agency of the material to your agency.
You apply the screening techniques through the colouring.

What about scales – do you work from a particular size?

SHAUN MURRAY
The scale of the drawing is from my position in the landscape.
I work with photographs of the context.
The backgrounds come from photographs and the photographs are my relationship to that context.
They are my engagement with a particular context and then I edit this context to privilege certain things that I want a relationship with and begin to manifest an architecture through.

Context is really important to me.
Someone talking about their relationship with the context …
that gets me really excited.
They are trying to describe in words something which is kind of indescribable because it involves their relationship to words
— for example, considering a rock face as a rock climber.

Words and drawings are two separate things.
The drawing is much more inhabited …
with the drawing I compose things as I move through them.

The drawing starts to rethink what is below the ground.
Ideas of exhuming things from below the River Thames, above the River Thames, and thinking about how we can construct things as a way of manifesting that tentative relationship between the above and below.

So, it is kind of a delicate dance of interacting parts
— it is always about editing; you are the editor of situations, and you are not the director of anything.
Editing and privileging things while you are thinking.
Even in the design of buildings, I am editing to get the best possible result out of a whole range of possibilities.

Riet Eeckhout
Sequential Depositions of the Image

BRYAN CANTLEY

Riet, you refer to the white wax pencil components as *thing* – a thing or things. I'm wondering if you could expand on what its *thingness* is, how you're determining it
from its field,
from its ground,
from other marks that are not part of its makeup.

RIET EECKHOUT

While I work,
the white pencil is a way of holding on to things. I use the white wax pencil to differentiate or privilege a particular spatiality generated from the graphite lines, and I build its presence up incrementally, as the drawing progresses.
But the use of the white pencil has evolved over the years, and sometimes changes within one drawing.
Initially I used the wax pencil as a notation, the development of a language, a visual communication – for example, I used the white in *Drawing Out Collapse* (2010) to differentiate particular dust clouds from other elements and so on. In the first instance, it had very much a narrative character, linked to the representational contents of the drawing's source material.
But now I use the white as a pure spatial device, the incremental build-up of spatial contents within the drawing.
Sometimes, the white defines the figure.
Elsewhere, the white defines how the figure merges with what is below, developing into a figured ground.
In some drawings, it is very much about sectioning the spatial configuration of the subject – the white sets the datum level of the drawing to then enable a more perspectival development, foregrounding and backgrounding the white. In other drawings it is about solidifying – substantiating a found configuration that needs to remain present and that can be developed in subsequent drawings.
But in any case, the white always sits in a spatial rhythm with the pale voids in the Mylar, on which I draw.

Take, as an example, the initial drawing, what I call the 'portrait drawing' of drawing set *The Space Between His Head and His Two Hands*. This drawing speaks about the temporal space of the movement between the hands of a man standing on one leg, making involuntary movements with his arms to remain upright. It is a movement that is unintentional but consistent, and it produces a spatial structure that I want to extract.
As an artefact it holds the intelligible and emotional disposition of what I want to point at, and that's why I call it the 'portrait drawing' of the project.
It is a starting point, an extracted spatial observation.
The portrait drawing demarcates the place of a particular moment,
place in its momentary status.
The pencil drawing traces the space described by the involuntary movement,
and the white wax pencil is an initial indication of what I'd like to look at in the drawing, of what I want to hold on to of this found space.
So, once I can draw its specificity and I make it white, it's present in the drawing and it starts demarcating the subject of the drawing, and I can work on the development of that found space in subsequent drawings.
At that moment, the space defined in white has released the meaning it had in its original or former representation, and goes off on a tangent.

MICHAEL YOUNG

The Mylar that you draw on is not being used for the ways in which the medium was intended or how it was developed over time in order to build up layers for sets of drawings.
You're not putting these on light tables to trace, you're projecting on to the Mylar with a projector – so, it could be an opaque medium. But the translucency brings a different kind of quality to the ground, a different kind of quality to this figured ground or however you define it. The Mylar changes the texture of

the drawing, yet it's not being used for any of the reasons people worked with it before.

RIET EECKHOUT

The use of Mylar is kind of a historical thing for me. I used to use it to trace information from photographs or prints, but once I had a projector that wasn't actually necessary any more.
But I kept using it for its qualities, in which texture and material resistance is suppressed. Mylar is mute, pale and smooth.
I like the paper I draw on not to present texture, allowing the pencil to slide over the medium with minimal resistance.

MICHAEL YOUNG

I wasn't aware of the role that photography played with Nat's or Shaun's work, or your work, Riet. I knew that you take photographs of your work and then project the photographs of the work to draw from. So, the photograph of the drawing becomes the genesis of a new drawing.
But this idea that you would keep the photograph in focus in some locations and purposefully put it out of focus in other locations, giving you a bit of wiggle room about the decision of when, where and how figured grounds become entwined.
That's super interesting and super weird also. And I mean, in focus and out of focus is a thing that happens with lenses. It's a thing that happens with photography. It happens with eyeballs too, but it isn't something we usually talk about when we think about lines, figures, grounds, drawing. And yet there is a generative idea within it.
I think there are also some connections with the ways in which Shaun and Nat have been using photography as an intermediary in their work.

RIET EECKHOUT

In principle I use film as it surrenders an abundance of spatial relational information on how something performs in context.
Also, the camera lens through which one views has a productive capacity to tease out spatial content.
When you take an oblique view through the lens of a camera towards the drawing, one looks at the same drawing, but the proportions of the spatial configuration change depending on the position and angle of the view towards the drawing. In this manner, some things are purposefully foregrounded and other things are pushed back – some things are sharp, other things retreat into the blurred speculative depth of the perspective.
And so, proportional distortion with a lens collaborates in a mediation process that informs the spatial performance of the drawing. And as I'm projecting the photographs back on to my drawing board to re-introduce and re-draw the same spatial information of lines, layers and surfaces, the drawing gains a different impetus, different speculative depth and spatial potential.

MARK DORRIAN

The oblique view is important in the work – it's really important to the process that it's a kind of low-level aerial photograph, and this produces two effects:
on one hand, a latent perspectival quality that one feels in the drawings, a kind of perspectival force that the oblique view produces;
and, on the other, a condition of differential focus, because of the splay of the image and depth of field effects that produces.
I have a sense – and this is maybe to do with the Jenny Saville photograph you showed – of the body pressing against the glass.
But, also thinking about your drawing of the peat landscape – of the cut section through the bog – thinking of ancient preserved bog bodies like the Tollund man figure found in Denmark and the kind of flattened figural deformations they show. It puts me in an archaeological mind in relation to your drawings that makes me think of the possibility of terms like 'deposition' to describe the serial transformation of the image …
that there's a kind of deposition of the image that the drawing is performing, as it shifts and moves.
The double sense of deposition is important here – firstly, the sense of something being put somewhere, laid down, placed; and secondly, the sense of something being

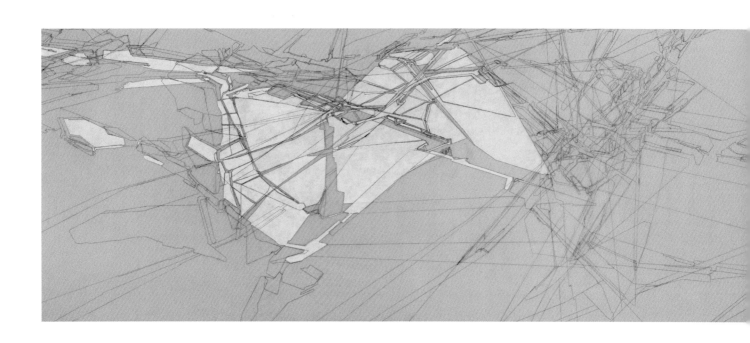

RIET EECKHOUT
Drawing Out Gehry II, 2018
Graphite pencil, white wax pencil on polyester film, 90 × 450 cm (35½ × 177 in)

de-positioned, shifted, and transformed.
The way the drawings build up, they feel like a record of processes.
They can only be a record because there are deposits in the drawings — or better, through the drawings.
At the same time, they're also a record of sequential de-positions, which are performed in various ways — partly through the video fragments, but also through your own photography, and then the re-screening of the images on to the drawing. It folds that archaeological process into itself.

C.J. LIM

I want to know, what is your sense of aesthetics? I wonder, with every single decision that you make, how you make it.
Is it intuition, or is there a rationale?
Is it something that comes through your imagination?
Because you keep saying there are details in the drawing, and you refer to the details of your drawing as something you want to look further into and develop in subsequent drawings. And it fascinates me. It makes me incredibly curious.
It's an incredible celebration of intuition and aesthetics, that nowadays, you know, we don't really discuss any longer. It's wonderful. I also wonder, how do you know when to stop?

RIET EECKHOUT

'When is the drawing finished?' is a question I'm asked regularly.
Mostly, I know it because I have the sense that the drawing is at rest.
Or rather, the drawing sort of speaks back. It is not requesting anything anymore, but rather is just being expressive of itself. You know, its autonomy becomes clear.
Regarding your question on intuition and reflection…
drawing is for me intrinsically a dynamic process, with periods where I am drawing intuitively with a certain speed, but then there are contemplative moments that are slower while I consider how particular parts will develop.
A lot of time is invested in understanding what it is, what the drawing is becoming while I'm developing it.

Also, my perspective on the drawing changes while drawing for months — the point of view changes, what needs to be further articulated changes, as does the sense of what is fine and what isn't, or what needs to be elaborated and what doesn't, what is on the edge of something and whether it needs to be kept there …

C.J. LIM

You're very precise —
and yet, you allow it to evolve organically. And the thing is, someone might say that the two things don't really scientifically match up. But I think it is the kind of precision of both your eye and your intuition that is remarkable.

NEIL SPILLER

I see these drawings as very much kinds of landscape drawing.
Further to your way of developing in sequences of drawings using photographs, maybe there is a kind of prima materia or 'prime matter' that you can keep excavating out of these.
And maybe with the aim of creating slightly more formal applications that then get pushed back into the terrain of themselves. I'm reading them all as beautiful terrains and I just want to see them inhabited with other Riet-type things.

RIET EECKHOUT

They might be seen as terrains — it might be a natural tendency to read these layered outlined surfaces through a pictorial association with a tectonic landscape, but it's not the focus.
For the past year, the drawings have revolved around the question of how to draw the figure into the ground to the extent that the figure is gone and what is left is a ground that speaks of the figure's passing.
The figured ground is established through the subtle exchange of forces between the figure and the ground — a situational event that left its traces and remains in the ground.
It seems to takes time, a slow process of one drawing being the draft for the next drawing, every time, at best, one step closer to the figured ground.

RIET EECKHOUT
The Space Between His Head and His Two Hands (portrait drawing), 2014
Graphite pencil, white wax pencil on polyester film, 90 × 110 cm (35½ × 43 in)

RIET EECKHOUT

Drawing Out Gehry IV (a), 2019
Graphite pencil, white wax pencil on polyester film, 90 × 140 cm (35½ × 55 in)

Pages 106–7: Oblique photographs of drawing details used as work documents

PERRY KULPER

I might have it all wrong here, but the way that this work has been talked about is in terms of an equivalence or a lateral set of relationships in it.
It seems like you're interested in various kinds of trans —
transcription, translation, transfiguration, transmutation, trans-substantiation.
Because, when you talk about them, it's about something leaving one state and moving into another, and then something else remaining in its previous state.
Is that not true?
That's why these drawings are hard for me to read pictorially, relative to horizons — because, as I listened to you talk, some parts seem like they're in their world seeking transfiguration. Other parts appear as translations, like you characterise them. So, they seem like they're in really different phase states to me.
Does that make sense?

RIET EECKHOUT

Yes, absolutely, Perry. That is correct.
It is transfiguration that I am interested in when drawing — how one thing leaves its condition as one thing, to become something else. This 'trans'-state allows the drawing to develop and remain in a state of flux.
Nothing is really settled, but everything is attuned to one another, in relation with and in response to one another.

NAT CHARD

Maybe the drawings are a spatiality rather than a space, giving critical analytical insights into a spatiality.
Just as with many movements in art, the insights in their representation, I suspect, change our perception of things, having seen the world through their eyes.
Think, for example, of how we conceptualise the world spatially having seen a map, as opposed to never having seen a map — the form of representation changes how space is thought.
And I wonder if, with these drawings, you've developed a practice that sees things in a particular way.
What sort of insights do these chronographic drawings beget from what you've learned through making them?
Typically, people learn how to project ideas by making analytical drawings of things that already exist. If you now have that knowledge, with your particular sense of spatiality, I wonder could you draw that spatiality without the origin?
As an architect, one might learn to draw a perspective of spaces which we inhabit in a very literal figurative way. That then would give us the skill to draw a perspective of an imagined space we would desire to be in. And then we could reverse engineer that perspective to ask, 'What would be the thing that will create that?'
Could you originate your spatiality and then reverse engineer it to understand your method — to find out what sort of space would we get?
Knowing this spatiality, can it be a projective method?

RIET EECKHOUT

Do you mean, without any other source material? Drawing freed from its subjects?

NAT CHARD

Yes.

RIET EECKHOUT

Well … the interest for me lies firmly in the ability to extract spatial content out of existing situations. Also, one has a certain way of drawing, and particular affinities. Having the source material challenges the spatial knowledge that the head and the hand know and draw. New source material and new observations trigger and re-structure the knowledge that has been built up, tacitly and explicitly.
The projective method is the manner in which I extract the spatial information, with the photographs and film frames.

MARK DORRIAN

It's very thought-provoking when you show us the whole set-up with the drawing board and the projection on the vertical plane.
It is interesting to see alongside Shaun's board and Perry's horizontal board and to think about the verticality of yours.

RIET EECKHOUT
Drawing Out Gehry VI, 2020
Graphite pencil, white wax pencil on polyester film, 50 × 19 cm (20 × 7½ in)

BRYAN CANTLEY
In terms of the verticality too, there's a gravitational and ever-presentness of the tool. I think in Perry's case and mine that we have parallel bars and so we have to establish a kind of a floating datum that we can pull all other geometric points off.
I mean, to reduce drafting to that crudeness of an exercise, you couldn't have that on yours.
At least I know in mine, there's the continual presence of the parallel bar as part of the dialogue of the drawing exercise. You don't have that.
I would find it an amazingly liberating act, to draw vertically.
Perry, I don't know if you find that or not, but the parallel bar is always part of the dialogue. As much as I'd like to ignore it, it is a player in everything that I'm producing.

PERRY KULPER
Sometimes I'll actually move mine up to the top of the drawing when I'm working on other kinds of things that don't have to do with its authority …

RIET EECKHOUT
I stand in front of the drawing.
It's also its size that demands that verticality.

MARK DORRIAN
One way of thinking about that verticality is that it gives the board, and the drawing, a more screen-like sense. We're also looking at it the way we might be looking at a window.

RIET EECKHOUT
Yes, the vertical drawing board is important to me.
When I am drawing, the drawing develops in front of me, vertical, at eye height, one to one and experiential. I want the drawing to move me.

RIET EECKHOUT
Drawing Out Gehry I on the drawing board, 2018
Graphite pencil, white wax pencil on polyester film, 90 × 155 cm (35½ × 61 in)

Keyword Phrases

C.J. LIM

QUILTING

Edwin A. Abbott created the two-dimensional world of *Flatland*, whose inhabitants consist of lines, points and polygons. Subtitled *A Romance of Many Dimensions*, Abbott's story, published in 1884, is both a mathematical treatise on dimensional perception and a satire examining Victorian sexuality and the class system.[1] Taking a cue from this work, each of the assemblages from *Virtually Venice* and *Short Stories: London in Two-and-a-half Dimensions* begins life as a two-dimensional sheet of paper. The paper is then cut, inscribed, folded and fused into a narrative, occupying a territory that is both real and surreal; cardboard cut-outs are spliced and woven into yarns with shadowy nuance to partially occupy the third dimension. Using paper, carbon and glue as ingredients, the stories construct a sequence of improbable marriages between reality and fantasy, laced with a healthy dose of myth and locational specificity. The making of these drawings is very much a collaborative process and has similarities to the intricate process of quilting. Teams of two to five would sit around one drawing and stitch together spatial architectural stories. Like the artwork described in Abbott's Victorian satire, the assemblages are 'immoral, licentious, anarchical and unscientific', yet, from an aesthetic point of view, 'glorious', 'ravishing' and 'a pleasure to behold'.

As with the poetic principles of quilt-making, this work takes advantage of the medium's inherent plurality – pieces of the assemblage are only ever half-subsumed into their new context, bringing with them a wealth of connoted meaning from their original time and place. We usually expect objects to exist in a singular location, but the elements in a collage or assemblage oscillate between existences like Schrödinger's cat, presenting a flexible vessel in which the reader is encouraged to deposit their own historical and cultural montage.

The ultimate purpose of the assemblage is to demonstrate that architectural representation need not be a neutral tool or mere picture of a future building, that drawings have a direct influence on the conceptual development of a project and the generation of form, and that there are alternatives to the reductive working methods of contemporary architectural practice. Produced by the majority of professionals in practice, the triadic system of plan, section and elevation are well-suited to the task of relaying information for construction or fabrication purposes, but they possess no qualitative narratives or phenomenological intelligence. And unlike Walter Benjamin, who emphasised that the most essential characteristic of the architectural drawing is that 'it does not take a pictorial detour', the assemblage and pluralistic nature of quilting argue that pictorial detours are essential.

1 [E.A. Abbott], *Flatland: A Romance of Many Dimensions* (London: Seeley & Co., 1884).

NARRATIVES

In *Invisible Cities*, Italo Calvino avoids a conventional sequential structure to describe the city of Venice, playing out the prose poem through a series of narratives recounted to Kublai Khan by the merchant Marco Polo: 'I could tell you how many steps make up the streets rising like stairways, and the degree of arcades' curves, and what kind of zinc scales cover the roofs; but I already know this would be the same as telling you nothing'.[1] When asked by the Khan whether he will repeat the same tales to his people, Calvino echoes Roland Barthes, explaining that there are as many versions of a tale as there are listeners, via the proxy of Polo. '"I speak and I speak," Marco says, "but the listener retains only the words he is expecting … It is not the voice that commands the story: it is the ear"'.[2]

It was not unusual for buildings to be constructed of and around narrative. Roland Barthes comments in his 'Introduction to the Structural Analysis of Narratives' that 'narrative is present in every age, in every place, in every society; it begins with the very history of mankind and there nowhere is nor has been a people without narrative. All classes, all human groups, have their narratives, enjoyment of which is often shared by men with different, even opposing, cultural backgrounds. Caring nothing for the division between good and bad literature, narrative is international, transhistorical, transcultural: it is simply there, like life itself.'[3] It is therefore disappointing that buildings and their drawings, as physical repositories of and monuments to human culture, now rarely signify anything beyond their quotidian function.

When, in 1830, Sir John Soane exhibited J.M. Gandy's bird's-eye watercolour of his Bank of England at the Royal Academy, it was accompanied by a quotation: 'I want to lift the roof of that wonderful national building. The interior will be revealed to you like a meat pie with the crust removed'.[4] Drawn from the popular novel *Gil Blas* by Alain-René Lesage, the quotation flickers with an ambiguous sense of human folly – perhaps, I like to imagine, reflecting Gandy's sorrow that the construction of the building was funded by the profits of colonialism, or a prophecy of the collapse of the banking industry that would occur centuries later. Irrespective of political statement, cultural discourse, or social commentary, there is an undeniable relationship between narratives and drawings. Narratives, especially of the drawn kind, can nurture the imaginative and even impossible creative voice to address a world in crisis, and to discover the true potential of our human conditions.

SHAUN MURRAY

EDITING SITUATIONS

I draw architecture as a dance of interacting parts that is always about editing situations to reveal the most curious. Becoming an editor of situations through drawing is about managing uncertainty between context and designing. This relationship is dynamic, like buildings, in that it is constantly being refined and reshaped by the broader environment and by participants in the environment of the drawing itself. To edit within this relationship is about negotiating and refining decisions, or different marks and shapes, as one discovers new information. Drawings in architecture should improve with time, if they are allowed to. To begin a project, I edit the context as I walk through it by sketching, studying, and reflecting on my intuition and intellectual 'active' purposefulness in relation to what I discover. I study the context through its histories and projected futures in order to define tools for determining the effects of interaction between space, participant and environment.

I see architectural drawing as an action coupled with the environment, and the outcome is carefully crafted. It is through the determining effects

1 I. Calvino, *Invisible Cities* (San Diego, New York, London: Harcourt Brace & Company, 1974), p. 10.
2 ibid., p. 135
3 R. Barthes, 'Introduction to the Structural Analysis of Narratives', in *Image Music Text*, trans. S. Heath (London: Fontana Press, 1977), p. 79.
4 Curatorial notes, 'A Bird's-eye View of the Bank of England', Sir John Soane's Museum Collection Online, museum no. P267, http://collections.soane.org/object-p267/ [accessed 28 November 2021].

of interaction within the system of varying powers that the architect can become an editor of environments and operate as a space-scribe. I consider drawing architecture to be a pursuit in which drawing and context are structurally interrelated, and I use it as a learning system through which to keep interacting with the environment. For example, by positioning oneself within an environment through the making of a drawing – as seen in the precedent of the Tibetan Buddhist sand mandalas, inhabited by certain deities – one can gain a different understanding of our relationship with it. There have been many attempts to gain insights into our environments and an important question would be: can we get instructions from the environment through experience?

The components of the thematic integration of ENIAtype, my practice, are context, design and communication. The relationship between context and design can be described as one of 'editing', while that between design and communication can be described in terms of 'reading'.

I look for coherence in the relationship between working drawings, participant and environment within context, design and communication – to be engaging and become wholly informed in all fields of knowledge and institutions that work with all sources of fieldwork data through the process of constructing our built environment. The role of the editor is to make a difference between our built environment and us.

When architecture can fully exchange information with natural phenomena, with a mutable field of quantum fluctuations, its capabilities for knowledge and communication will be far deeper and more extended than presently understood. It will also blur the boundaries of our individuality – our very sense of separateness from the built environment.

SYSTEM OF LAYERS

Physical layers in my drawings allow an exchange of ideas, forms, shapes, and lines, enabling redesign back and forth as an 'open system' drawing – thus allowing drawing to establish stoppages in designing ecologies. The drawings are composed of five layers, including the ecological, notational, instructional and aesthetic.

The 'ecological layer' is composed of two strata – the base and the first acetate sheet that reveals shifting relationships within the existing context. Here I take photographs of the context and use this as a guide to privileging certain parts of it. Every step in the communication of my drawings involves the addition of information to an already existing system. The ecology of the projects not only specifies their structural changes, but also which disturbances from the environment trigger them. One is the notion of an architecture existing in the form intended as a result of complex interrelationships with it, through it and on it, where the drawing itself exists through the relationships between things, and not through the things themselves.

The 'notational layer' denotes rhythm in the outside world, the self-absorbing intuitive and poetic acting out of a battle with the elements. Notations in architectural drawing are mostly taken as given, a neutral code towards the design. I aim to challenge and reverse this well-worn assumption and design notations to suit a new vision of how we can communicate our architectures – as a scaffolding of an architecture before the architecture, and not something derived from the arbitrary specifications of the notation itself. Notations can be spatial and embedded in our environment. Such physical notations are incredibly important in understanding how we perceive environments, and mediating the experience of the design towards architecture.

The 'instructional layer' reveals the editing of situations as a process of managing uncertainty – the 'in', 'off' and 'by' spaces of the drawing. The edges of a design project are not redefined through a computer screen, but rather through a vast web of relationships. Drawings can become the space to edit the environment through the reader of the drawing. Working with the idea of drawing as being embedded 'within' the environment, we can begin to describe the event before the architecture as architecture. A sequence of prompts or combination of prompts in a drawing would enable an infinite sequence of spatial notations – as a reflex for future architectures playing out as a response to whatever has already occurred or is now occurring.

The 'aesthetic layer' reveals the consequences of the design, depending on the elements involved in the three other layers in the drawing. This layer is where the reader of the drawing notices difference between the others. The reader of the drawings is encouraged to describe this relationship through the final composition. Are we developing the reading based on our experience of the environment, or are we establishing a reading of the environment through a drawing? The action of reading a drawing should be focused on transferring knowledge and encourage discussion. We should not delude ourselves that *we* construct the architecture; instead, we merely put readers in place to translate the complexity and beauty of the world.

RIET EECKHOUT

PLACE IN ITS MOMENTARY STATUS

The phrase 'place in its momentary status', relates to the demarcation of a relationship between time and space. I use situational events, encounters and the coming-together of circumstances, to investigate and substantiate the performativity of space. Circumstances take in space as they unfold over time. Space is viewed here as a dynamic notion, in flux and experiential. And it is within this passing of time that a spatial performance takes place in which the specific circumstances of the event are enacted in all their complexity. The 'portrait drawings', as I call them, are residues of a process of extraction, drawing out an essential spatial disposition of the situation from a particular point of view, involving the space of movement of and between parts, tracings of fluctuating interstitial space, and the spatial-geometrical implications of the cause-and-effect exchange of forces.

Spatial-relational content is traced from films and photographs of events, projecting the footage on to a screen of Mylar on my vertically orientated drawing board. This set-up allows the space of the momentary to become present and to be viewed with precision and in a state of immersion. Things appear in durational overview, frame by frame, in their matter-of-fact disposition.

There is an interest here in the evolutionary aspect of how one thing morphologically gives rise to another, in such a way that form and change can be studied simultaneously without being in opposition. When using film fragments, looking at a situation frame by frame, every iteration both arises from and supersedes the previous. The spatial-relational condition is where my focus lies, as opposed to an object-directed perception of space. Form matters to me, but less the form of things than the form between them.

I use the term 'portrait drawing' because the drawings are portraits of events – they intend to contain the essential spatial presence of the event, rather than just a moment frozen in time. This drawing operates as an augmented device, beyond the operational mechanics of the situation, positioning the momentary in relation to a 'before' and 'after' in the relentless maelstrom of life.

SPECIFICITY AND THE CONTENT OF FORM

If only we had trusted our eyes, if we had just looked at the images instead of turning our back on them, remarking that they were mere fetishes, fetishisations, surfaces, the semblance of something that lay concealed behind them: essence, the law, the principle that held the key to the proper understanding of appearances. When we see dead bodies, we are confronted with the death of actual people and not some principle of death; when we come face to face with torture victims, we must investigate their torturers and not evil as such; when we see ruins, we must study the blasts or ravages of time that laid them low, not some transhistorical law of impermanence.[1]

When I project film fragments or photographs of situational events on to my drawing board, and draw from them, it is the particular morphology of how subjects present themselves and the specific space in which they develop over time that I am interested in. This bottom-up visual exploration of spatio-temporal specificity and consistency in images and film frames by means of tracing brings to the surface particular aspects of the portrayed subject that escape the generalisations of top-down analytical and enculturated understandings. While both readings are inextricably connected, this bottom-up retrieved content resists verbal articulation, although it can be recorded and sensed in the drawing. I refer to it as the 'content of form'.

Whether it is through examining footage of a NASA helicopter crash that informs a particular figure-ground transformation through the observation of an exchange of forces; or scrutinising the space taken in by the involuntary movements of a person balancing on one leg; or exploring a sectioned bog landscape in Ireland in order to unearth the dynamic exchange between a farmer and his ground – once locked on to a subject with conceptual and cultural interest, I spend time with its visual information by tracing its consistent aspects.

When we look at visual information, we decide quite quickly what the value and content is of what we have in front of us. By projecting representations, film or photography at a (sometimes unrecognisably) large scale on to my drawing board, and sitting at the pixelated end of the image while drawing, I linger with and map the formal morphological disposition of the visual information. When I am immersed in detail without synoptic overview – copying and tracing boundaries and pixel colour differences of lines and surfaces, noting intensities, proximities, densities and depth – symbolism and cultural meaning can be momentarily discarded and intelligible coherence deconstructed, allowing me to reside temporarily with the formal qualities presented by the footage in order to extract its content.

1 Karl Schlögel, 'The Work of the Eye. Trusting Our Eyes', in *In Space We Read Time: On the History of Civilization and Geopolitics* (New York: Bard Graduate Center, 2016), pp 222–6.

THE AGENCY OF DRAWING

Inquisitive Drawings

Nat Chard

PETER PAUL RUBENS
The Apotheosis of the Duke of Buckingham, before 1625
Oil on oak, 64 × 64 cm (25 × 25 in)
National Gallery, London

The most common form of architectural drawing – those made to enable production or to give a pictorial likeness of how a project will appear – is produced by the architect to communicate knowledge of their proposal to others (for instance to the client or builder). That knowledge is accumulated through the architect's education and practice as well as their research into the particular project. To show this knowledge to other people, these drawings describe the material thing and often the rhetorical aspects of what it proposes to achieve – the explicit performance of the architecture.

    Architects also make other, often more private, drawings. The purpose of this work is not to show but to discover, and its audience is primarily the author. The knowledge such drawing creates can productively remain in the tacit realm, for there is no application that needs to be communicated to others. Often this takes the form of the sketch, especially when working through a practical idea related to a project. Many architects also develop their sensibilities and conceptual grasp of the discipline through a parallel practice of drawing. During the late 1970s and early 1980s, when so much of the architectural discourse was played out through drawings, some people denigrated this practice as 'paper architecture' – yet it is noticeable, in retrospect, how the buildings these so-called paper architects subsequently produced often gained their power through the sustained investigations by drawing that had preceded them.

The nature of architects' inquisitive drawings is wide-ranging. Le Corbusier habitually painted before going to his office and the resonances between what he painted and what he built are apparent. Despite the complementary concerns and themes that relate to his architecture, however, his paintings have an autonomous presence as art. Other architects – such as Piranesi, Boullée, Lequeu, Sant'Elia and Chernikhov[1] – have used the conventions of architectural representation as a means of speculation. While the character of their drawings is distinct, their speculative works rely on the relative or absolute projections typically used to illustrate architecture. Other architects, including contributors to this book, occupy sites in between these poles that learn from a combination of art and architectural practices, as well as some scientific methods of inquiry.

Michael Webb's drawings, which explore the interstices between perception and its spatio-temporal modes of representation, exemplify such a practice. The relationship between the content and method is so intertwined that it is hard to determine whether the means is a way of studying the thematic content or whether that content is a vehicle to study the means of representation. Webb's 1987 *Temple Island* exhibition at the Architectural Association in London gave equal importance to the iterations of development drawings as it did to the more polished renderings. An intensely poetic premise is explored through a series of studies that approach the content from a variety of directions, each played out with precision and rigour. The analytical description of both method and content in both the studies and the propositional drawings appears to make so much sense that, although what it adds up to is never conclusively stated, the observer is led to build their own understanding of the work. Architecture touches many fields, and often architectural research follows the methods of one of these disciplines rather than finding its own processes. Webb's (ongoing) *Temple Island* project establishes architecture's own voice in the realm of research.

One of the pleasures of architecture and one of the challenges of being an architect is that it is a place of intersection of many diverse concerns. Other contributors tease out architecture's capacity to gather seemingly incompatible things and ideas. Mark West's recent drawings blend photographic images of often quotidian but irreconcilable things and, through this process, strip them of their signification to reveal an underlying character. He then overdraws a print of this assembly to find apparently seamless transitions between things that would normally seem allergic to one another, making local judgements about how one element might coexist with another. Where so many architects have resorted to reductivist practices to synthesise disparate entities and ideas, West's drawings revel in irreconcilable conditions, where differences become pleasures enjoyed through local and specific negotiation. These delicious associations are beguiling but appear implausible until one remembers West's constructional alchemy with his fabric-formed castings.

If West negotiates the relationship between different figurative entities, Riet Eeckhout has invented a common visual currency through which seemingly unconnected events can be discussed on equal terms. If D'Arcy Wentworth Thompson's diagrams isolate the critical differences between similar species, Eeckhout's drawings allow the controlled crash test of a helicopter to exist on equal terms with a Frank Gehry drawing or a gymnastic or dance routine.[2] She has developed a method of distillation and interpretation that finds a common language through which we can visualise the associative possibilities between otherwise disconnected stories.

In Perry Kulper's *David's Island* drawings, the nuanced graphical characterisation of entities provides for conversations between choreographies, fields and material objects. In his *Fast Twitch* series, the drawn line is ambiguous — we are not sure whether it delineates a thing or an action, such as a tool path. The inclusion of traces of the geometric construction of the line, including tangents and radius points, emphasises the logic of the line as much as what it delineates. The drawings gather a sense of *how* and *why* in addition to *what* is drawn.

In these examples, the way the content is drawn is as important as the formal appearance of the drawing, and that content is discovered through the act of making the image. In each example there is a method that is modulated by intuitive decisions made by the drawing's author. These decisions are a core part of such drawings. While architects justify their work to others by professing an explicit knowledge of what they are doing and about the agency of their architecture, much of architectural knowledge is not explicit. Instead, it is personal or tacit knowledge, gained from experience and from rehearsing ideas. The medium or process with which the architect works can provide a critical resistance to their ideas, especially as exemplified in the practices touched on earlier, when that process or medium has a resonance with the content under discussion.

In my research that helpful resistance has been provided by an element of the apparatus of perspective — the picture plane. My research discusses our engagement with the built environment beyond what is predicted in the programme — the conditions of indeterminacy and uncertainty that form so much of our experience of architecture but which, by their nature, cannot be predicted. This is a relational question and the most common form of relative drawing used by architects is perspective. The picture plane is an active ingredient in the perspectival mechanism, an intermediary surface that artists have, at least since Leonardo, manipulated to make their images appear more true to life. This malleability also allows the person drawing to manipulate the picture plane to make a critical reception or projection of an image.

In an interview with David Sylvester in 1960, the painter Philip Guston stated,

We were talking yesterday at the studio about the picture plane, and to me there's some mysterious element about the plane. I can't rationalise it, I can't talk about it, but I know there's an existence on this imaginary plane which holds almost all the fascination of painting for me. As a matter of fact, I think the true image only comes out when it exists on this imaginary plane.[3]

Guston's paintings, even his early figurative work, are far from slavish in their adherence to the conventions of perspective. Guston is not talking only about the geometrical agency of the picture plane, so what might he be articulating here? I suggest it is the idea that the spatial ordering of the picture, the structuring of picturing, is as important a carrier of content as the pictorial character of the image. We see this in the spatial gymnastics of some of Pierre Bonnard's still-life paintings (for instance *The Table* [1925], but there are other examples), where items in the foreground such as a plate on a table are seen almost in plan whereas the bottle just behind it is painted as if almost in elevation. His skilful modulation of the picture plane constructs an image that makes perfect sense while articulating different spatial associations for each of these items.

If a picture reaches out into space, as with Baroque ceiling painting that melds pictorial sky with a material interior, we can see how similar manipulations of the picture plane can sustain an inventive spatial narrative without collapsing the pictorial illusion. Peter Paul Rubens' oil sketch for such a painting, *The Apotheosis of the Duke of Buckingham*,[4] at first sight appears to make sense, as almost all the figures relate to the central figure of the Duke, whom we see foreshortened from below. If we examine the secondary relations of the peripheral characters, we are drawn into a sequence of subplots with a variety of horizons and vanishing points. Through his dexterity in handling the picture plane, Rubens is using an understanding of the underlying structure of picturing to introduce content and relationships that could not be held by picturing through a flat picture plane – and perhaps here we find a resonance with Guston's statement.

When conveying formed ideas to others, the standard pictorial projections (relative or absolute) are wonderful tools – but when exploring possibilities of what an architecture might be about and what it is doing, the modulation of the underlying structures of picturing, assembling, interpreting or delineating (picking up from the earlier examples) can tease out as much content as the picture itself.

1 Giovanni Battista Piranesi (1720–78); Etienne-Louis Boullée (1728–99); Jean-Jacques Lequeu (1757–1826); Antonio Sant'Elia (1888–1916); Yakov Chernikhov (1889–1951); all architects best known for their drawn work.
2 The diagrams in D'Arcy Wentworth Thompson's book *On Growth and Form* (1917) articulate the formal differences of common features between different animals from similar species.
3 David Sylvester, *Interviews with American Artists* (New Haven: Yale University Press, 2001), p. 87.
4 The sketch was painted before 1625 and is held in the National Gallery, London. It is a preparatory study for a ceiling painting commissioned for the Duke of Buckingham's London home. The ceiling was destroyed by fire in 1949.

Bryan Cantley
Media-specific Impregnation: the Drawing as Subject

BRYAN CANTLEY

Some of the topics that I've been playing around with in these specific drawings are looking at markers of architectural graphics and information sets,
which include basic things like the architectural graphic scale, HUD systems, architectural notation systems, fiducial markers…
What happens if they become architectural events, rather than side notes to the drawing? In a typical drawing, these kinds of things might be set aside for designating materials, or be about demolition zones, or carry safety warning graphics.
I'm interested in the deconstruction and repurposing of any kind of structural grid, notations, etc.
As I draw, I wonder how these elements might manifest themselves in an architectural identity or language.

NAT CHARD

You have been refining the way you make your drawings for a while, Bryan, and through them you have been developing your own logics, which also rest on other logics that we can recognise.
In your drawings you use quite a few figures and numbers and the development of those figures also comes through a history of refinement and through the sub-logics of the tools used to cut the wood blocks to print them, or the other techniques of printing. Your more recent drawings appear to be charged with these sub-logics that go beyond describing something material or describing the sequence of assembly, for instance.
It seems that there is something inherent in the nature of how you draw that describes something beyond the object-ness of the thing.

BRYAN CANTLEY

If I look at some of the earlier work, there have been these architectural conditions — I won't call them architectural objects — but architectural conditions that had a graphic identity associated both with them and with denotations that describe them. What I tried to do for this particular series over the summer is to take the graphic logics of those drawings and extract them to try to make drawings of the graphic logics themselves. It is not so much about the objects that generate the drawings, but about the logics that generate the drawings.

NAT CHARD

Paul Virilio said of the accident: 'When you invent the airplane, you also invent the plane crash'. You, Bryan, seem to be saying that when you invent the drawing, you invent also this other thing, this other consequence of the drawing which is beyond the thing that the drawing originally set out to do.

BRYAN CANTLEY

Exactly. It's always been about the consequences and residues, not the initial event itself.

NAT CHARD

Yesterday Michael [Young] was talking about some of his earlier work where every line beyond its given hopes had a tangent that provided another life. I really enjoyed your talk, Michael — we are all sitting around here in one of the most generous groups of people that I have experienced, talking about the soft underbelly of their work but even so, there are things going on in all of our drawings that are at a layer beyond either what we want to talk about or what we can talk about.
And you Bryan, you are trying to make a systematic way of acknowledging those things in your drawings and asking where they come from and what they might give — this seems like a nice conversation to open up.

Bryan, can I ask, in this drawing you have a gas cylinder attached to a pair of compasses? [laughter]

BRYAN CANTLEY

Well, I get the question a lot during lectures or on social media: 'What app or programme are you using to produce these drawings?', which I find to be hilarious because I am maybe 10–20 per cent software-driven.

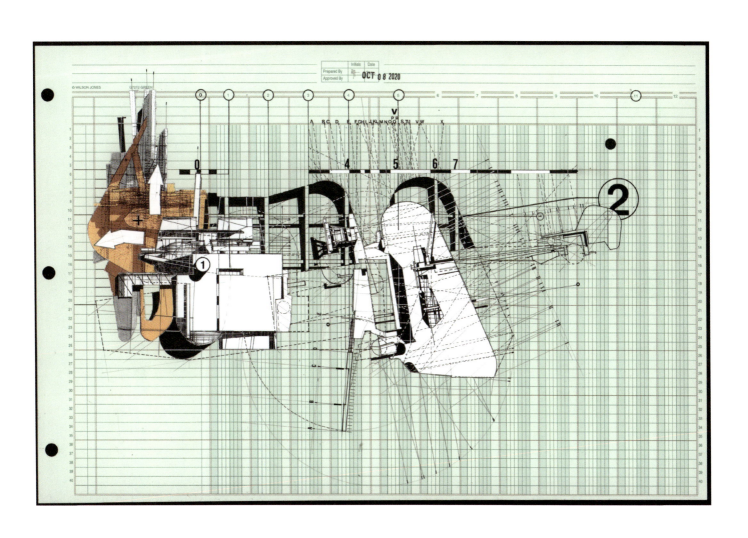

BRYAN CANTLEY

Myth-Appropriations, 2020
Ink, collage on ledger book, 28 × 43 cm (11 × 17 in)

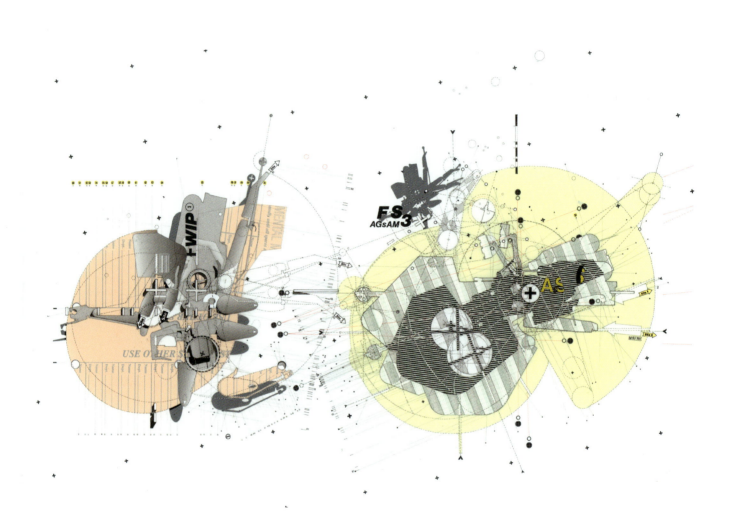

BRYAN CANTLEY
Other Side First, 2019
Ink, paper, transfer media on duralar, 50 × 76 cm (20 × 30 in)

So, these are some of the active tools that were lying around my desk. And I had this notion of this romantic, antiquated, custom-driven, incredibly analogue machine that breaks down and leaks ink on the page.

I was trying to explain to the students what an analogue drawing was, and I was getting the idea that they were not certain of what that meant. So, I thought, I'll get together these incredibly old-fashioned tools that meant something to me in terms of the tactility of the process of making and of residues — a bit tongue-in-cheek.
I think some of the students may have gotten the joke. It has become one of my favourite images because I think this represents the physical and more importantly the conceptual space in which I construct the work.

MARK WEST
That's an old telephone cord attached to the gas cylinder?

BRYAN CANTLEY
Exactly.
It also talks about the issues of connectivity prior to the ubiquity of being wireless and having to have that physical connection to the drawing.

The idea of the temporary or disposable nature of what the drawing might be …
I like the idea that the nature of drawing is universal in its geographical placement.
It can occur at any place any time
and it is not workplace specific
nor necessarily project specific.
There is a series of tangents and overlaps that occur in many places and different types of residues can be produced.
Media-specific impregnation on an aesthetic and also on an intellectual level.

MARK WEST
So, it sounds like the subject of the work is the drawing rather than the drawing being a reference to anything outside your drawing.

BRYAN CANTLEY
Yes, that's correct. It's rare when the drawings are only looking at the physical reference.

MARK WEST
And yet, the drawings, the affect of the drawings, at least as I receive them, seem to refer to a technical world like an actual world and not the world of drawings.
Well, obviously it refers to drawing —
it is so drawing-like because you are actually interrogating drawings, but it also has an affect, kind of like space craft, the android world of dimensional precision.
So, it is also referring to a world outside itself and I am wondering if that affect matters to you or if that is just something that I am picking up.

BRYAN CANTLEY
It is a good observation.
If you think of a music band that releases their first album and they have a sound that is unique to them …
that may not be a conscious effort,
it is just a sort of reflection of everything they've filtered in their journey of life and constructing music.
I think I am the victim of that same condition.
I am painfully aware of exactly what you are talking about.
On the one hand, it serves me well because it is something I am familiar with.
On the other, it is something that I think I'm struggling to edit or partially remove from the drawing, as it limits it to a certain aspect. It limits the ability to only deconstruct those particular artefacts and I think there is a next level of not starting in that position.
But to be quite honest, this is where I initiate these fantastical, not-responsible, non-pragmatic architectural conditions.

MARK WEST
But any really good drawing that is alive seems to have a life of its own.
Is it a John Lennon quote? — I don't know …
'Life is what's happening while we're busy making other plans'.
Sometimes the drawing that you are making is the drawing that is happening while you were making other plans for it, if you see what I'm getting at?

BRYAN CANTLEY
Yes, that's a very good way of putting it.

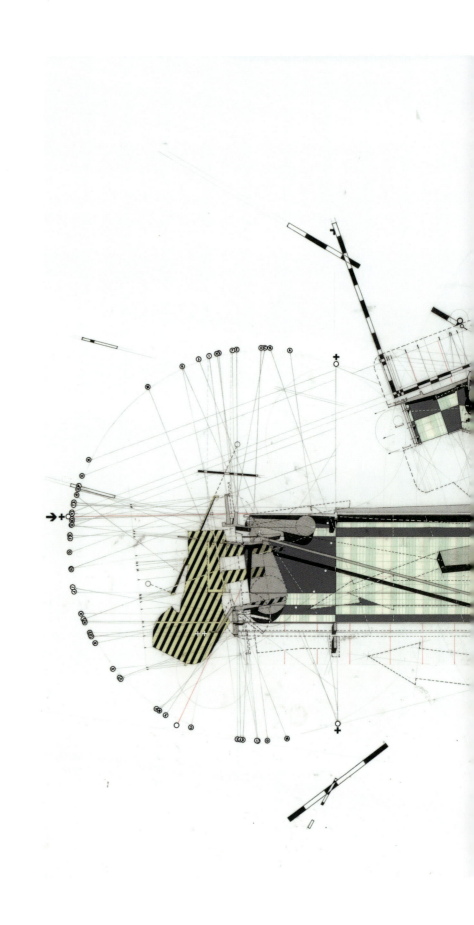

BRYAN CANTLEY
Fiducal Shifts 01, 2018
Ink and media on duralar, 51 × 76 cm (20 × 30 in)

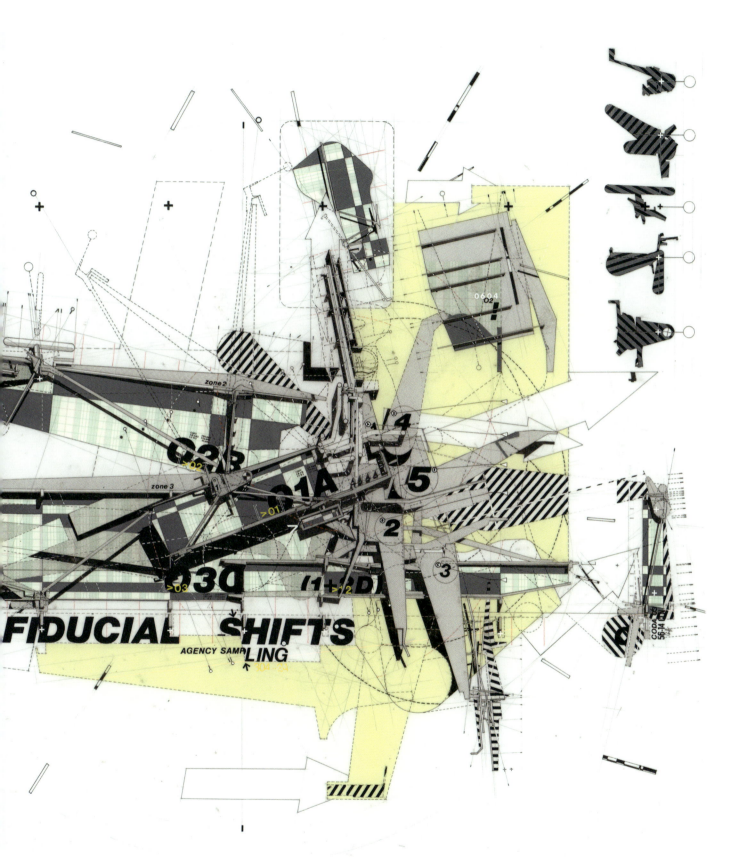

BRYAN CANTLEY
Fiducal Shifts 02, 2018
Ink and media on duralar, 51 × 76 cm (20 × 30 in)

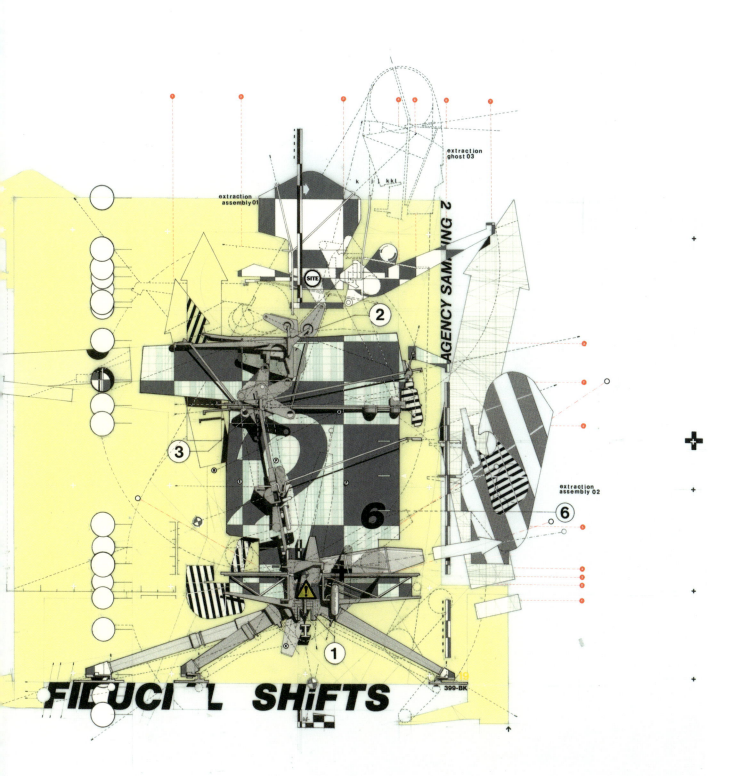

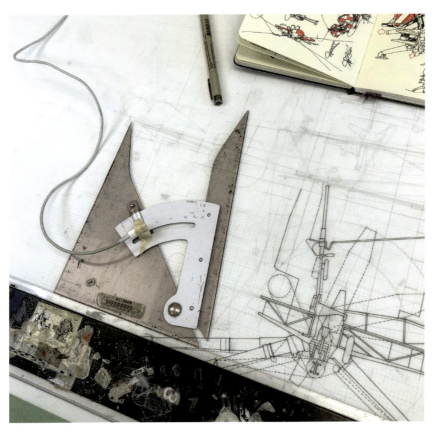

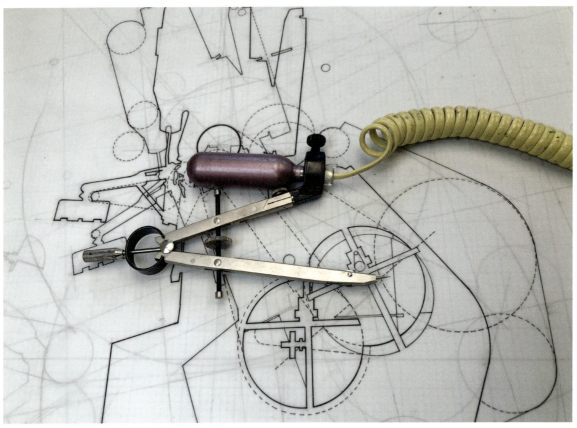

BRYAN CANTLEY

Photographs of gas-cylindered drawing, 2019
Ink on vellum

MICHAEL YOUNG
Earlier today Neil brought up the idea of dislocating the creative self,
and to me this seems a bit like that.
I wonder if you see it this way?

Taking certain aspects, trades, tricks of architectural drawing notations and asking how you make it talk to itself, as if those things were not there for us to interpret the drawing
but for the drawing to interpret itself, distancing its relationship to either the author creating it or to the audience that typically the architectural drawings are made for.
Am I making sense?

Because this is maybe a little what you're trying to do in terms of, when you say 'deconstructing', or the harvesting of data from one drawing in another.
It seems to be an effort to find this dislocation.

PERRY KULPER
Bryan, if you were to turn up at two o'clock in the morning in the drawing room,
would there be things happening in that drawing of their own volition – I mean, in terms of how we might think about the work conceptually?

BRYAN CANTLEY
Absolutely.
The way I envision these is that I don't see them as static entities.
Not to say that they are alive, but they are event spaces, the events are constantly repurposing themselves and interacting with each other in dialogue. I like to call this 'line politics'.
I see it as a very kinetic kind of condition of the graphic elements.
I think at any time, when I show up at the drawing room, I am going to get events that sometimes are shrouded.
I like your condition at two o'clock in the morning when they are playing when no one is looking … very much so.
That is the way that they are constructed.
That is the headspace that I am in when I construct them.

PERRY KULPER
Would at two o'clock in the morning the drawing know that something was referring to a shadow, for example? I'm trying to see if there is a way to get around the drawing being seen as an architectural event – because that is our referential structure.
The shadow allows us to apprehend or through reference to say, 'Ah! This has some technical or spatial consequence'.
But would the drawing know stuff like that?
Like a shadow refers back to a human being and the referential condition that we would link to and say: 'Ah! That is shadow and that means depth'.
What would the drawing know – in terms of its drawing and undrawing of itself?
What would the drawing recognise of itself?

BRYAN CANTLEY
I think initially the drawing would recognise shadow as an indicator of what it is, but parts of the drawing would after that realise that shadows are now shapes and forms and membranes for other graphic impregnation and they would recognise that the definition of shadow and the chronology of shadow would no longer be sacred and no longer standard and that new definitions are meant to be continuously happening.

PERRY KULPER
Bryan, I wonder if you might think also of the drawing as an evidence field?
If you worked more like a detective trying to invent or tease out the possible crimes of the drawings and perhaps the devices and instruments or notations enabling a probing of those pieces of evidence, if you could also extract yourself, if you authored from other geysers, an archaeologist setting up the ways in which the drawing would be scrutinised or a crime scene or whatever. The other thing I wonder is if the drawing could set up resistances that didn't allow you to encounter things that are more familiar or native to your arsenal …

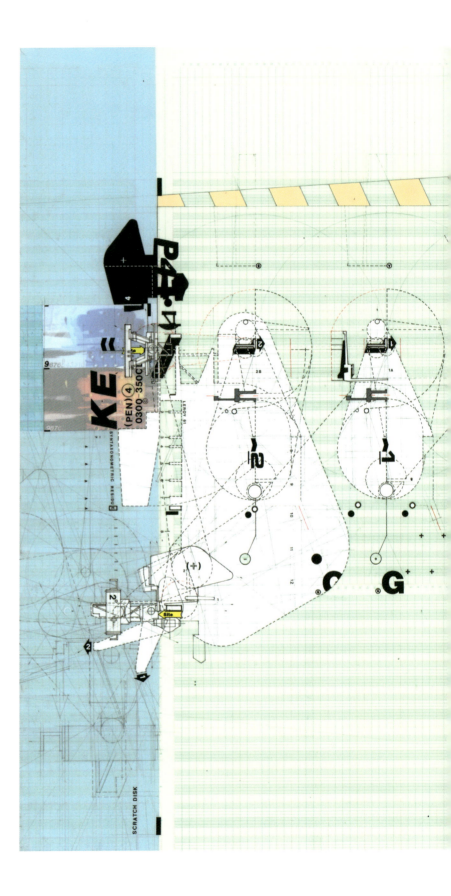

BRYAN CANTLEY
Syntaxonome Residue 01, 2019
Ink and media on duralar and ledger-book paper, 50 × 76 cm (20 × 30 in)

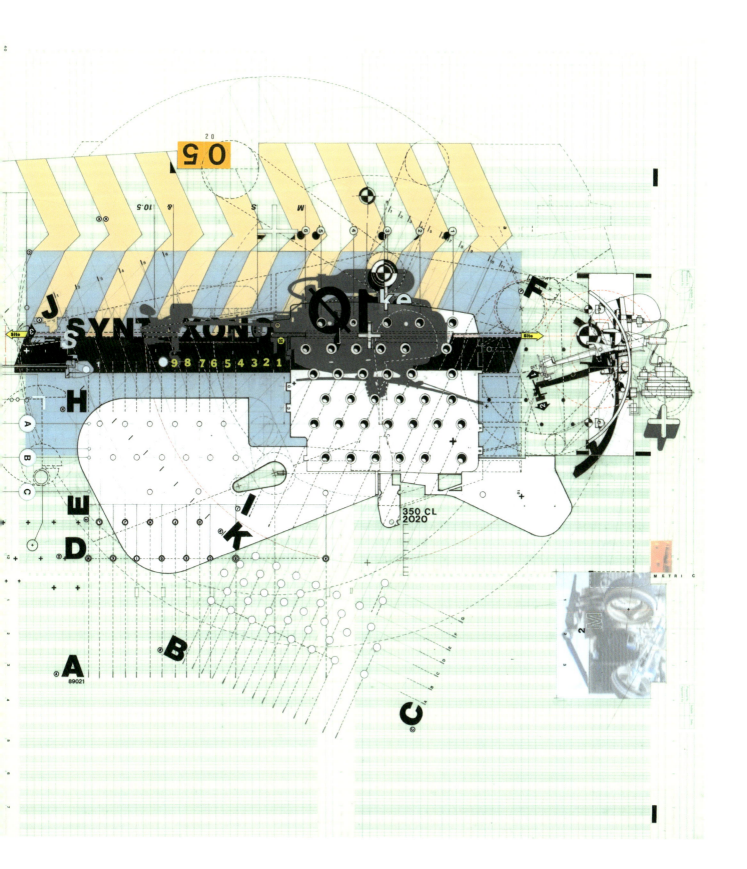

Perry Kulper
Multiple Languages of Representation

PERRY KULPER

Architectural drawings have allowed me to think in broader terms about how we work as architects and designers.

There's a body of thinking that I've explored through seminars and studio work with students at SCI-Arc and Michigan, and in my own work, trying to understand the etymologies, the ethics, the operational protocols, the references, and the directness and indirectness of design methods with respect to spatial production – to become more agile and more plastic in my world, more able to move conversations around.

So, the architectural drawing came first, and opening that up afforded me the opportunities to think about the primary means by which we work with design methods.

This drawing, the *David's Island Strategic Plot*, I often talk about it as the most important drawing, in terms of my development.

In the early days, I was doing a handful of things with drawings, trying to open up the ways in which I had been trained.
Orthography.
Parallel projection.
Perspective.
I was trying to find a way to keep multiple languages of representation, and sometimes heterogeneous ideas, in play, simultaneously. To invent ways of working on things that I otherwise didn't know how to work with. This allowed me to visualise things that were quite complex, things I had a hunch about or that were flat-out shots in the dark, and things that I was certain about.
As a result of this drawing, a whole series of drawings was made to elaborate things I understood and was trying to discover about my work.
The *David's Island Strategic Plot* is the most important set of drawn marks that I've made, where I began to understand the conventions of drawing that, in 1996 when this was made, didn't allow me a way to work on certain kinds of interests.
So, I set up a sort of prototype set of marks which are familiar now where I was trying to use notation, indexes and figurative mark-making, trying to build a world which talked about temporal changes, in different phases where things might occur.
And that was probably the pivotal moment for me in terms of our discussion about architectural drawing.

At that time, I couldn't figure out a way to hold the range of heterogeneous ideas in place simultaneously for a project.
So, in this drawing, the *Central California History Museum: Thematic Drawing*, I just said:
Well, why not?
Why not try to produce a visual archive, a diary, or repository of the things that might belong to the discussion of the development of this museum?

This drawing moves between figures, notations, indexes and quotations by others, to trading on the Greek muses as inspiration for a contemporary museum. And then the cryptic drawings, one of which is here, is a kind of DNA, a genetic or chromosomal drawing for the same project.
The marks are not yet formal, but they have a sort of loaded-up intelligence.
They're relational algorithms in terms of what they might enable in the production of spatial accounts, relative to the thematic interests of the project.

MICHAEL YOUNG

I'm so happy to see the real thing! We've all had this experience where you live with something for a long time as an image in a book or as an image on the screen. And then you actually see the real thing – and I don't have some kind of fetishised fascination with material reality or am somehow sentimental of things 'touched by the hand'…
but it's really funny, things like scale matter. And the ephemeral shifts of the Mylar.
I remember during my first job I worked on Mylar at a landscape office, drawing hexagons

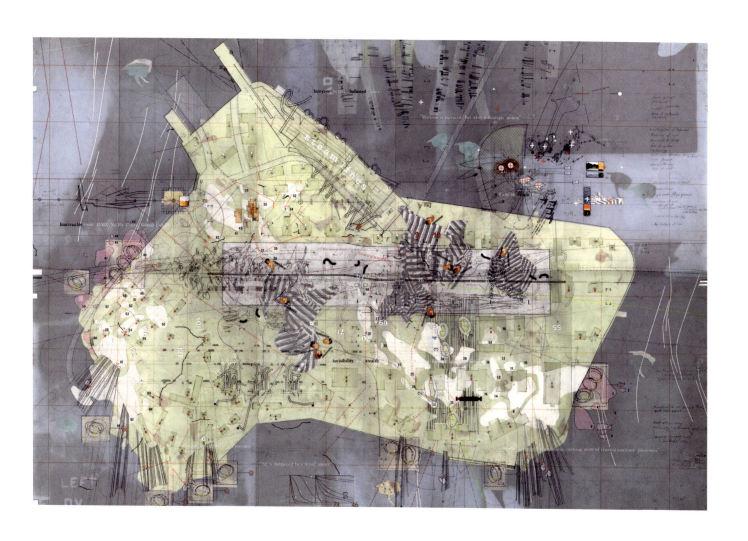

PERRY KULPER

David's Island Strategic Plot, 1996
Mylar, text, found imagery, X-rays, foil, photographs, transfer letters
and film, cut paper, tape, ink, graphite, 61 × 91 cm (24 × 36 in)

PERRY KULPER
20.80, v.02, 2021
Mylar, found paper, tape, graphite, 61 × 91 cm (24 × 36 in)

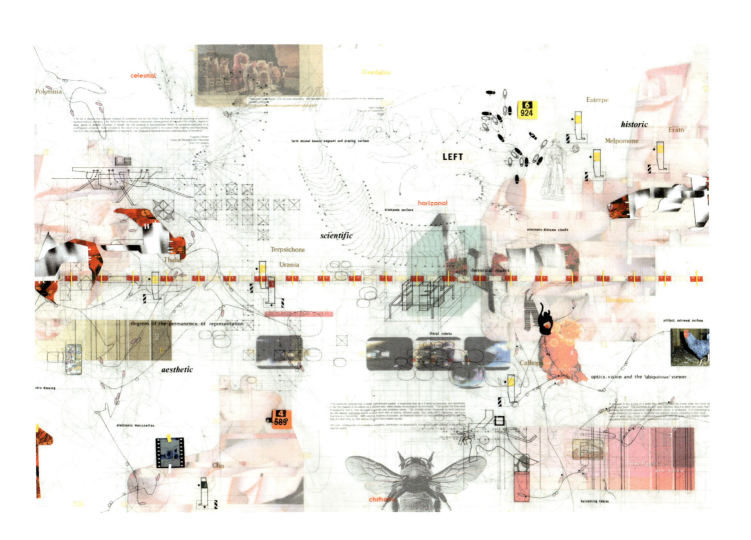

PERRY KULPER

Central California History Museum: Thematic Drawing, 2001
Mylar, assorted found imagery, cut paper, acetate, transfer letters,
tape, graphite, ink, 61 × 91 cm (24 × 36 in)

for other people to fill in with information about plant species. But I would get into the Mylar layering because you get these soft-focus shifts, so it's a totally aesthetic fascination.
Is this the one that you feel launches this set of investigations?

PERRY KULPER
Well, there's a second desert house – you may remember the *House in Borrego Springs, C.A., Aspectical Probes* that I made in 1992. They started to open up the drawing a little bit. But the *David's Island Strategic Plot* is the one where I realised I could hold multiple languages of representation in place, simultaneously.
I could work as a designer by working out diagrams, that might talk with appropriate font types, which was black, which was white, which could talk to pictorial images, and other things.
This was something that I could never do in perspectives, sections or plans.

MICHAEL YOUNG
You need the plane.

PERRY KULPER
Yeah.
So, these marks got made before the other things on the drawing.
I also like that things could be in and out of phase with one another.

ANTHONY MOREY
The way you're describing the process, how much of it is pre-set and how much of it is developed?
You have people like Bryan [Cantley], he does little things separately, and then he puts them all together. The last pass is to bring it all together and edit the drawing. Or, you have other people that just work on the whole and – like wrangling squirrels, you know – they're just trying to control the chaos.
When you worked on this, was it part of a series of, say, ten drawings that you were working on before this, or was it all figured out here, in this one drawing [*David's Island*]?

PERRY KULPER
The way I worked on it was to research islands for about two and a half weeks, everything I could lay my hands on, without making heavy judgements. The competition was for an island. Then I identified 14 key ideas that I wanted to work on, like:
panoramic and panoptic vision;
remoteness;
things to do with nautical cartography;
mythical sea folklore;
military suppression and regimes.
These were the kinds of key ideas.
I tried to set up the drawing to work on those things. This was when I realised the ideas I had would require a temporal choreography of some kind.
I thought, I need to figure out a way to get that in play, early, as a genetic prototype for the drawing so that it could emerge. I also used the drawing to invent programme-like elements and relationships to carry and structure engagement with the ideas for
the project.
I was inventing programmes such as the 'silver shell surface', an 'axis of mutiny', 'no-fly zones' and 'polished metamorphic rock gardens' that refer to the great Zen Garden, Ryoanji, 'landings for mythical sea travellers', and so on.
There is also a kind of geo-fluidic landscape condition that floods tactically selected things that was part of the equation.
For that, I spilled water on the floor, mapped it and dropped the mapping on the drawing because I needed a kind of lack of my control, relationally. I wanted to work that out through the drawing ...

ANTHONY MOREY
Really?

PERRY KULPER
Yeah, you know, on the vinyl floor in the kitchen,
spill the water and map that, and then just drop it in the drawing wherever it hit.
I worked with that.
I was just trying to work out how the water might behave. I also dropped black-and-white striped fabric on a Xerox machine because I knew I wanted camouflaged surfaces, for example. So, I added fabric ... I was Xeroxing

PERRY KULPER

Central California History Museum: Thematic Drawing, 2001
Mylar, assorted found imagery, cut paper, acetate, transfer letters,
tape, graphite, ink, 61 × 91 cm (24 × 36 in)

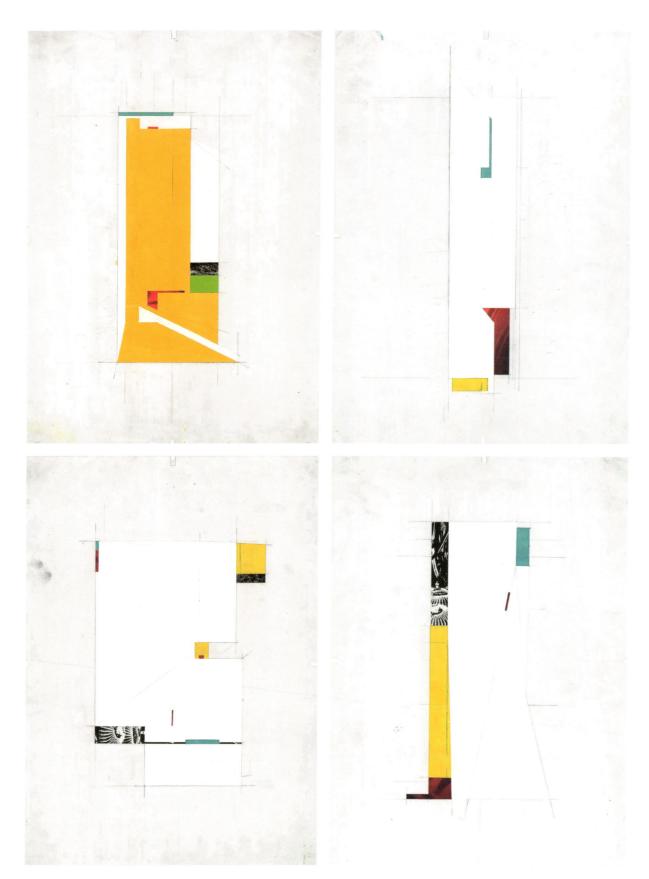

PERRY KULPER
House in Borrego Springs, CA, V.02: Aspectival Probes, 1992
Mylar, found paper, gesso, acrylic, graphite, 61 × 46 cm (24 × 18 in)

that, cutting things out, scaling things, Xeroxing again.
So, working things out through the drawing.

ANTHONY MOREY
There are many physical layers to the drawing.
At what point can you make the decision in that process as to when an object is behind and an object is in front of the Mylar?
You could have done all that as one, solidifying it into a singular thing.
At what point was the decision made to keep it as solid back paper with Mylar on top to produce transparency?

PERRY KULPER
That's just something that I bought, 50 sheets of Mylar, and somehow that gets installed and becomes a kind of default register for that kind of decision-making.

NATALIJA SUBOTINCIC
Is the back layer X-rays of animals?

PERRY KULPER
Yes, those are animal X-rays.

NATALIJA SUBOTINCIC
Can we put it up against the light on the window?

PERRY KULPER
They might fall apart but we can surely try and do it. You could just put it against the clear window …

ANTHONY MOREY
Secret X-rays.

PERRY KULPER
I also have about 80 of those 8.5-by-11-inch yellow notepads that accompany this drawing as I am working through the project.

ANTHONY MOREY
Are there any more hidden secrets within these layers? It looks like they've got another X-ray there.

MICHAEL YOUNG
I think they probably all have some hidden secrets.

PERRY KULPER
Like these figures, I used to cut out all the parts of the drawings by hand.
I might also selectively cut some things from another drawings, and might think, well, that's an interesting part of a surface …
I also occasionally pick up random pieces that might be lying around. Well, that could be quite an interesting part of another surface realm. But that's not a secret really.

MARK WEST
Does anyone else feel anything like what I feel?
I'll describe what happens to me when I look at Perry's drawings.
I feel it in my body somewhere here [points at his stomach],
a tremendous disturbance and tension.
I don't know, this doesn't happen to me under normal circumstances when looking at a drawing.
I can't describe — it's a bodily experience that I can't describe properly.
I can't describe it in language, but I'm vibrating all over when I look at these things.

It's almost like there is a tease, there is something that I could satisfy if I could just get at it.
It's a physical reaction, a real physical and mental emotional thing.
I am emotionally agitated in the presence of these things, in all of this stuff.
All of that stuff too.
I don't know …
I'm sorry to be so inarticulate,
but I'm curious whether anyone else has anything like this reaction,
or is it just me?

ANTHONY MOREY
Perry, what I'd like to know is how do you regard your drawings yourself?

PERRY KULPER
I remember having a conversation with Neil Denari. We were talking about the drawing just allowing you to do certain kinds of work on certain kinds of things.
The drawing for me has become more artefactual over the years.

So, the artefactual qualities interest me not so much in terms of what you see, but as having potential as an artefact, regardless of a designer's intent.
So, that is something else that is changing over time. But that's how I think about the drawings, they just let me do *stuff*.

MARK WEST
Do you have your own sense of authorship about them?

PERRY KULPER
No.

MARK WEST
I didn't think so.

PERRY KULPER
I make the drawings,
but I'm in a total world.
There's no external world when I'm working on them, and I don't feel like I'm authoring.
It is little bit like the drawing is blossoming, emerging.
You know, it's not intuitive, but I am in negotiation with it.
I don't think of them as top down.

MICHAEL YOUNG
Part of this is it being a thing, it being authored, but not authored to determine its interpretation.
Mark's nervous sensorial excitation might be because the drawings become worlds to and of themselves.
These marks here on the drawing — circular or elliptical forms working off tangents that are continuities that allow those lines to become controlled as they meander and wander.
But then suddenly, I'm over here and I'm seeing that, at a miniscule scale, the same language is going on and these now are the …

PERRY KULPER
… these are the Greek muse references …

MICHAEL YOUNG
These are the beginnings of a figurative image.
They are the start of the bird motels, they are the start of those kinds of figurations and yet they're absolutely linked back into the original marks of the drawing.

PERRY KULPER
Those marks that you're referring to, Michael, those are muses. They operate in and through the museum. Here they are still cryptic. You can see the floating bird on top …

MARK WEST
How many years are there between the bird motels and the *David's Island* and museum drawings?

PERRY KULPER
David's Island was worked on in 1996, if recollection serves, the museum was worked on in 2001. The bird motels are the last three years, so that would be 15 years between the two.

MARK WEST
So mysterious and weird where these things come from.
I don't know if I'm speaking a bit for myself, but I'm imagining that it's a similar experience that these things arrive seemingly of their own volition, although obviously we're making them make decisions.
But they arrive.
You recognise them as something meaningful, useful and real — you keep them and then years later …
Somehow there's this weird power that just keeps coming. A premonition, like Nat Chard's flung paint … you go back to those earlier drawings made with, you know, a super-controlled airbrush, and now you see in retrospect that he was channelling drops of paint or something.
I mean, we're not alone in having this experience, I think.
It happens to lots of people who work in this way, which is where you cut the mooring lines to reason just enough for you to determine that there's this other capacity.
It's a capacity of human *sensorium* or imagination, or whatever it is.
It is generative, surprising, mysterious.

PERRY KULPER IN COLLABORATION WITH KYLE REICH
Triptychs, Domes + Still Life(s), Ryoanji, Reconstruction, 2021
Digital file

PERRY KULPER IN COLLABORATION WITH SAUMON OBOUDIYAT

El Dorado: Floating Bird Motel, Peachcraft'd Overtones: Embellishing Shaped Evidence, 2016
Digital file

PERRY KULPER

Mark, would you say that habituation or having habits would flatten the things that you're after in terms of certain kinds of vividness?
I would argue that, perceptually, habitual participation with things moves them into the background?

MARK WEST

Habit is the enemy

PERRY KULPER

In your world.

MARK WEST

Habit is the enemy that never gives up.

PERRY KULPER

But could you deal with habitual things and keep them alive in your world? That would be an interesting thing ...
repetitive acts, pieces of evidence that trigger themselves over and through time and only through acclimation to them do they release energy.

Among other things, I'd like to understand knowledge and what's being constructed by the recursive acts in the practice that I've tried to produce.

I'm also interested in word play and trying to identify other kinds of tendencies within things like the architectural drawing.
I often return to Wallace Stevens's poem *Thirteen Ways of Looking at a Blackbird*, both numerically but also cumulatively – the point is that the stanzas are always talking implicitly about a blackbird and somehow pointing to the blackbird in enough ways to reveal the possible relational assemblies to which a blackbird, as a thing, belongs.
And so similarly I'm now trying to think about and design 13 bird motels, in which I use the 13 bird motels of different kinds to talk about the ways in which I practise, teach and frame my own engagement with the world.

Natalija Subotincic
Stabilising the Evanescent Thought

NATALIJA SUBOTINCIC

I have been fascinated by Sigmund Freud's work rooms, the consulting room and study. Freud would work during the day in the consulting room, and in the evening, he would work late into the night in the study. He smoked cigars – so these rooms would have smelt of cigars.
Next to cigar-smoking, he said his greatest passion (or obsession) was collecting.
He arranged all of his collection, over 2300 images, objects, antiquities, paintings and photographs, only within these two rooms. He also never really wrote about the collection.

So, I am interested in looking at what he chose not to speak about.

In his earlier scientific days, Freud drew a lot and I find the drawings incredibly spatial, including the notes that went along with them.
As I started reading his writings, and looking and discovering his work, I found his drawings.
I think they are just great drawings. He drew less later in his life when he developed his psychoanalytic practice, but by then he was well into collecting.

And then the thing that got me very excited was discovering all the drawings he did of the different rooms he lived in.
I thought, oh my god, he is totally connected to the space that he is in.
A lot of these drawings are in letters to friends. In one letter written to his fiancée Martha Bernays he drew the plan of his room and gave it plan titles – the 'animal side' and the 'vegetative side'.
So, I started drawing his rooms.

I went to both museums, measured the rooms in Vienna, measured the objects in London, and I put the objects and the rooms back together again.

Because the rooms and the objects don't exist together any more, this reconstruction of mine is mostly based on Edmund Engelman's 1938 photographs of Freud's Vienna rooms. These show the height of the collection, just before he moved to London.
While drawing the plans and the elevations, I discovered all this stuff that was going on in the rooms, that had to do with how he choreographed the patients in relation to where he'd put particular objects.
Then I thought, I've got to do another set of drawings that start to unpack the discoveries that I made while doing the drafted plan, section and elevation drawings.
Because the rooms are full of colour, everything is very tactile in the spaces and I just didn't feel that drafting could help me explore what I found. So, I felt I had to move out of drafting and into painting.

Freud developed three architectures of the psyche, as he calls it, three realms.
There is the 'External World', which exists outside our bodies, but is perceived and sensed by the body.
There is the 'Inner World', which exists within the deepest recesses of the body and is understood as the unconscious.
And caught between these two is the 'Outer World' – the space of consciousness. Freud was always labelled a dualist, but I think he is mostly fascinated by what hovers between things.
The Inner World, or the space of the unconscious, according to Freud is strictly spatial and time is absent here, which drove me crazy, and I tried to think of what this would mean …
Have I ever experienced a purely spatial world?
As well, he clarified that within the unconsciousness concrete concepts can exist but impressions of them have to arrive at a level of consciousness, and until they do, you can't articulate them verbally.
In other words, there are no words in the unconscious … it's spatial.
There are no ways to speak about the unconscious – it is only when things return to a level of consciousness that we can then articulate them verbally.

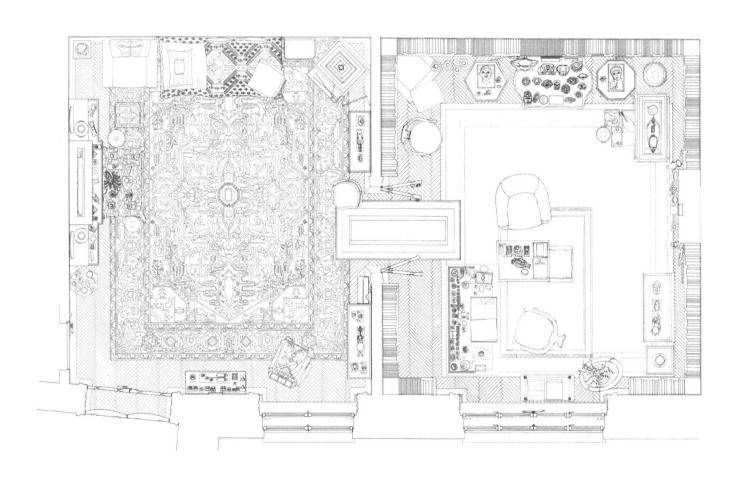

NATALIJA SUBOTINCIC

Plan of Sigmund Freud's Cabinet – Consulting Room and Study at Berggasse 19 in Vienna, 1998–2001
Ink on Mylar, 1:10 scale, 91 × 122 cm (36 × 48 in)

NATALIJA SUBOTINCIC

The Scholar's Constructions in Analysis, 2012
Photocollage and acrylic on canvas, 56 × 99 cm (22 × 39 in)

So, I started making paintings of the rooms and the relationships I discovered that were going on in these rooms.
I had photographed and documented everything before making the drafted drawings of the two rooms.
So, when I began the paintings, I drew everything right on to the blank canvas, but this took a very long time for each painting — especially the carpets. Later on, I began to use photographic collages printed on to the canvas as a base, and then I would paint sections in, or I painted large sections over.
The reason I was doing the paintings was that I was imagining making a film with them.
I had stills and photographs of the paintings, but I felt there had to be motion in these.

LAURA ALLEN
Was there a storyboard for the film? How was the film structured?

NATALIJA SUBOTINCIC
I didn't really have a storyboard, I wanted it to be like a dream.
The storyboard turned out to be the paintings themselves — they each depict different scenes.
I photographed the paintings in lots of detail.
I also photographed the paintings coming into being as well, first sketch-like for the underdrawing, and then later more precise as they got painted and finished.
I wanted the film to be like a dream without any clear narrative. The drawings and paintings were used to create a short film in an attempt to become more immersed in an animation of this terrain. I wanted the film to wander through the paintings and for the paintings to suggest connections to each other.
I just had this strong feeling that the paintings should move, that the images should move and not be still.
Or for you to be able to feel or sense the texture of the fabric, the carpet, as a way of being in the space, as a way of bringing people into the space more than just looking at a painting on the wall.

MARK WEST
Didn't Freud talk to the objects?

NATALIJA SUBOTINCIC
Yes, he greeted the ones on his desk every morning. He referred to them as his audience and he got to a point where, when his family would go away on holiday during the summer, he would bring a large portion of the collection with him.
He could not work without them.
So, they would rent a house out in the countryside and they would always have a separate room for him to work in.
He really could not write without them being around him. The antiquities were essential to his writing.
For him the collection was a way of folding the Outer World and the External World into his inner sanctum — into the world he was actually constructing here within these two rooms.

Freud talks about 'construction' being a more appropriate word than 'interpretation' for what he is doing. He says that 'construction' is an assembly of a number of elements, structures, memories and associations.
And for me, this suggests an open and relational space of assembly, which to a large degree is what the rooms are about.
They are completely a relational space of assembly.

I recently came across this quote by Gregory Bateson, which clarified things for me and resonates with my understanding of this work and its current trajectory.
He said, 'The observer must be included within the focus of observation, and what can be studied is always a relationship or an infinite regress of relationships. Never a "thing".'[1]
I see these drawings and paintings as constructions being done in order to better understand the role Freud's rooms played during the analytic sessions for both his patients and for Freud himself.
And I use the term 'construction' in a Freudian sense.
For me, the activity of construction ponders an open and relational space of assembly, as opposed to the term 'interpretation' which hones in on an individual element, subject or object.

NATALIJA SUBOTINCIC

Sigmund Freud Pens Athena's Castration, or Silenced, 2011
Acrylic on canvas, 41 × 51 cm (16 × 20 in)

Initially I understood my work as a drafting, drawing, painting project.
But lately, my understanding is sort of moving towards understanding drawing as a material practice or situated practice — because the constructions that I am making have literally drawn me into a situatedness within these rooms …
To be within Freud's rooms is to sense the relationships of the experience that these rooms had, with the materiality, the effects of light and colour, the physicality and the psychological aura of the assembled collection.
Where he and his patients were able to experience these rooms directly, I have only experienced them remotely, through the objects and by drawing and painting them. The painting studies have helped me to conjure a certain embeddedness or immersion into the nature of his rooms, and an awareness of their importance to Freud himself.

Freud had explained to Hilda Doolittle, who was a patient of his in 1934, that the statues and figurines are a way of stabilising the evanescent thought or keeping it from escaping altogether.
During a session with a patient, he would go to his study, pick up one of the statues and come back and talk using the statue to illustrate or hold on to the thought.
The statues were essential to him, not only to his writing but in relation to how he discussed issues with his patients.

MARK DORRIAN

I have the sense there is a kind of mediumship with the statues, so that the speech moves through them. The logic of transference is partly to do with not being able to visually see the source of the analyst's voice.
It seems like the objects transform into the visual counterpart.

NATALIJA SUBOTINCIC

Yes, the objects are the stand-in.

NEIL SPILLER

It is also that the statues are like elements in a memory theatre. When you touch them, you link into some sort of rhetorical expression.

NAT CHARD

Also, with these statues on his desk, there is an ontological shift so that those things that were made as statues with a certain possibility 2000 years ago become instrumental didactic tools of a brand-new science of psychology. Is there a parallel in that to the ontological shift in the readymades in Duchamp's work? The sense of an unintended possibility of things.

MICHAEL YOUNG

The readymades as the sacralisation of the profane and Freud's statues as the profanation of the sacred. You are pulling one thing out of one realm and revaluing it by pushing it into the other.

MARK WEST

All of Freud's objects involve an old mythology, so there is a fixed story and fixed attributes that carry forwards with different meanings. But they are not disconnected from their stories and their attributes and powers.

NEIL SPILLER

Mythologies are always about various aspects of the human condition, which are more enduring than the societies they came from.

NAT CHARD

But in the case of Duchamp's urinal, its original purpose is not insignificant either.

MARK WEST

It's a much shorter story, I thought, the one of the urinal.

NATALIJA SUBOTINCIC

Well, they are both human conditions …

PERRY KULPER

I was thinking about the withdrawal of Freud and clients, and the objects themselves constructing kinds of cosmologies that are maybe independent of his memory theatre. And I am wondering if anyone began to draw from the world that they construct at three in the morning when Freud was sleeping elsewhere? They have a set of accounts as well, that don't have anything to do with a patient coming in and him picking up one of them and so on.

I was just wondering on a representational level if the things that you do still have to do with an account of pictorialisation and dream-like states back through Freud or through some parallel construction to him. If the body was withdrawn, if the object were dreaming about worlds that don't have anything to do with the way we might understand or reflect on things scientifically, about how dreams are constructed, and so on … It just seems like there might be a rich representational territory when a point of view is withdrawn.

NATALIJA SUBOTINCIC
Or the point of view is from the objects themselves.

PERRY KULPER
There might not be views in such a realm if there is no human being.

NATALIJA SUBOTINCIC
The paintings are a physical depiction but also a psychical depiction.
They are trying to reach out to the psychic terrain that Freud has set up, especially looking at the kind of objects and what he put in what groupings, and where these groupings are in relation to his position, or in relation to the patient.

RIET EECKHOUT
Nada, can you elaborate on your collection of objects, the chicken bones, the sticks? How does that sit in relation to your interest in Freud's relationship with his objects?

NATALIJA SUBOTINCIC
Well, collecting things myself and studying his collections has contributed to moving my practice from a strict drawing practice towards drawing as a material or situated practice. When Covid hit, we were all essentially confined to our houses, so because of this my work turned inwards. I'm also a lifelong collector and my collections have never been far from the Freud drawing project. My own passions for collecting are partly responsible for my initial attraction to Freud's collection within his rooms.

For seven years, I collected the bones of everything I ate, with the full intention of using this culinary refuse to create further projects.
The reason I started collecting these was that I looked at my dinner plate one evening and I thought, these are so beautiful, why am I throwing them in the garbage?
After a few years of collecting and cleaning, down to each individual bone, I asked myself: 'What am I doing?'
By cleaning the configurations I found on the plate until they fell apart to individual bones, I was in fact denying the configurations that attracted me to collecting in the first place. These dinner remains or configurations had something to do with me, held hidden evidence of how I ate, and what was left of that act on my plate. So, then I stopped cleaning until they fell apart and started cleaning the configurations but kept them intact.

RIET EECKHOUT
There is a certain point in your book, *Never Speak With Your Mouth Full*, where you talk about the collection of these bones and that you rendered them mute, decapacitated, unable to perform.
There is something about allowing the bones, how you arrange them, allowing them to be expressive in a different manner compared to when they were inside the chicken.
When I see you talk, draw and produce a film about Freud's object collection, I am wondering, is this a way to find your own relationship with object collections?

NATALIJA SUBOTINCIC
Well, one of the reasons I started reading Freud was to figure out why I was collecting bones …

RIET EECKHOUT
Interesting notion you mentioned when you considered the bones you collected over all those years, you said you rendered them mute and later made them expressive again when you made the dining table.

NATALIJA SUBOTINCIC

What Is Not Heard but May Be Seen, 2012
Photocollage, acrylic and PanPastel on canvas, 96 × 122 cm (38 × 48 in)

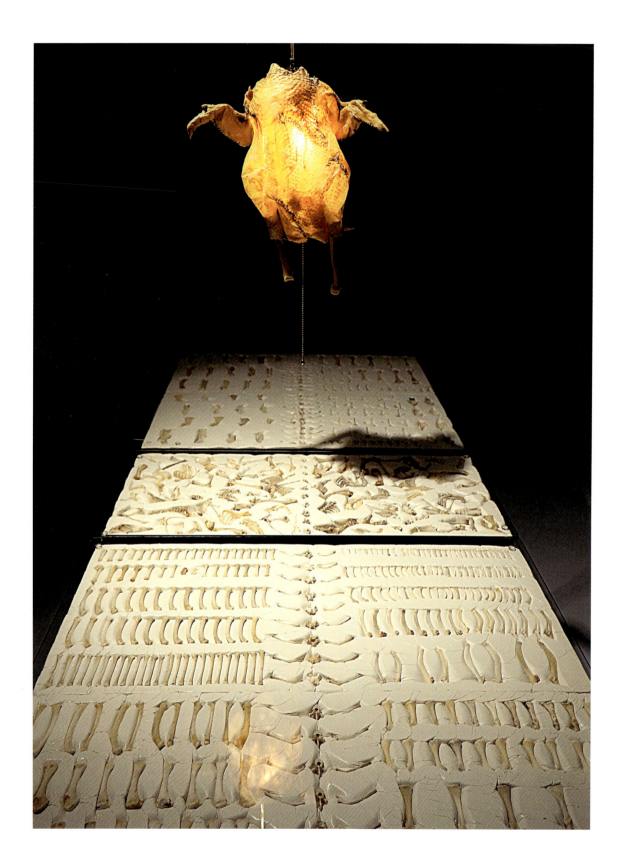

NATALIJA SUBOTINCIC

Chicken Bone Dining Table with Lamp, 1989–96
Chicken skin and bones, white Portland cement, glass, 203 × 81 cm (80 × 32 in)

NATALIJA SUBOTINCIC

Yes, the bones were rendered mute because they were just sitting there 'silent' in their storage boxes, in separate little compartments with cardboard separations.
And I thought I have to stop collecting and do something with these now – so the first thing was to take a taxidermy course. I X-rayed a chicken that I bought in the grocery store and then I peeled the skin off, froze it and then I proceeded for next ten weeks to macerate the flesh off the carcass. It is a procedure where you keep it in a solution that rots the flesh so you can peel the meat off the skeleton.
I did it this way because if you put it in a bug house – this is how you normally do it – the chicken will fall apart into its individual bones and you lose all of the tendons and cartilage that hold the bones together. Again, I wanted an articulated chicken carcass.

Before I began to macerate the chicken though, I made a plaster cast of it, and injected that with expanding foam.
So, I ended up with a foam chicken, in the identical shape of the original chicken I started with.

After the skeleton was clean, I took the skin out of the freezer, tanned it, and stretched it back over the foam chicken and let it dry. So, the skin now looked like the original chicken. I took all the foam out and then put the bones back inside the skin and placed a light on the inside of the skeleton, so the bones were projected on to the skin of the chicken. This became our dining lamp.

NAT CHARD

I have looked at lots of taxidermy, but I have never before come across an example of a taxidermised oven-ready chicken!

NATALIJA SUBOTINCIC

I took the store-bought chicken into the taxidermy class I was enrolled in at this small eco-college that I was teaching at. Everybody in the class was working with road-kill animals, and I came in with my plastic wrapped chicken, and they all looked at me and said it was disgusting …
The next obvious project, following the lamp, was to make a dining table for my family. I decided to make it entirely out of the chicken bones from my larger bone collection. So, I laid out the individual bones anatomically on the table with the posterior and anterior along the long sides going from the head of the table at one end to the tail at the other, with the spine bones running down the centre. The special panel of the cleaned configurations sits in the middle of the table interrupting this 'scientific' anatomical layout.

RIET EECKHOUT

There is something about the agency of the objects and how you view and evaluate them and bring them back into the world again.

NATALIJA SUBOTINCIC

Or how I construct a world out of those objects …

A few years ago, while walking my dog, I began collecting little sticks that washed up on the shore with the tide.
Small, insignificant objects that we usually don't even notice …
And I hadn't noticed them until then.
I was intrigued by their figures and was moved by how they reminded me of my bone collection, and even Freud's statuettes.

In March 2020, during the Covid confinement, I began mounting my collection of bones and small sticks. This past fall, I acquired several storage cabinets to house this growing collection. Because of their fragility and sheer accumulation, I needed to protect them.
As I began filling the cabinets and arranging them in our house, I realised the next step of this project should actually be to assemble my own room.
Even though I never set out to make a room, I think the situatedness of my drawings and paintings that I spoke about earlier pointed me in this direction.
And I can't help but wonder if the room has partly come about because of my desire to also somehow situate the Freud drawing and painting explorations within a context beyond themselves.
My habits of collecting, and the Freud room

NATALIJA SUBOTINCIC

Cabinet of Consulting, 2020–present
Room construction and assemblage of Freud paintings and the author's
personal collection of sticks and bones, 300 × 300 cm (118 × 118 in)
Ceci n'est pas un musée, Montréal

studies, have been lifelong parallel partners that are now converging in this room, which I see as a prospect or meditation on the latent tactility of drawing.

Overall, in my work with the collections and rooms, I've noticed a slow and progressive dissolution of attention on things moving towards assemblages or relations between things …

For example, from the individual bones to the configurations, or from Freud's objects to his assembled groupings and rooms. And now from my individual drawings and paintings to their assembly within this new room, which I am calling the *Cabinet of Consulting*. In unpacking Bateson's infinite regress of relationships, I am searching for what is disguised or hidden by our attention to individual things, especially, between the thingness of a drawing, and its situatedness within a larger ensemble.

In this new room construction, the *Cabinet of Consulting*, I'm trying to grasp at what exists between Freud's assemblages and my own.

1 Gregory Bateson, *Steps to an Ecology of Mind: Collected Essays in Anthropology, Psychiatry, Evolution, and Epistemology* (Chicago, IL: University of Chicago Press, 2000), p. 246.

Keyword Phrases

BRYAN CANTLEY

KINETIC CARTOGRAPHIES

I use the phrase 'kinetic cartographies' to describe the fluctuating natural system of implied movement that effects (if not produces) the drawing linguistics. This is *Mechudzu* – a term that lightly outlines the dichotomy of the organic growth pattern of mechanical systems.

The *work* is animate in structure and nature ... as are the *components* ... as is the *drawing* itself. Though the artefacts are technically static, they describe a set of conditions, chronologies and politics that are envisioned as continuously peripatetic, never singular in time, nor at rest in their field of denotations. They are drawn and intended to be read/occupied as a set of kinetic circumstances and timings, a biologically influenced dance of synthetic apparatuses and (their) notations. These drawing typologies are impacted by what I call 'line politics', a system in which each component either acknowledges, resolves, or confronts conflicts and frictions within this society of two-dimensional cacophonies.

The notations (the taxonometric, or *live* data that define each factor) are equally driven by their own set of kinematic ruling structures. Both serve as an autonomous group, the policies that empower the overall drawing. They are agents that dynamise the atmosphere, conceived as the flickerings of a constantly metamorphosing spatial condition around, in, and on each drawing element. They might be seen as reverberating clouds of pulsating data that simultaneously demarcate and obscure the intelligibility of each constituent of this thickened dance.

Nothing is at rest. Each drawing contains 'circulation' and at the same time is circulating, on and within itself. The attempt is to create a depictive arena that we might anticipate transforming at the blink of an eye – one that constantly refuses a stabilised compositional stance but at the same time takes place on a flat surface with only physically inert components. It is the plane of denotation, detonated.

It is hoped that the reader/inhabitant of the drawings understands that there is nothing static, nothing rooted and nothing stable to offer a completely definable responsive framework. The context itself is in flux – it adapts to and provokes adaptation by its inhabitants. It is not unlike water. It assumes the shape of its vessel, and yet can erode the most solid of materials over time and with immense force. Even the most obstinate yields. The drawings attempt to denote these somewhat elusive components and their equally slippery governing systems. It is only through these graphic kinetic implications that such ideas of drawing inertias, motile contexts and their pulsating notational conveyances can be manifested. Information fields in the drawings repurpose themselves as they engage in complex spatial (and therefore) graphic politics. One entity is always aware of the trajectories and implications of the others, although levels of interactions and deformations are not always calculated events.

These drawings are mappings of such interactions and explorations of the zoning of fluid positioning and malleable identities.

GRAPHIC (IL)LOGICS

Some of the rules can be bent, others can be broken.
Morpheus, *The Matrix*

There has always been a set of organic logics that resonate through, inform, and deform my drawing. The ruling systems that code, generate and shape the work are as much a component of the drawing as are the strokes and figures. The symbiotic relation between the graphics and the environment in which they operate are critical to the development of the work.

The logics/rules of their construction are copious, but we can identify two main kinds:
1. ordinances established before the drawing; and
2. rules that develop as the drawing is cultivated, examining new associations that materialise from the exploration.

Both logics assume the conditions apply to the drawing as opposed to only any identifiable object that may be part of its pursuit – the drawing of a drawing, as opposed to the drawing of an object.

Type 1: Established constraints
These graphic experiments always start with a set of policies, which are typically fleshed out in various sketchbooks and writings. These establish the parameters in which the drawing will operate – a system of guides, maps, definitions, proposals and constraints that require the drawing to respond to an externalised set of issues (not vastly different from programme, site and code issues in construction). They do not dictate the language of the drawing per se; rather they provide defined controls, goals, and attitudes adopted by the drawing and its components. Any community needs laws and rules of order to thrive and be harmoniously productive. These are the codes of the drawing; they are the seeds carrying the DNA from which any given speculation can emerge. They attempt to balance the equation. They are equivalent to the staff in musical notation.

Type 2: Evolutionary procedures
In addition to the pre-established conventions, each drawing births a secondary set of rules – these develop from the discoveries of new legislations, frictions and engagements that are constructed as the drawing evolves. They are mutations of the original code, amplifying and contradicting original programme commands. These rubrics respond to ebb and flow – they are highly organic, reacting to the emergent conditions and often challenging or breaking some of the stratagems established within the first set. Ultimately, they work in harmony to support the pursuit and evolution of the drawing's potentialities and inquiries. They create unbalance in the equation. These are the notes that can break free from recognised patterns of structure, and that can respond organically to harmonies previously established.

It is perhaps the disharmony of the two (il)logics that animates and gives force to the work. Or perhaps a better way of thinking of this might be that the logic-conflicts provide an opportunity for inquiry free from the burden of proof.

RELATIONAL STRUCTURING

As a term, 'relational structuring' is connected to the principles of actor-network theory, advanced by Bruno Latour and others. ANT asserts that all 'things' in the social realm and natural world exist in dynamic relations, in constant states of flux. Similarly, I've thought about relational structuring linked to temporality, the largest organisational structure that holds the universe, or universes, in constant play. The interest emerged at a time in my life when I heard – and I still do with some frequency – many people talk about things 'relating' to other things, without being specific about what kinds of relations they were referring to. I was much the same.

I am trying to come to terms with: the types, kinds, or species of relations in any given situation (a tricky word here); the strengths, weights or magnitudes of those relations; and the duration, or temporal performance of those relations – the changing nature of the relational assemblies, a kind of temporal calculus. This relatedness is always in some ways indeterminate and provisional, because it is situationally specific. These relations are not only linked to a present, but to anything – in various degrees of communicative potential – that belongs to, and helps to 'construct', a situation. Here, situational thinking is not simply related to immediate phenomena or spatial conditions, but to a range of relational 'evidence', or attributes, that might move between material and spatial evidence, to conceptual conceits, to histories, to things lost and never to be found, and so on.

For example, a Ticonderoga #2 wooden pencil, with an eraser, is 'made possible', or is structured by a range of conditions that include: practices of deforestation; the history of writing; censorship (the eraser); mass production and advertising; relations to other objects in the world that dematerialise over time; the advent of writing instruments; the gestural structure of a body; and so on. These, and other relational properties of the pencil, interact with the multiple conditions that structure any given situation – which will include things like one's attention or intention (both explicit and implicit) – to bring to the fore possibilities for action and communication. This field is negotiated through a fluid intersection with the agencies afforded by our memory, senses and imagination, enabling navigation in a complex world.

If spatiality, architecture and spatial visualisations can speak, and – from a design perspective – relational structuring is useful in setting up the potential of varied forms and gradients of communicative potential, then relational structuring could play important roles in design, situated in relation to varied audiences, linked to understandings of cultural perception, and speaking, in reciprocal negotiations and constructions, with 'the body'. Remembering that situations can comprise different levels of reality, this understanding, coupled with broadened awareness, and discretionary implementation of techniques of representation and design methods, might afford spatial realms greater cultural durability and consequence.

ASPECTIVAL DRAWINGS

The development of the aspectival drawings, and their subsequent framing, was a response to an earlier proposal I made for a small and un-built desert house. While these visual prompts emerged partially in relation to changed ambitions for the house, they were equally a result of rethinking design through the conventions of architectural representation, particularly perspective, advanced in the earlier house proposal. These drawings are distinct from the coordinated and synthetic logic of perspective drawings and instead structure aspects, or tendencies – critical fragments as it were – of/for possible spatial configurations. As a result, they are referred to as 'aspectival drawings' and foreground the distinct aspects of a spatial realm, as opposed to 'perspective drawings', which are synthetic and continuous. This kind of drawing type was also developed to challenge the certainty, or lateral relations, of most conventions of architectural representation, enabling the key aspects of a spatial setting, or object, to find representational status, without recourse to producing representations of contiguous space.

While having a sense of coherence, and occasionally alluding to relations of proximities and distance, the aspectival desert house drawings are structured by a series of fragments that are ambiguously flat and deep, simultaneously: a flat-deep recess; a bracketed and stretched cactus surface; a trapped and intimate red object; white parallax; a folded, artificial and limited horizon; and so on. They challenge the continuous spatial preferences established through perspective constructions and open the potential for phased or punctuated spatial make-up.

Among other things, these studies also revealed the possibility for an incomplete architecture, one not unfinished, but triggered by spatial catalysts, or attributes, relationally structured, but not necessarily spatially continuous. The empty, evacuated, or transitive space between tendencies, or aspects, also became interesting, ideationally, spatially and particularly in relation to representational techniques. Here, there might be gaps in the drawings and gaps in a projected spatial realm. The phased, or emptied space of representation enabled the structure of the drawings to trade on non-figurative spatial aspects, and, looking back, I see they subconsciously informed my later interests in erasure as a representational and architectural activity.

In retrospect, it's clear that the deep background, or the larger project, of the development of this drawing type came from a concern to open the architectural drawing to alternative potentials, to develop visualisations that might be more effective in particular phases of designing, and to augment the 600-year-old protocols of the history of linear perspective – the controlled roles of the picture plane and a viewing subject, or the station point 'I'/eye. The aspectival drawings served as catalysts to unpack what spatial drawings might discuss, and how they might do that in ways perhaps not ordained by the traditions and histories of representation. In a larger context of cultural production, these drawings and the subsequent species of drawings that I have made, owe a real debt to Marcel Duchamp and his readymades such as *Fountain* (1917), which opened questions about what qualified as art and who could produce it. For me, this raised the possibility that the architectural drawing might have other agencies, in addition to those usefully proffered by conventional drawing typologies.

RELATIONAL SPACE OF ASSEMBLY

The observer must be included within the focus of observation, and what can be studied is always a relationship or an infinite regress of relationships. Never a 'thing'.
Gregory Bateson, *Steps to an Ecology of Mind*

Drawing and painting Freud's rooms made me aware of how carefully he curated the collection, and the importance of his constructed assemblies. The act of drawing made them more tangible and drew me into a corporeal understanding and situatedness within these spaces. Many scholars have dismantled Freud's assemblies in order to focus on the symbolic significance of individual antiquities in connection with his writing – his expected form of expression – but, in doing so, overlook the importance of the relational space that the assemblies create. Likewise, displaying my Freud images in a gallery seems to undermine their ability to converse with each other, losing the 'intimate and infinite regress of relationships' that so strongly defined his rooms. What seemed necessary was to find a way of situating the drawings and paintings in a 'relational space of assembly' of their own. Moving from explorative images to a construction, the *Cabinet of Consulting* gathers my images of Freud's rooms together with my own personal lifelong collection. This conjoined betwixt-and-between room invites the observer into a liminal space for 'consulting' relations between the known, unknown, hidden, forgotten and suppressed in this expanded assembly.

Upon first encounter, the cabinet portrays a recognisable domestic space – a comfortable room with display cabinets, paintings hung on walls, and carpet-covered couch and floor. As an ensemble, it exudes a warm, tranquil and stable atmosphere – an apparent interior. On closer inspection, this semblance soon dissipates into an internal/external, seething, vaguely familiar, strangely unsettling, transitory atmosphere, whose lifelike theatre leaves one dangling between Freud's world and mine. The assemblies and their sheer density overpower any ability to pay attention to individual pieces on the shelves, immediately thrusting one into a collective realm, in which Freud, myself, the observer, and the collections effectively become the 'field of observation'. One witnesses oneself amidst a cacophony of reflections generated by the glass fronts and mirrored backs of the display cabinets. What appears in one place one moment reappears in another the next, through intimate, manifold, and fragmented visual exchanges that implicate and entangle the observer in this oscillating ebb and flow of relations. This contiguity, or spatial connection (Freud considered this one of the essential principles of the processes of association), elicits a kind of reciprocal space of exchange for a transference/countertransference between his world and mine. My collection of profane sticks and bones acquire a discrete sacredness, whilst Freud's sacred, venerated antiquities assume a subdued profanity. Just as with Freud's rooms, my cabinet exhibits private visual musings not unlike those found in dreams. And like a liminal dream, where one is neither fully awake nor asleep, this physical, psychological, threshold chamber allows one to encounter and appreciate how this relational space of assembly also loops back to offer a prospective meditation on the latent tactility of drawing.

THE AGENCY OF OBJECTS AND THE EVANESCENT THOUGHT

Many thoughts cannot be uttered through words but require alternate forms to assert their presence. Architecture is often about realising these kinds of presences. Evanescent thoughts, dreams, memories and ideas can be held in place through drawing or the objects we surround ourselves with. For me, the 'agency of objects' is their ability to provoke reminiscences and associations through our perceptions of them.

Freud referred to his collection of antiquities as his 'audience', especially the statuettes adorning his writing table that he greeted each morning. His consulting room and study not only defined the space of psychoanalysis for his patients but also provided a spatial framework for his 'unconscious thoughts'. Hilda Doolittle, a patient in 1934, wrote: 'He said his little statues and images helped stabilise the evanescent idea or keep it from escaping altogether'.[1] Likewise, dream images keep the evanescent from escaping altogether, which is perhaps why Freud was so intrigued by them. In recounting dreams, his patients would reach into the abyss of this sea of evanescent thought and return with fragments that allowed him to lay a forgotten piece of their early history before them in a psychoanalytic 'construction' that brought thoughts, memories and associations together.

Freud's collection and its arrangement provided him with a 'pictorial language' that he pondered, considered, free associated, speculated and dreamt upon. This may well be why he never really wrote about the collection – it just didn't come to him in words. This is the Freud we know so little about, whose assembled collection constitutes his silent thoughts, and who, by not writing them down, protected them from outside scrutiny. Perhaps the assemblages presented Freud with a venue for secretly continuing the apparently terminable self-analysis presented in his book *The Interpretation of Dreams*. Or alternatively, as each piece earned its place within his developing working universe, their tangible presence, and spatial relations brought certain thoughts to life in a much more intuitive, corporeal way than his text on a page ever could. He understood that concrete concepts exist in the unconscious and it is only when impressions of these arrive at a level of consciousness that we then become able to articulate them verbally.[2] So, perhaps this assembled collection provided access to his 'inner' unconscious world. The evanescent that furtively slips away can sometimes reappear … I was too young to sit at my grandparents' dining table. Instead, I would circle the table, calling out in my limited words, 'mesa, mesa' or 'meat, meat'. My calls would be rewarded by extended arms, offering vestiges of meat on bones. I would gather these treasures and retreat away from the noise and chatter to devour them among the forest of legs, in the intimate space I had found underneath the table.

Many years later, while building a dining table for my own family from the chicken bones I had painstakingly collected over a seven-year period, this memory unexpectedly resurfaced. Was it the bones, the dining table, or both, that brought this about?

What would Freud make of this?

1 H. D. (Hilda Doolittle), *Tribute to Freud* (Boston: David R. Godine, 1974), p. 175.
2 Sigmund Freud's thoughts summarised in E. Jones, *The Life and Work of Sigmund Freud – Volume 2: Years of Maturity 1901–1919* (New York: Basic Books, 1955), p. 326.

THE LIMIT CONDITIONS OF DRAWING AND OTHER DISCIPLINARY CONSIDERATIONS

Spectral Mediums

Michael Young

FRANCESCO BORROMINI
Lantern, S. Ivo alla Sapienza, 1649–52
Graphite on paper
90 × 37 cm (35½ × 14½ in)
Albertina Museum, Vienna

Some architectural drawings possess a soft, ghost-like glow, which fuzzes figures into a shallow ground, not exactly the background, but more akin to something harboured in the skin, in the dermal celluloid within the surface. The effect is one of suspension, as if what the image depicts is held in a translucent medium, layered in a cloudy translucency or veiled haze of accumulated matter. At one level, this is a question of the representation of depth, one of the longest-standing issues for all drawing and imaging media. Yet the qualities described here are not resolved by discussions of perspective, or shading, or occlusion. Instead, I will suggest another term: they are *spectral*.

The meaning of the word itself hovers. It could mean the electromagnetic spectrum: infrared, visible, ultraviolet, X-rays, all are designations bracketed by different wavelengths of radiation and can be used to create images exceeding and extending what human vision has access to. They show something else, something more, or possibly even something in-between what we typically see. Spectral mediums use chemistry, electricity and magnetism to gather information about the energetic world and then translate it toward our sense of sight. In doing so, they bring to the visible image artefacts from the other spectral ranges. For instance, an X-ray sees through the skin to tissues, organs and bones that lie within. But it does not do this with complete transparency – as much as it clarifies, it also clouds. An accurate determination of depth in an X-ray is not at all clear. And this leads to another aspect of the spectral. Without diving too far down the tunnel of spiritualism, ghosts and parallel dimensions, it is important to note that 'medium' is also the term used to describe those who channel between the material and immaterial worlds. As François Bonnet writes, 'It is the province of the spectral world to draw the contour of this limit-point. This knot of confusion between the world of facts and the world of dreams, which reciprocally cut across one another to form the world of lived experience.'[1] Most architectural representations attempt to clarify, to reveal, to define, to firm up the specificity of material dimension in depth. Images that are spectral, however, float into an undecidable, ephemeral space between. They can still be precise, but they often spring from a desire to see the flat and the deep simultaneously, the inside seen through the outside, a superimposition set in motion by embracing the effects of drawing through accumulated layers.

This practice of drawing through layers is so common that it would seem to require little comment. Layering has ties to compositional concepts in painting such as 'underdrawing'; to Beaux-Arts analytical exercises in architectural pedagogy; is prevalent in modernist design techniques through iterative developments on tracing paper; was a necessary technique in the reproduction of drawings as blueprints; and is an integral management menu in every design software. However, common as the use of layers is in daily architectural practice, there are side effects that significantly shift aspects of architectural representation. Some of these are conceptual in that elements of a drawing are free to be displaced in relation to others on different layers, a technique resonant with collage and montage. Other aspects are aesthetic, as layering is variable in opacity, cross-fading forward and back in shallow simultaneity.

Emerging in Europe towards the end of the 16th century, the pencil is an often-overlooked paradigm shift in technologies of mediation. As opposed to the two previously dominant modes – ink and charcoal – the graphite pencil was more responsive to subtle changes in pressure, able to range between dark and light marks along a single stroke. These changes in tonality encouraged a layered approach to drawing as the draftsperson would recursively go over previously drawn lines to firm up emphasis on elements under consideration. This also created halos or veils as lighter earlier marks hovered around heavier darker markings. Another crucial difference of graphite was the ability to erase, not only allowing the removal of errors, loosening the hand and the willingness to take chances, but also altering the entire process of deciding what counts as 'error'. The noise of residual traces could be revalued as important qualities in themselves.

Francesco Borromini was one of the first architects to draw with graphite.[2] The drawing of the lantern spire on top of the dome of Sant'Ivo alla Sapienza is the product of a pencil mediation exhibiting many of the traits discussed above. In this drawing, Borromini does two very odd things. The drawing should be considered an orthographic elevation: the front exterior face of the lantern is drawn conventionally, but the back face of the exterior elevation is also drawn, superimposed on the front. This makes some sense geometrically, as it verifies that the spiral is continuous in its rise, but it also seems to further emphasise the spiralling motion of the total body, even if it could never be viewed in totality. The second oddity is that there is another set of lines, darker in their emphasis, which indicate the volume of the interior space as a section cut floating between the front and back surfaces of the lantern. This means that the drawing collapses multiple depths into a singular X-ray view of the front, back and interior of the architecture.[3] The surfaces of the building are all present, illustrating relations not possible to experience physically by the senses, but operative in the concepts and aesthetics of the design. This drawing may just be the first spectral image in architecture.

Another crucial development for the spectral image was the medium of a translucent drawing surface. Many of our contemporary layering techniques developed alongside drafting linen, vellum, tracing paper and Mylar sheets. Drafting linen emerged in the 19th century, valued not only for its stability as a drawing medium, but also for its translucency. Synthetic plastic materials (there are several, but for ease of conversation I will just refer to these as 'Mylar') replaced other mediums around the middle of the 20th century on account not only of their cost and uniformity, but also for their increased and even translucency. There are many reasons to use a translucent medium for architectural drawing, but they are all in one way or another tied to techniques and technologies of reproduction, to the creation of copies, duplicates and traces.

A drawing produced on a translucent medium can be mechanically reproduced by passing ultraviolet light through it to make a copy (the diazo process). Commonly known as blueprints, these are a species of photogram, spectral images where a line drawn on Mylar casts a shadow stored on a chemically sensitive paper in direct contact with it – a template transfer via projected light, with the veracity of the transferred information assured by the absence of physical depth between the original and the copy. This process allowed multiple layers of Mylar to stack, each with their own notations and information. This separation of layers was tied to divisions of labour, where primary design geometry could be on one sheet, while dimensions, specifications, notations, entourage and other symbols could be on others. This separation literally means that different people could work on the same drawing in different locations at the same time, the final print an accumulated shadow of multiple temporalities brought together. Although this process reinforces distinctions between design labour and technical labour, the division is more than simply professional pragmatism and bureaucracy because it also lends the print an artefactual quality – it becomes a document, the synthesis of shiftable, shuffled, exchangeable layering. This aspect allows architects to extend the allusive and associative possibilities of their representations by exploring combinations of figures and notations outside of logical intentional control. The automatic cut-up processes of Surrealism, the dialectical montaged conflicts of Dada, and the accumulative material detritus of Art Brut found entry into the technical architectural drawing.

There is another interesting visual effect that emerges as dark lines change to light shadows, the image of lines glows. This effect tends to suggest that the lines are not on the surface but illuminated from behind, a precursor for the lines as light in digital display screens. Also of interest is the soft luminous haze as light bounces in the tooth of the slightly roughened surface of Mylar, an effect very similar to the ghosted render setting in digital modelling software. Ghosted views allow the designer to see the surfaces of the object under design as an entity, but also to see through the object to the interior and back faces. The ghosted view has become in the first decades of the 21st century one of the most prevalent visual appearances for modelling software. This can be understood as the outcome of centuries of architectural desires, a spectre of our own spectacles, released by desires for the diaphanous, for the world seen through *and* looked at. In doing so there is always a remainder, a ghost, a spectral image, often more latent with meaning than the built reality it attempts to mediate.

This brief essay relates to the work of a number of the contributors to this book, each of whom in their own way explores aspects of what I have been describing as spectral images. I'm fairly certain that none of them use this term, nor that they would particularly find these qualities the most important in relation to what they do. This is not the point, however. The purpose of this discussion is not to explicate intentions. What I am discussing here has to do with two things only: conventions of representation and aesthetic affects. The most innovative work often happens when these two are in tension with each other. The aesthetics of the spectral image in architecture have been operative for over 400 years. Layering in architectural representation is likewise centuries old and conventional. In the kind of work of which I'm thinking, the effects of translucency are used to challenge the conventions of how depth is represented, not just phenomenally, but also the relations between the appearance of a surface and the surfaces of appearance. These are philosophical provocations for the discipline of architecture. They are innovative in how they extend the possibilities of representation as a conceptual space for architectural speculation. They engage conventions yet challenge a viewer on how those conventions should be interpreted. They are also extra-disciplinary in their allusions to artworks and imaging technologies and carry cultural associations typically excluded from architectural representations. And ultimately much of their interest comes from the precision with which, initiating spatial ambiguity, they look through the world as spectral mediations.

---

1 François J. Bonnet, *The Infra-World* (Falmouth, UK: Urbanomic, 2017), p. 69.
2 James Ackerman, 'The Conventions and Rhetoric of Architectural Drawings', in *Origins, Imitation, Conventions: Representation in the Visual Arts* (Cambridge, MA: MIT Press, 2002), p. 295.
3 Joseph Connors, 'Borromini's S. Ivo alla Sapienza: The Spiral', *The Burlington Magazine*, vol. 138, no. 1123, (October 1996), p. 673.

Mark West
Estrangement is Critical

MARK WEST
I would like you to be at the back of the room, at a distance from the drawing,
as if you were looking at a 19th-century European painting.
From a distance it reads as a certain kind of figure or image, and as you come closer, that image de-structures, and other images and figures appear.
That is how my drawings are drawn.
I'm drawing at a distance and I'm drawing from very close.
I'm drawing in between one and the other, constantly moving.
In fact, now I draw in a wheelie chair, so I can kick back and go back in.
The figuration is designed to arrive in part, and change.

PERRY KULPER
You work on the drawing that way?

MARK WEST
Yeah, for sure.

PERRY KULPER
You're looking at the drawing from 50 feet?

MARK WEST
As far back as I can get and as close as I can get, and anything in between …
The figures belong to each distance,
each distance produces a different figuration. It's like looking through a microscope.
You see a bug, and then you look through the microscope and you don't see a bug any more, you see some weird hexagons or something, right? So at each scale, in
and out …

PERRY KULPER
But it's not *Powers of Ten* by the Eames, that's not what you're doing right?
That's an arithmetic progression. These don't seem to involve arithmetic progression in that way.

MARK WEST
Yeah, the *Powers of Ten* are just a device for going in and out. What happens when you go in and out is a natural phenomenon and one of the structural things that's happening when I make the drawings is that I want that always to be the case.
The drawing will not be done if, at a certain distance from it, it falls flat and I can't see anything new. Then it's like OK, well that's not good enough, I've got to work on that.

So, that's one … that's kind of an important thing that I wanted to make sure was grasped.

ANTHONY MOREY
Can I ask, are these the actual drawings or are they prints?

MARK WEST
These are the actual drawings. So, this is coloured pencil on a printed photo collage. When you get the oblique light, you can see the density of the coloured pencil (and the difference in reflection).
Prismacolor pencils.
It's printed on Strathmore 500 Bristol, the only paper I draw on because it is bulletproof. You can erase on it, you can work it and work it and work again, and the surface doesn't care.

Sometimes I'll use turpentine on those little paper sticks [tortillons], the ones you use to move graphite around. I dip those in turpentine, and that will dissolve the coloured pencil. Depending on the pigment, some pencils don't dissolve, and some dissolve really well. So, it all depends on which pencil you happen to pick up.
But sometimes I'm simply burnishing the pencil, and at other times I would want it to appear that you see the pencil.

One of the things that happens in the presence of the actual drawing, which doesn't happen when it's reproduced, is this special enigma that causes you to say:
'What is this made of?'

MICHAEL YOUNG
I was asking myself exactly that question!

MARK WEST

A Night Out on the Town, 2019
Coloured pencil and PanPastel on paper-printed photomontage
64 × 56 cm (25 × 22 in)

MARK WEST
Everything Falls Apart. Blackout Drawing, early 1980s
Graphite on paper collage, 74 × 64 cm (29 × 25 in)

MARK WEST

So, it becomes a surreal object at a material level because you don't know what it's made of.
Which is a thrill to me. So, I get the drawing to that point.
In some of these you can see traces:
'Oh, OK, now I see this is actually changed, this is actually a *made* thing,
I see pencil marks'.
So, there are hints left in the drawing.

The origin of the method comes from collage.
Photocollage, à la Max Ernst, Hannah Höch and Raoul Hausmann.
Those people and Eric Dolphy and Ornette Coleman opened my mind and my eyes.
So, that's what busted me out of the incredibly uptight lessons that I learned at Cooper Union when I was in that monastery.
After graduating I attacked my education through collages.
You know how it goes,
you can't really control them,
you wait for serendipity.
In a way, the major decision you make is whether you glue it down or not.
And in that I started to learn to see things not for what they were but for what they might become, or their phenomenal qualities rather than their name or what they refer to as objects in the world.
And that was truly liberating for me.

From the collages,
which are largely matters of getting right with chance and learning how to get right with chance, this is a photograph of a collage that is blacked out.
I couldn't bring the original thing because this is from the mid-Eighties – it's really fragile and just falling apart.
You can see here, there's a line between two photographs, and another one here.
These are like Chinese cuts.
You lay them on top of each other, you make the cut, and then they fit flush. And that way you can draw across it with a 6B pencil.

The blackout is with a soft graphite pencil that reveals figures and images that were in the photographs all along, but you couldn't see them when you recognised what it was you were looking at in the original image.

So, the first thing to do is get rid of all that you recognise,
all the faces,
all the hands,
all the things that would key you in to what the original subject of the photograph was, and then that releases the forms and images that are hidden inside it.
When I discovered this method, I felt that I had discovered a secret of the universe, because I already – by the making of collages – had altered my perception of the world.
I wasn't looking any more at, let's say, images or photographs for what they were, I was looking at parts – like, 'This is really interesting, this is potent, for what it could become'.

I was already pulling the world apart when everything had a name and everything was what it was.
And then this started opening up ideas of renunciation – that if you renounce certain things, especially those things which you already know, then that thing that remains is opened up in a new and unexpected way.

PERRY KULPER

So, the estrangement is critical?

MARK WEST

Absolutely critical. This is where I'm trying to get to, talking about the practice and techniques of drawing.
To have the ability to open or close or alter your perception of the world.

MICHAEL WEBB

How many images did you take to make that up, bulk part estimate?

MARK WEST

Let's say 20 images.

MICHAEL WEBB

Well, 20 pictures, let's say that was one of them [pointing at the collage]. It is already in a collage-like form. So where do the images come from?

MARK WEST

This one here is the Metropolitan Museum of Art in New York from above; this is an image from World War Two; this is a Roman sarcophagus. I don't remember what this one was. This is of World War Two paratroopers; this is an African sculpture … I've added some paintings from the Metropolitan Museum.
So, it's like, they're good images, you know – for the collage I need good images.
It's like going shopping for really good food.

And then you wait to see.

So, first is the labour to get rid of all this stuff that you recognise.
For example, you see this putto here, a little baby angel in the collage? Turn it upside down and take the face out, and maybe a leg, and all of a sudden it's released into … well, now we don't know what it is. It seems to be either vegetal or biological.
And then the discipline is to draw only what you've already seen. And that's the hallucinatory work part.

It's the same technique that you use when you look out if you see these beautiful cumulus clouds on a sunny day and stare at them.
You see animals or faces, right?
And they are so clear.
And the weird thing is that of course it looks exactly like a dolphin but it's not shaped like a dolphin but like a cloud.
And yet, I can say: 'Hey, look, see the dolphin?', and you go: 'Where? Where?'
'You see, the nose is there!'
And then it pops in and you see the dolphin. That's even weirder, right, that it's inter-subjective, and we could see the dolphin out of something that doesn't have a dolphin shape?'

MICHAEL YOUNG

There's a Greek word for this, for seeing things in clouds: *pareidolia*.

MARK WEST

Ah, I didn't know that …

So, I discovered the technique, and I was intoxicated with it.

You know I really love Roberto Matta's paintings, especially from the mid Forties. That stuff makes me crazy.
And as I was studying Matta, I read this interview with him in which he described his method.
It is the same method!
And then I said: 'Oh, right, the youngest Surrealist, it is a Surrealist method'. And then he referenced Leonardo da Vinci who gave exactly the same advice.
But Leonardo says stare at a water-stained wall and then marvellous things will come to your vision.
I said, 'Ah, that's that, as old as the hills'.

So, this is a capacity that is innate to the human sensorium.
We are pattern-seeking animals, and given the slightest provocation we start to see.
And mostly you see faces. Faces are really easy to see, they happen all the time, heads and faces happen all the time. I don't draw them because they are too easy. All I would ever see would be faces …

An interesting fact about the Chauvet cave in France is that they know what the people who were making those drawings ate because they have carbon-dated middens that have the bones of animals in them. So, they know what their diet was and their diet was overwhelmingly ibex …
80 per cent or something of the bones are ibex bones.
And yet there's only about one ibex drawing in the cave, and the rest are bison and buffaloes.

So why were they not drawing this really important animal?
I don't know why, we'll never know why. But there's a choice made about what you draw.
And this gets back to this discussion I had with Nat Chard.
Nat, you were pretty rough with me sometimes when I would say, 'I only draw what I see'.
I said, 'I set up the circumstance, I set up the Petri dish, and I wait for the thing to arrive'.

PERRY KULPER

But you have a particular term that you use
for that and I'll never forget:
'The drawing volunteers itself'.
That's what you said to me the first time
we talked:
'It volunteers itself'.

MARK WEST

Like the dolphin volunteered itself out
of the clouds.
That's what it feels like.
I don't want to be spooky about it, but this
is what the experience is like.

So, because of this conclave of ours here and
because of Nat's grumbling over this question
of authorship, I figured I should do some
thinking.
It's true that my experience of doing the
drawings is simply recording and clarifying
what comes to vision, but this is not a fixed
thing — because as soon as you start to clarify,
say the dolphin head, as soon as you put
something down, you're not looking at the
same Petri dish anymore. It has changed.
What you see is changed.

PERRY KULPER

Even when you draw something there, you're
seeing the whole drawing differently.

MARK WEST

Yes, the whole context changes. That's right,
the whole thing is different.
So, it's not like I see a dog, I draw a dog.
No, it's like, you see a dog, you start drawing
a dog and the dog disappears,
because it becomes maybe a void and this
other thing is arriving.
The whole thing is in motion!
It is a fantastic pleasure, an amazing pleasure
to draw like this.
And then I don't feel that responsible for
what happens.
And I don't know where it's going.
I don't know what the drawing is of.
And I actually don't know what the drawing
is discussing.

However, having thought about it — because
there's the conclave context, and also Nat's

around, and I didn't want to be beat up in
public — I realise, being a little more self-
conscious about it,
that I do make some very precise structural
decisions [laughter in the room],
very structural decisions.
I really was not conscious of that.

I put colour down on top of the print. You can
still sort of see some strokes and make the
strokes disappear. You can burnish it, which
was how I used to do it. Or you can take the
turpentine to it. It becomes like painting.
It's like drawing with watercolour pencils and
water, it does the same thing, except if you
put water on this paper, you've screwed up
the paper.

I make collages on the computer.
And because I have to print them, I
photograph stuff in large, high-resolution
files. Just an exposure with the camera won't
hold up.
To have a photograph in very high resolution,
I have to split what I photograph up in tiles,
and put them together on the computer in one
big file. I keep those in a library and I'll use
my collection to collage in Photoshop.

PERRY KULPER

Do you make all the photographs from which
these come? You are not downloading images
from internet sites?

MARK WEST

No, no, I'm collecting my own library.

PERRY KULPER

Ah, that is interesting, because the
ramifications exceed the resolution of images
downloadable. You are curating what you see.
Once you capture, we see how you see the
world, what you focus on, and so on.

MARK WEST

Plus the world becomes much more
interesting to me, because I'm always looking
for, 'Oh, this could be good …'

PERRY KULPER

But you would not photograph, for example,
a Donald Judd piece, I'm guessing.

MARK WEST

The Incubator, 2019
Coloured pencil on paper-printed photomontage, 57 × 48 cm (22 × 19 in)

MARK WEST
Probably not.
But 19th-century European painters?
Yes.

PERRY KULPER
Of course, yeah.

MICHAEL YOUNG
But this question of resolution is an important one I think, because of the question of the seamlessness of the collage in its layering and juxtapositioning.
There are shifts between resolutions.
For example,
two pieces of the collage operating at different resolutions,
and sometimes it might be the movement between what has been Prismacolored and what hasn't ... I'm not sure.
But I find it really interesting that it's at multiple resolutions.

PERRY KULPER
The resolution is out of sync sometimes with the photograph and the contribution, right?

MARK WEST
Yeah, that's right. The photographic resolution, when it's in focus, is the highest. I can't achieve that with the Prismacolors and the turpentine, so there's always that one.

And so you're right, there's this question of at what resolution something appears in the drawing, and also, would you like to expose the game of the photograph and the drawing?
Which is one way to do it.
Or, do you want to hide it so you don't know what this thing is?
And then you can use out-of-focus photographs, which is a whole other thing.

PERRY KULPER
Yeah. And you can sharpen them.

MICHAEL YOUNG
That's one way in which the final piece is made available to the viewer, the desire to go to different distances that is being introduced.

MARK WEST
Yeah. They're also primary structures that are revealed from different distances.
Those structures are apparent at this distance and all of a sudden, they are not real any more at another distance.

PERRY KULPER
There are primary things, that from 50 feet are not detectable at all — they dissolve and don't appear till you get back in.

But it's not just an optical proximity — there are structural shifts as you move through different distances in relation to different things ... it's shifting.

MARK WEST
So, this gets to the point that I would like to make about the way that I make the structural decisions, like choosing to draw buffaloes instead of the ibex.
And the choice of things is for me a search for what I would call, for the time being, 'a proper realism'.

So, since we moved to Montréal, we're meeting lots of new people, making new friends. And they would ask:
'What are you doing? How do you spend your day?'
'Well, I draw a lot.'
'Oh, you draw? What kind of drawings do you make?'
'Well, they're kind of hard to explain.'
And they said:
'Well, is it abstract or realist?'

I got this question about three or four times when we moved.
Abstraction or realism?
And thinking about what I said:
'You know what? It's realistic.'
Yes, these are realistic, but a 'proper' realism, which would be based on a set of rules for 'a proper realism'.
And I wrote them down, so I could have the beginning of a list of the rules.

I'll name a few.
One is that 'All matter is particulate but always connected, interconnected'.

MARK WEST

Emblem of the Forest Floor, 2014
Coloured pencil on paper-printed photomontage, 46 × 69 cm (18 × 27 in)

MARK WEST
Emblem of the Forest Floor (detail), 2014
Coloured pencil on paper-printed photomontage, 46 × 69 cm (18 × 27 in)

Another one is that 'All matter is prodigiously active, always'.
Another one is that 'Context is also content'.
And the other one is that 'A thing is always a gathering'. It's not elemental, but it's a gathering of other things. And as you go into the thing, which you see as apparently unitary and elemental, it turns into a kind of theatre composed of characters. And you go in further and each of those characters turns out to be a theatre made of other characters.
And that's the structural way that the world unfolds itself to our perception.
And so, a realist rendition of the world should also have that structural and scalar density as well.
So that's another thing, which is why I decided to do that, my decision.

This relates back to the fact that I have now spent more than 10 per cent of my life living on an otherwise uninhabited island. When we step out of our house, you're on the forest floor.
And the forest floor is chaotic according to a certain idea of what order and chaos is, but in fact it is so deeply ordered that the forest floor becomes the reference point for something which is actually, you know, highly organised and the matrix from which everything else comes.

ANTHONY MOREY
Is this work art? Do you consider it art?
And is that the worst thing for an architect to hear?

MARK WEST
I think for me it's self-evident.
Of course it is.

PERRY KULPER
I would say it's not. Because there are relational properties being distributed from all kinds of disciplines here.
I think as among many of us here in the room, for me it is just relational structuring.
And for me,
relational structuring has nothing to do with disciplinary boundaries of knowledge.
It's not that I'm picking the pockets of other things,
it's just that structuring is cross-disciplinary by nature.

MARK WEST
Well, it's not that interesting a question, because you may ask, is it architecture? Or is it not?

ANTHONY MOREY
Yeah, but I mean … I guess it's the same question.
It has come up earlier today, where you say, 'being at an arm's length from architecture', or 'I get closer to architecture', or 'I am on the fringe of architecture'.
That has come up and everyone has been OK with having that conversation included in the way that they discussed their work.
But if you're on the fringe of something, you're obviously heading towards somewhere else. So, there's obviously a map of points or nodes, and that distance implies proximity to others, right?
There is no distance if there's no relationship.

MICHAEL YOUNG
I'd say this is architecture too.

PERRY KULPER
It is not architecture. I would say it is spatiality.
It refers to spatialities, which is to me a more consistent, more generous terminology.
Architecture has very specific cultural expectations and disciplinary definitions.

MARK WEST
I want these things, these drawings, to be as much like life as is possible.
They are analogical and as much like life as possible, clarifying what life is like.
That's an incredibly valuable thing for me.
So, to start thinking about elements composed in free space … what sad, poverty-stricken fiction is that? But that's how I was taught to think about the world in architecture school.
So, for redefinition, this work and a bit of free jazz has made all the difference in the world, you know, made it possible for me to see the world in a way which was capacious and deep enough that I could perceive the order of the

MARK WEST
Happy Town, 2016
Coloured pencil on paper-printed photomontage, 53 × 53 cm (21 × 21 in)

forest floor, for example, without studying ecology or biology.

MARK DORRIAN
Another way of talking about the dividing line between what we call 'art' and what we call 'architecture', is understanding the context in which it emerges as an issue.
It seems to me that one of the predispositions we might have, whether it is a disciplinary disposition or not, is that architects often are interested in talking about the productivity of the image, in a way that artists are not necessarily concerned with.
The image not as an end in itself,
but what it does,
or what comes from it,
or what it gives rise to,
whether that is some kind of construction or some kind of further elaboration or pursuit of the image, it never seems quite settled or finished or finalised in itself.
In an architectural context that question haunts the image or the drawing or the representation in a way that it doesn't necessarily in other contexts.

Clearly there are artists for whom that is an issue. But I think it is particularly poignant in an architectural context.

Somehow,
looking back at our work,
what strikes me in a way that didn't before was that really a lot of the way it was developed was very much about the operational aspect of the drawing.
Drawing as a material thing,
as something that is put into play through its material instantiation.

Michael Young
The Speculative Territory Between Image and Drawing

NAT CHARD
How did you invent the flowers?

MICHAEL YOUNG
We took botanical flower specimens and then we took animals, because we were interested in flowers as sex organs for plants and the fact that we would give them to our grandmothers.
We were interested in flower vases as assisted suicide devices where you would elongate death for your pleasure.
We basically 3-D-modelled botanical, geological and animal characteristics to learn how to do the flowers.
Then we mapped images on the 3-D-models and we tried to build up these species.

The question here is about realism,
realism as an aesthetic position,
realism as something that produces tension between reality and its representation.
Not as copying, but as how you could produce that sort of tension.

The question I started thinking about is, if one can do that through the world of painting and the world of imaging and the world of photography …
I was reading through a lot of photography – all the Thomases, Thomas Demand, Thomas Struth, Thomas Ruff – and I was getting in to arguments with people about the difference between images and drawings.
And my position was that we're all dealing with images.
This is the world we're swimming in.

MARK DORRIAN
What does 'image' mean for you, Michael?

MICHAEL YOUNG
This is the catch.
To me all these are images.
Only some of them are operating within conventions of understandings within painting.
Others are working with photography.
Others with the conventions of drawing.
So, could you take drawing as we would understand it as architects –
axonometrics, planimetrics, low perspectives, lines, *poché* –
and begin to defamiliarise those in a way that would allow me to have an argument with my friends and, somehow, I would be able to stop them saying, 'You're just working on images, man, you should really be working on drawings'.

MARK DORRIAN
So, the question would be, what is the limit condition of an image for you?

MICHAEL YOUNG
Well …
I don't want to say that it's all images and that drawing doesn't matter.
Drawing matters immensely,
but drawing matters now more as a mode of work and as a way in which architects make disciplinary arguments.
Less within the techniques of – it must be drawn by hand, it must be a projection, etc.

MARK DORRIAN
Would you say there are some kinds of drawings that we probably wouldn't describe as images and there are certain kinds that we probably would?
If I have to draw a line …
I'm not sure if I would describe this [drawing] as an image,
but if you tell me for example that it's a weather map, it really becomes an image, it starts to have a referential attachment.

So, maybe I'm wrong,
but I would suppose that there is some kind of immanence that is determinant here …
Things we tend to describe as images are things that we anticipate being of something, or that could be of something,
or that we know are of something.
This condition is not always there in a drawing or other mark-making – unless we wanted to say that a drawing is an image of its own making.
Is this something you might accept?

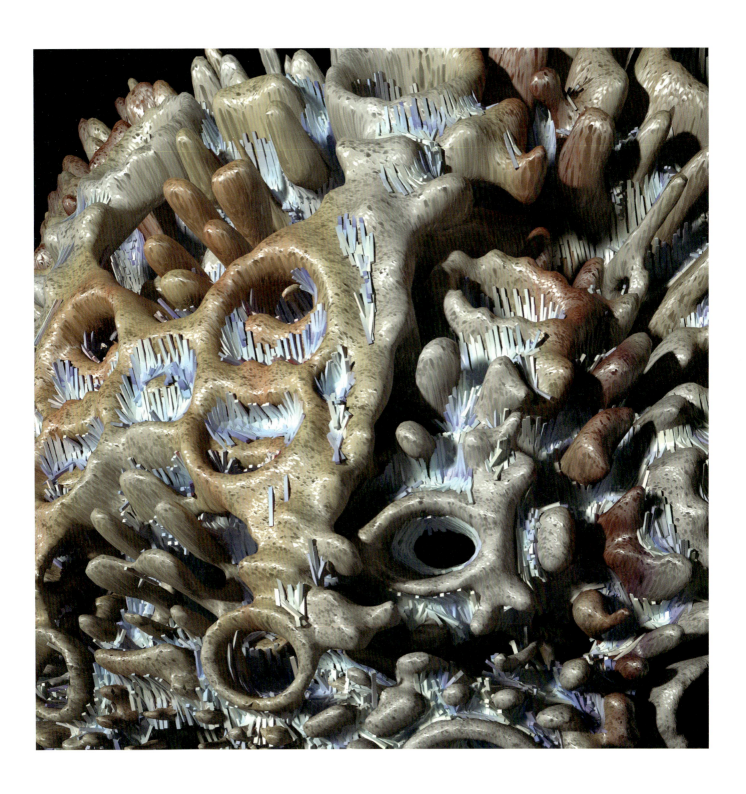

YOUNG & AYATA

Base Flowers, Lignum Agri, 2016
Digital drawing

MICHAEL YOUNG
An image is more descriptive or depictive within this distinction or definition? And a drawing more speculative?

MARK DORRIAN
I think what the choice of the term does is that it establishes some kind of relationship that we have with the thing we're talking about.
I would not say that an image is something that is simply representational in relationship with something that we know …
I think we use the term when we anticipate it developing an attachment with something besides itself.

MICHAEL YOUNG
Maybe it has something to do with the question of finality. That there is something within our continued use of the term 'drawing' that has within it a kind of discovery and exploration — or a mechanism of not knowing where it is going.
At a certain level I am saying everything is an image to try to get over the hump.
I view those as exploratory drawings, as speculative, driven by trying to find out something I don't know.

So, to me the way that people usually use image is to say that it is depictive or pictorial, and is of something known.
To me, the thing you have to get out of then is that some people will produce images that look like drawings in order to make an argument against images.
If it looks like a drawing,
if it looks like it's been done rigorously,
if it looks like it's been done abstractly,
if it looks like it has been hard-lined, sometimes very minimal,
it begins to say 'I'm being disciplinarily rigorous'.

This drawing, as preliminary as it is, is in a way, me trying to fight back, somehow saying,
'So, here are your terms: I'll make it black and white, I'll work within shallow projection, I'll draw axonometrics … but can I push them to understand that the importance of the drawing is not that it looks like a drawing, but the way in which it can become part of an argument, part of a project, part of the development of an idea?'

About a decade ago, we started doing these things that we claimed were hovering between drawing and painting as a way to abuse and misuse our software, all done digitally in Rhino (Symmetry Series No.7). There are lines and only lines, but we're manipulating hundreds of thousands of them in ways that we at the time argued were closer to painting than to drawing because none of the lines were associated with the bounding contours of an edge.
Instead, there were things like marks and a matrix of colours and saturations, driving optical depth and trying to blur distinctions between what was in front and at the back, what was figure, what was ground. And so, we found this as a way to experiment with digital technologies at this intersection between drawing and painting.

A lot of these are to do with questions that I've been asking in my work about traditions extending from the Beaux Arts into contemporary digital imaging, around three words, three terms the Beaux Arts would use for the conceptual arguments about the aesthetics of rendering:
entourage, poché, mosaïque.

What I'm interested in is the observation that the three terms are not dead.
Entourage initially referred to landscape plantings, but later the term referred to things like fixtures and furnishings, and then finally, in the 20th century, to things like scale figures, people. More and more often, architectural imagery is being made as a form of a collection or aggregation of entourage, especially in the 20th century, when it merged with montage.
So, the photomontage now is, I would argue, our kind of dominant mode of thinking through *entourage* and the creation of architectural imaging.
Almost to the point now where there's an architecture that is made completely out of the assembled entourage.

YOUNG & AYATA
Symmetry Series No. 7, 2012
Digital drawing

YOUNG & AYATA
Donkeys & Feathers: Sinew Pair, 2014
3-D printed powder

Poché is that pocket of space hidden in between the interior and exterior – a sort of space behind the space, hidden between or within. In our world of photogrammetry and LIDAR scans, it essentially becomes everything that is outside of the electromagnetic range that the scan is collecting.
All of those photons, that energy, is scanned and stored, and given three-dimensional spatial depth, but everything that exists outside of that range, be it behind, or actually outside of it in terms of its energetic spectrum, is not collected; it exists in a hidden zone, the kind of thing we would formerly call *poché*.
Be it the couch, the wall, the floor, the shadow of the curtain rod, all of those things are now outside of our technological photon mediation of the surfaces of the environment.

The *mosaïque* is the articulation of surfaces, the ornament and decoration in the ways in which it became conventionalised to communicate things like decor, atmosphere, programme, circulation, all of the kind of inscriptions and renderings of the surface.
All that stuff is collapsed and completely fused because a photogrammetry scan or a LIDAR scan does not know the difference between a car, a person, a trashcan or a building.
The surfaces as they are collected are a form of digital mosaic. They are simply XYZ and RGB. And because that builds up our world known in many ways, through everything from satellite scans to Google street views to self-driving cars, and all the other kinds of scanning technologies of our environment, we maybe as architects should take it on as something that we can screw with.

I scanned the Ludovisi sarcophagus in Rome. This was an experiment in how low could I actually get a model with the fewest number of images to composite it.
I think a lot of us maybe have this within us, when we start to learn a new tool, a new technique, a new technology, a new mode of making representations, we try to break them.
So, this is me at some level trying to figure out when and where and how things fall apart.
I got interested in the ways in which the model at a certain distance away from it would look incredibly photoreal, with a bas-relief three-dimensionality in terms of the ways in which the forms and figures are kind of suggesting a shallow depth.
But as you got closer, things got stranger and stranger and textures would kind of evaporate and go into almost like burlap.
So that proximity did not increase realism. Proximity increased abstraction.
It shifted the associated qualities created through these photogrammetry techniques.

The other thing I scanned was Piranesi's Santa Maria del Priorato church. The scanning in its shadows begins to present a totally different understanding of what is and what isn't an edge. This goes back to the *poché* question. This is that statue of St Basil, the altar from above.
So, we're looking down through the head of the statue of St Basil, and everything black is in 'shadow', meaning everything which was not available to the camera.
I didn't climb on top of the altar and take photos or scans from above, I could only scan that which was available to the camera. But this gives us a totally different kind of sensation of space in the things we're looking at. The thicknesses are gone, because we're only looking at points describing surfaces.

So, when I start to see through St Basil's head to his face from behind, we're in a kind of different relationship to the ways in which these tools of representation describe spatial, formal and figural ideas.

When do things start to get strange? When does the modelling and imaging technology itself begin to push back and change things? And how can we understand it as a medium?

Relevant questions in this regard drove the exchange between myself and the artist James Casebere when we started collaborating in an attempt to try to have a conversation about shared terms between art and architecture and the ways in which we work on forming space.
Working back and forth with photographs James took of physical models he was making

in his studio and my remodelling of them with photogrammetry software, the exchange provoked questions on edge conditions of the techniques and their speculative capacity.

If it's only light that is being collected by the digital camera, just photons in an array, what happens if you make a model out of black? Once something was black, the photogrammetry model could no longer build a surface for that set of information.
What we started to figure out is that different lighting conditions, different backgrounds, different assemblages, especially different colours in relationship to the different lights, began to get very different effects.

And then this question of how do you work with millions of points?
An overwhelming question at first.
Because I can work with lines and move a few lines and be able to structure some relationships between space and form. But if I've got a million points, which point do I move first? Almost a meaningless question. But because of the ways in which the photogrammetry model works, it's essentially just working off collected colour data of points in space.
And so, we started working on isolating different colour spectrums, and then building new models by assembling different colour spectrums as opposed to assembling different shapes.
When you begin to manipulate the model, you're no longer looking for edges, you're looking for thresholds of colour ranges.

This led to a number of different experiments where the drawings started looking a little bit like the images I was doing at the start a decade ago in Rhino, with questions of array, depth, dynamic vibrations and the luminosity.

BRYAN CANTLEY
I'm really intrigued by the relationship of the initial placement of the camera that photographed James's physical models. When we get back to the discussion of *entourage*, as something that is present in the performance and in the relationship with the space, I'm wondering if the device that enables the recording has an opportunity to become a condition within the conversation, if that makes any sense.

MICHAEL YOUNG
It totally makes sense.
And I think the way, for me at least, it is in there, is in this question of this re-evaluation of *poché*.
Because for instance, in the photogrammetry images, you can see elements that look like a shadow, it is a shadow, but it's simply a shadow of occlusion from where a set of four photographs were taken.
So, if I had all 50 photographs, the shadow of occlusion would be gone, or would be submerged within a whole other set of imaged information.
The image is made by fragmenting and what I'm starting to call 'interleaving'.
I'm taking the raw photographs,
I'm screwing with them,
and then I'm bringing them back together to build new photogrammetry models, meaning I'm adjusting the colours before the software builds this three-dimensional reality.
The camera is not physically present as an object, but its actions are present in terms of shadows on the floor, which are just simply occluded flaws, but also directionality of mark-making with the camera position.

Furthermore, as one collects through a series of photographs, something that's focused on that sculpture, one is also collecting the background …
all this other kind of ephemera that's been captured by the photograph and then modelled by the software.
So, this also means that you can begin to collage them and start to fragment and remodel three-dimensionally, through different pieces at different levels of colour.

And this led to a number of other experiments into what happens if you start to break the series down in different colour ranges.
And that this may be a way in which one could build a new model, a new space.
Because essentially, we're capturing the environment through its imaging, and

MICHAEL YOUNG
Ludovisi Sarcophagus, Study and oblique detail, 2020
Photogrammetry experiment

MICHAEL YOUNG
St Basil from Above, 2020
Photogrammetry montage

fragmenting the model to remake new models,
new spatial ideas,
new formal ideas,
new relationships between figure and ground.
The shadow is the *poché* in this case,
and it's as interesting to me as the thing casting the shadow.
That interrelationship is what I'm interested in.
I was looking at a lot of Josef Albers. I was trying to do it on an almost pixel-by-pixel basis.
I was thinking about it like Ken Price, his sculptures,
the kind of inlaid colour variations within the sanded-off forms that he would work with.

We've developed such a kind of strong history of the ways in which we work with lines, but we're at a kind of disadvantage in trying to find ways in which we work with points and how we can bring those into architectural discourse.
I think this is, at least for me, an important question.
How do we work as architects in a world that's not primarily described through hundreds of lines, but through millions of points? And what are our modes of engaging in that?

And then there's also this idea that because essentially these are collages that we're looking at, they're collages of thousands and thousands of coloured points, but they're still collages. So, what about the question that always comes with collage about the seam? And how could one find new seams or remove seams?
If you wanted to turn this into something else, what would be the ways that we would do that, because it would no longer be analogue?
The cut of a knife against a photographic edge would be the cut of a range of colour.

I'm interested in painterly effects. I'm interested in materiality in terms of illusions of things that are not there. And I'm also interested in ephemera and accidental things, accidents that begin to lead and become the start of a project.

Ways of misusing the technology, ways in which the technology begins to create associations with other forms of media and representation.
And how do we then feed that back into our work as designers, as architects?

When making these investigative drawings, there are moments when, for one reason or another, I get excited about a kind of breakthrough.
For instance, one of the things I've been interested in is this false dichotomy that we sometimes hold between abstraction and realism. As if we want to position these two things against each other – like,
19th-century artists made realist art,
20th-century artists made abstract art.
Or renderings are photoreal images and drawings are abstract concepts …
I've always been uncomfortable with those kinds of binaries.
I've always thought there's much more play in weirdness between them.
Somehow with these photogrammetry models, there are moments that look photoreal, and then moments that look like abstract-expressionism.
But the movement between them is all to do with questions of resolution, colour, angle of view, layering of information and collaging of different sorts of sampled models.
And I find that this for me is interesting, to move between abstraction and realism in a way that I hadn't before.

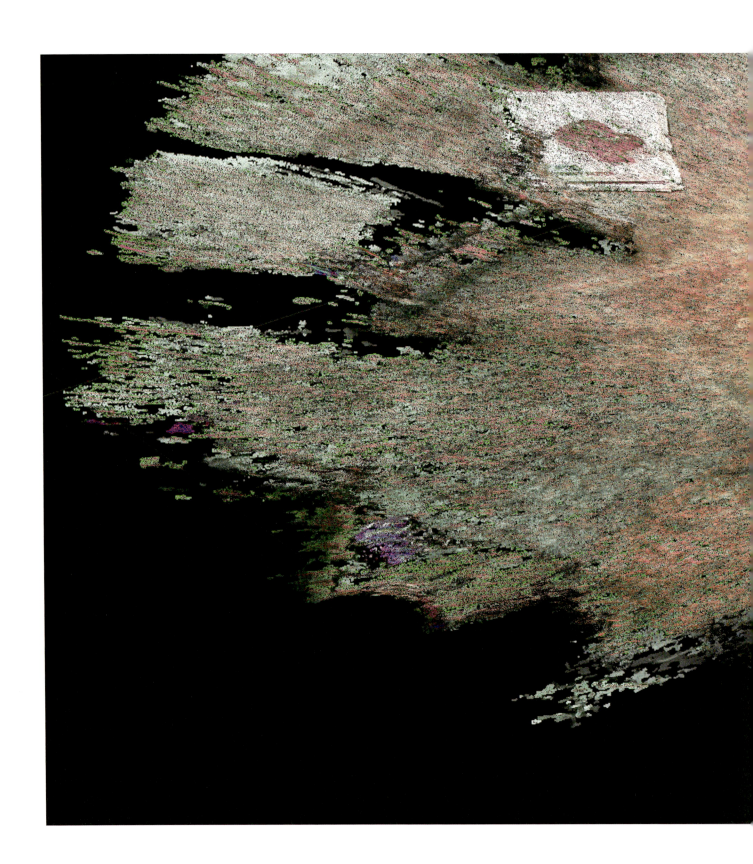

MICHAEL YOUNG WITH JAMES CASEBERE
Reality Modelled after Images – Study 7, 2021
Photogrammetry montage

Metis:
Mark Dorrian + Adrian Hawker
Between Drawing and Model

MARK DORRIAN

Making this model felt like drawing on a thick surface.
To me this model always seemed to be like a drawing, and I don't think it is because of its low-relief quality but something about the way it was produced and made and the use of digital tools, in which, as you know, you're defining the tool paths for cutting and etching and for the development of the model.

And I suppose one of the questions it raises for me is: in what way does a drawing become spatialised?
Is drawing inevitably something on a flat surface?
I guess it is about the kind of things we decide to call drawing and why we chose to use that term.
It was interesting hearing Michael [Young] talking about his experience of the use of the terms 'drawing' and 'image' in the particular context of the Cooper Union
and the investments that exist in these terms. It seems to me that often these words are less useful as descriptions of what things actually are, than as symptoms of the kind of relationship we have with things that we do. Also, the ways that we want to situate these in particular discursive situations by the way we name them.

The model is part of the production for an urban design competition for Verona.
At the time we were very preoccupied with the material substrates and conditions and codes of particular kinds of drawing.
We were interested in making drawings that could be manipulated and used in particular ways, so the drawing is not something that appears on a flat sheet but is something that is put into motion or action or operation in a way. In fact, there were a number of drawings for this project that were destroyed in the process of developing it because the drawings became performative agents or, in a way, actors and got worn out.

A lot of the time the kind of drawing and the character of the work is very much driven by the programmatic conditions of the brief, but also by the kinds of terminology that are used in the briefing materials of a competition.

Whenever you do a competition, you're given a particular archive of materials, which may be historic maps of the site and may be site photographs etc., and — maybe also because of the speed in which you have to work — they form a kind of horizon of knowledge. You are expected to elaborate a certain understanding of the site from this limited information, and I suppose we are interested in the unexpected or the unintended consequences of that.
We are interested in the interference in the images, for example the particular quality of differentials that exist in the images and information that are supplied in a competition brief with the possibility of re-reading these,
almost in a naive way,
against the grain —
the possibility of paying attention to things that are effects of particular modes of representation rather than the objects that are supposed to lie behind them or the reference to which the information points.
Working with this idea, the Verona project, for example, developed through the idea of 'copying strategies' which would select elements from the existing city and translate them through representational techniques into the site.

Part of the pleasure of doing this is working with physical drawings in which the paper becomes spatialised by cutting, tearing and folding.
I am actually not very clear if this is a process of drawing or a process of modelling, or some sort of combination of the two.
In the case of the Verona project, the excessive length of the city wall in relationship to the site, and the kind of compaction it necessitated, became part of the pleasure of this particular process.

The projects that we produce are very much about the materialisation of a kind of

METIS: MARK DORRIAN + ADRIAN HAWKER WITH
RICHARD COLLINS AND AIKATERINI ANTONOPOULOU

Railyard Zone, Mimetic Urbanism, Verona, Italy, 2000
Laser-etched base, hardwood and plywood elements, wood veneer and paper infill

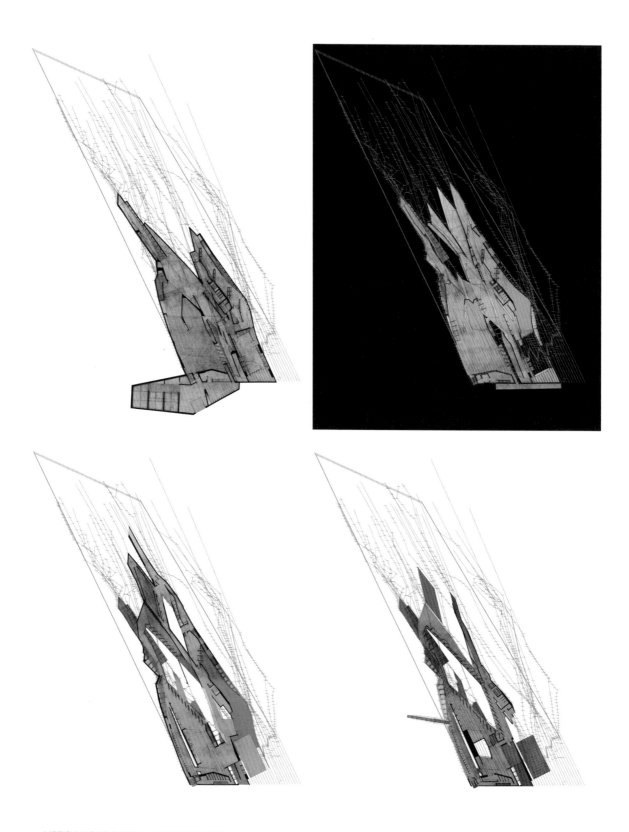

METIS: MARK DORRIAN + ADRIAN HAWKER

Project for Nam June Paik Gallery, Seoul, South Korea, 2003
Digital file from pencil drawing on tracing paper/collage,
103 × 80 cm (40½ × 31½ in)

drawing or drawing as an operative mobile material thing.

MICHAEL YOUNG

Mark, I have to think of Vitruvius's term *ichnographia*, when I see the drawings.
It refers to a plan, but a plan as a 'cut' is a convention we didn't have until Bramante.
Ichnographia's history is much more tied to surveying and markings made on the ground.
And it seems that you are very interested in surveying,
tracing,
ground movements,
ground flows,
ground patterns of walks, etc.
I almost see this as different psycho-geographic walks where, instead of stitching or cutting, you are working with traces.

NEIL SPILLER

Can we talk about the shapes,
the shapes you make?
For instance, in the Verona project,
the kind of infills you make between the wall and the project site,
the spaces between the walls.
They are nice shapes …
There is this kind of Le Corbusier purist thing about the forms within the wall and a kind of Libeskind-like engraving.
Are these two particular things you enjoy, as I do?

MARK DORRIAN

Yes, absolutely – part of our framework of references.
Libeskind was incredibly important for us – *Chamber Works* in particular.

I guess it is hard to talk about,
it's a kind of compositional thing …
but it's also a sense of the body language of the forms and the sense of pressure that they put on one another and the way they dynamise particular kinds of relations.
They elicit a kind of imaginative occupancy of them.

The timber pieces on the model were thought of as drifting elements,
which pass through a texture and get caught or clogged.
I suppose I like to use the term 'clogged' and am very aware of the way the use of words guides and shapes thinking in the design process.

We've always enjoyed the kind of physicality inherent in the way Peter Salter talks about his architecture, and particularly the Thai Fish Restaurant project that he made for Toyo Ito.
Peter talks about the timber shell vessels that form the dining spaces as, on the one hand, in communication with the volcanic landscape outside but, on the other, as also having an affective quality in the interior because of the way they act as blockages that put pressure on the interiors and squeeze space between them.

You inherit these ways of thinking, and part of that is inheriting a vocabulary as well, and when there are two of you working together, there are words that you use to talk to one another about the work that gain a kind of density.

NEIL SPILLER

Establishing common ground by precedents and references.

MARK DORRIAN

Absolutely, and that becomes incredibly important to the way you think about the forms.

NEIL SPILLER

You use the word 'marquetry', which I have never heard used in relation to an architectural model, and yet it seems so obvious …

MARK DORRIAN

I've mentioned the 'low-relief' quality of the model.
'Marquetry' is the lowest of low-relief in the way it wraps and moves.

In a way, here in the Verona project, it was partly a response to this big concrete railroad goods yard – the feeling was that this was something you were not going to dig deeply into. There was something about the hardness of the surface. This marquetry, like a timber mat on this hard surface, had a kind of potentiality in that space.

Talking about marquetry was a way of talking about the intensification of that surface – making ground scores through an increasingly complex use of materials, but working in a shallow depth.

NEIL SPILLER

All the walls are the same height in the model. You were not tempted to make some higher than others?

MARK DORRIAN

No…

I suppose we were thinking of it as a single structure like a room with a ceiling or sky at a given height.

It is probably a reference nobody likes now, but we've always appreciated Aldo van Eyck's Sonsbeek Sculpture Pavilion in Arnhem, with the parallel walls and circular footprint. There is something of that in this project.

When we are working on a project and trying to understand the dimension of how big something might be, we often go and find a similar place in the city in which we live. Thinking about the closeness and the tightness in this project, we think of Edinburgh's incredibly tight structure of closes, the little slot-like lanes that branch off from the medieval High Street.

Sometimes you can touch the buildings on opposite sides of the close at the same time with your arms spread out.

There is that feeling of the body caught in the compressive quality of the architecture, but at the same time in relationship to some sort of expansive condition – the sky seen overhead, or the sea at the end of the vista …

It is that idea that is reflected in the rigid structure of the walls.

The Nam June Paik gallery project, outside Seoul in South Korea, was also developed by thinking about the representational documents that were supplied during the competition stage.

We were interested particularly in Nam June Paik's *Electronic Opera*, and the way he distorted and re-performed television images by manipulating the electron beams in a cathode ray tube with a powerful electromagnet.

We misread the topographic map of the site as an electromagnetic field, developing a process of interference between cathode-ray-tube-like scan-lines and the topography, and then re-screened the distorted image into the site.

Drawings were developed through a taxonomy of the scan-lines and what happens to them as they encountered the field pattern of the site. Through that drawing process, the project is really embedded within the landscape, and the landscape is condensed into it. With the production of these drawings, the building is 'found' within the planar condensation of lines.

In the competition for the Egyptian museum, we were interested in the Flinders Petrie trigonometric survey of the pyramids at Giza, which is often said to be the first accurate survey.

The way this project developed is to do with shadows and the mythology of the shadow of the pyramid. But again, also the idea that one might, in a sense, take the representational documentation as itself the site of the project. The speculation was that this geometrical network might be redirected to capture things other than the geometry of the pyramids. The figure of the pyramids is inscribed within it, but could it also act as a net to pick up other elements?

Working with the photographic material we had received from the competition brief, the idea was that the net could begin to pick up the inscriptive shadow lines and, through a series of folds and manipulations, transport those to the site and sediment them as a kind of spectral shadow landscape that is formed in relationship to the pyramids but dissolves the image of the pyramid and picks up something else.

NAT CHARD

You mentioned yesterday the story of measuring size and scale of the pyramids, mediated through the shadow …

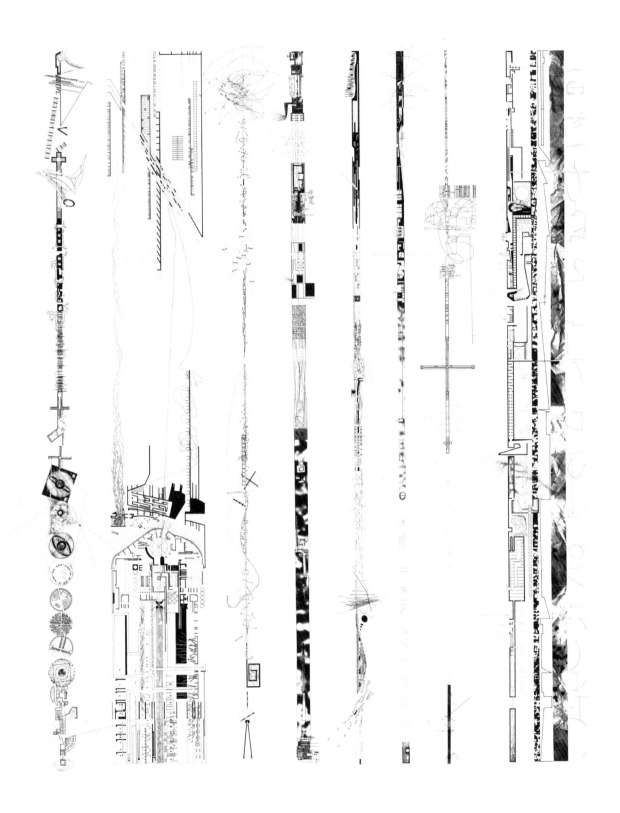

Previous page:
METIS: MARK DORRIAN + ADRIAN HAWKER WITH
RICHARD COLLINS AND AIKATERINI ANTONOPOULOU

Metis retrospective exhibition 'On The Surface' (Aarhus, Denmark), showing the section of display with the Museum of Egypt project, 2014
Digitally printed textile, digital prints on watercolour paper, laser-etched wooden model with 3-D printed elements

This page:
METIS: MARK DORRIAN + ADRIAN HAWKER

Narrative strips, Micro-urbanism, Ottawa, Canada, 2001
Digital file from ink drawing on tracing paper, 69 × 56 cm (27 × 22 in)

MARK DORRIAN

Yes, that was very important – there is an essay by Michel Serres called 'What Thales Saw ...', based on a story about the measuring of the pyramids. This deals with the shadow of the pyramid and a kind of enigmatic interiority that exceeds the apparent transparency of pure geometrical forms. He talks about things being 'infinitely folded into one another ... like the stones and objects of the world'.
This motif of enigmatic interiority occurs time and time again in Western thinking about the pyramid. It is there in Hegel's *Aesthetics*, for example.

I suppose the thought was that one might reorientate that toward a kind of shadow topography, which was less about what was held within the contours of the pyramid than something more distributed and inscriptive. As the shadow develops, it becomes a kind of writing on the surface.

In the context of the project, the shadow-marking process produced the possibility of a kind of archaeology-to-come of this topography that was captured in the moment of the photograph.

From the aerial photograph we redrew the shadow forms of the pyramids' oblique shadows, the tombs of the priests and also the topographic features. We traced everything within the topographic web.

PERRY KULPER

A lot of the marks have the quality of a kind of divination or a geomancy, maybe indexical, and I wondered the degrees to which the drawing-forth of the divining lines can impact a different kind of programmatic thinking.

It seems interesting that the drawing and the divination of that would have that impact ... and so you wouldn't say 'this is a convention centre' or 'this is a library'. There is something about the way you are working, the process of drawing and the drawing-out, that is summoning hidden ciphers or indexes that then have other kinds of effects.

Those lines, the shadow net and so forth, they are there in some hyper sense. I am interested in degrees to which things like drawing can begin to impact typologies or impact programmatic thinking, and the work you make seems to offer that.

MARK DORRIAN

It is difficult, isn't it?
I'm not sure if I have a good way of describing it, but
whenever one is doing this
one is always trying to hold a kind of latency or immanence within the work,
which is less about conclusively ascribing programmatic conditions to the things that we find than it is about allowing a certain kind of attachment to emerge between programmatic requirements and the spatial architectural conditions that are being set up.

It is almost as if you have two forces, two kinds of vibrancies brought into contact with one another. One is the material and spatial condition that is appearing through the process, and the other is the force that is coming from the programmatic demand. The two are placed in a relationship of interference, of tension, but also some kind of accommodation with one another. Whenever you are working on this, whenever you are thinking through this, you are aware of a kind of latency or potential, and for sure it affects the way that you think about particular ways that the work is developed and certain discussions that occur.

You are always trying to alienate your relationship with the work in order to find something.
The process is like losing one's route, and re-finding it, or finding another.
It involves a sort of proleptic understanding, a kind of leaping forward at times ...
You have this sense that some ways of drawing, some lines of investigation will be incredibly productive, and that some others will be arid and run dry.
But you don't necessarily have a way of rationally describing that.
It is like a kind of foresight, in a sense.

PERRY KULPER
The drawings seem like fertile lines.
It seems like they might then produce a whole set of other kinds of occupations or lines or divinations ...
I was thinking as a form of urbanisation, a kind of urban morphology.
The lines' indeterminacy, their potential in other kind of lines.

I wonder if you think of that?
This form of drawing and drawing-out might end up cryptic,
quasi-indexical,
quasi-spatial?
It is not a *tabula rasa* thing at all,
nor is it a zoning.
There is something about it that seems to almost have an ecological potential that I could take up and work with,
or others in the room.

MARK DORRIAN
Well yes, I think if the project has done anything,
if we've been able to do anything at all,
it is always because of something that was there before,
which sets in motion some kind of relational thinking.

PERRY KULPER
You are insistent on that actually, aren't you?
That there is still some dependence on cultural grounds, density and history of ideas and so on, which is super nice.

MARK DORRIAN
Because we have the impression of 'choosing' ways of working
we often don't think about the general complexity of what inheres in them already and the way histories are concretised in the instruments that we use.
There are capacities and values and orientations that are embedded in our hands and our bodies through training and acculturation.
I feel we always have something of that shock of difference when we look at a historic document – I think of cursive copperplate script, for instance. Probably no one in this room could write like that now, but it was second nature for 19th-century schoolchildren.

And maybe this is a question that comes up when one looks back at the objects of one's life.
'Who was I then?'
What array of things came together in this material trace that I left behind?
That is a kind of open line of thought because it is just so complex.
But endlessly interesting and instructive to think about.

BRYAN CANTLEY
I'm interested in the chronology of the generation of images. You seem to be bouncing back and forth between drawing and object-making and back to drawing.
Is there such a thing as termination of this, and if so, where does the termination reside?
As architects, we are typically trained to draw and then make, and I rather like the fact that you are oscillating between the two.
I'm wondering if you consider the terminal point to be the fabricated object, or would you conclude with a set of analytical drawings of process if that makes sense?

MARK DORRIAN
Well, when you are working on a competition there is a kind of forced termination point, the time of the submission.
But personally,
I don't think of any of the projects as completed or terminated in any way.
It is partly because of the intensity of the way one imagines the project and its spaces as you are working on them. One is always aware of the possibility of going on to unfold the project further – but also about different unpursued futures that different stages in the design process pointed to.

I tend to say that a design process is fundamentally a chain of representations. Something has to be carried between those representations in order for it to be a process. We do something and then we do something else in relationship to what we have just done to find out and elaborate a little more.

METIS: MARK DORRIAN + ADRIAN HAWKER
Sequential unfolding of the cartographic montage
Cabinet of the City, Rome, 2002
Digital collage with drawn elements, 76 × 56 cm (30 × 22 in)

METIS: MARK DORRIAN + ADRIAN HAWKER

Episodes from Rabelais: The Whale (Book Four, Chapters 33-34), 2022.
Digital print on folded watercolour paper, 76 × 56 cm (30 × 22 in)

But equally, it seems to me that, at each of these points, things are left behind. Often in what we make, like drawings or models, we do things we were not intending to, which shift — or have the potential to shift — the making or drawing.

I feel quite strongly that, within that kind of process, what we have is actually not one single project but a multiplicity of different ones — in the sense that you could go back and examine any point and anticipate different futures from it.
There is a kind of archival sedimentation of material that has a latency that can always be returned to, which is proof against any single conclusive end-point of the project.
And I suppose we enjoy that, and try to remain open to it.

Nat Chard
Drawing Instruments

NAT CHARD

I have been looking into territories of indeterminacy and the uncertain. There are two sides to this — firstly the side that would tend towards the sublime, which deals with occurrences that one cannot predict, and secondly, the very straightforward fact that we all experience the world differently.
The world is available differently for each of us. This is partly explored by a series of 'body projects' that took the sites where architecture and the city claim to have the tightest relationship to the human body, adjusting the performance of the human body in relation to those sites (hygiene, heating and cooling, digestion, waste, etc.) and asking the question if, by doing so, we therefore also change architecture and the city?
And could we take possession of it, each of us on our own terms?

I have made a series of drawing instruments to try and address this question of uncertainty in an architectural condition.

What I hope to do is to employ drawings in a way where they are spatially active, addressing the question of what role the picture plane is playing in our individual reception of a common event.
How can the drawings be active provocateurs in that situation? Historically, artists have folded the picture plane to make their images appear more realistic. I have been folding the picture plane to receive images critically, so that you can receive them in one way and I in another.

My drawing instruments, as they have evolved, have become more architectural and more spatial, becoming propositional things in their own right.

The first three instruments investigate the potential of the folded picture plane — the possibility of the surface providing a critical reception of an idea.

Instrument Four was the moment where I went from throwing light to throwing paint. Previously I was working with optical projection, with light projected on to the picture plane. The folding of the picture plane was working very well, but with optical projection I had complete control over how the light was received.
There was no uncertainty,
it was self-defeating.
And so, I thought, well ...
I've done all this work on the folded picture plane, how can I use this?
And the answer for me was to change the projected medium from light to latex paint, which is much more mischievous.
The drawing comes from the collision of the material and the splatter, rather than optical shadows, where you always get the figure, whatever geometrical alteration you make.

When I threw the paint, it all happened rather quickly, and what I was missing seemed important.
So, I started taking high-speed flash photographs, learning from people like Arthur Mason Worthington and Harold Edgerton.
The first flash I used wasn't nearly quick enough, so I employed a faster flash and it started revealing all sorts of productive surprises. I see the paint throw and its collision with the model as an analogue for occupation, where the architectural model is adapted to acknowledge the paint in place of bodies.

Very stupidly I thought,
the paint is like light, it will hit the thing, and then it will cast a shadow.
The flying paint that misses the model obscures the splatter, the very thing I'm interested in.
The noise obscures the signal.
I address this later in *Instrument Seven*.
I use a latex paint, a non-Newtonian fluid, like blood.
There are digital and analogue techniques for forensic scientists to derive narratives from patterns of splattered blood.
Analogously, I'm using a medium that could work from this knowledge.

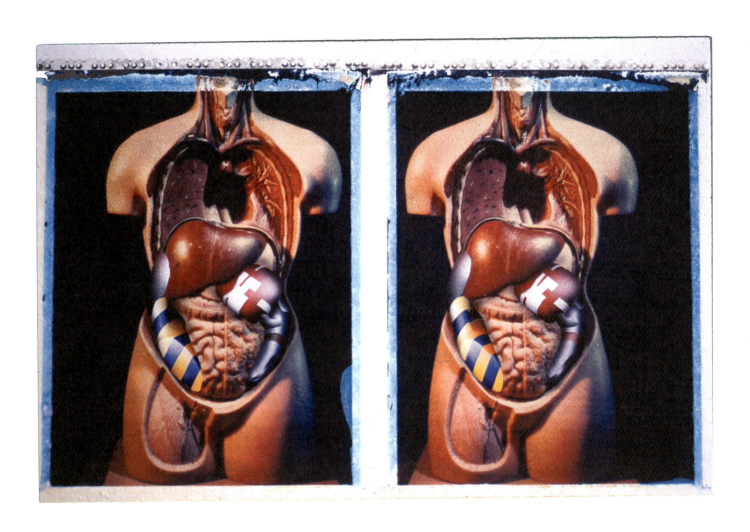

NAT CHARD

Body Architecture 2 (House), Layer Four (of eight), c.1996
Airbrush on Polaroid transfer (stereoscopic pair), 12 × 20 cm (5 × 8 in)

NAT CHARD

Instrument Five, c.2008
Latex paint in flight, high-speed flash photograph of drawing in action

MARK WEST

Is that a rubber band holding the spoon down?

NAT CHARD

Yes, the spoons are propelled by rubber bands and the power can be adjusted by the number of bands.
I had never made a paint catapult before and I was surprised by its accuracy in terms of line and length.
But very pleasurably, each throw is completely unique.

A while back, Perry and I were having a conversation by email about *Instrument Five*.
I was trying to explain what I was doing and discussing the pieces that the paint was thrown at.
I described the space as being a little bit like the interior of a submarine,
where the whole space is made by programmatic elements.
Perry wrote back and said: 'I've never been in a submarine!'
So, I put together a couple of photographs stereoscopically that I had taken in the *Argonaute* submarine at the Parc de la Villette in Paris.
And when I sent them off to Perry I looked more carefully and saw this strangely annoying floating blur,
which I suddenly realised was exactly what I'd been looking for.
What happened was I had taken the left-eye picture and the right-eye picture to get the parallax for stereoscopy, but having a flash on the camera, there was a second parallax for the shadow. This constructed a floating shadow, a sort of paradoxical shadow, the very thing that I had been trying to play with in *Instrument Two* and *Instrument Three*.

So, I dropped everything to build *Instrument Six* to be able to become Peter Pan and float shadows in mid-air.
When I see the floating shadow, my perception sees the shadow floating in space, but my consciousness says, 'This is naughty' because I've got a very obedient consciousness that tries to put the shadow back where it should belong. While observing the floating shadow my perception made it hover and my consciousness tries to put it back on the screen.

MARK WEST

So, with *Instrument Six* you made the floating shadows with an actual object in real time rather than photographic evidence?

NAT CHARD

Yes, before your very eyes.
You need to use polarising glasses and filters to see the floating shadow. It also works photographically.

In *Instrument Seven* I located the picture plane adjacent to the trajectory of the thrown paint rather than behind it. So, I only capture the signal (splatter) and let the noise (paint) pass through.

Instrument Eight was born out of a transatlantic conversation Perry Kulper and I were having.
This long-distance communication via instruments resulted in two versions of the instrument, Perry's version and mine, throwing paint at each other and playing out our conversation.

Instrument Nine calibrates that depth of the floating shadows that just developed in *Instrument Six*.

Here are three drawings of some chairs I'm working on that depict the same instant.
The slight variations in them could be down to one being a reality, another a memory, another the construct of one of the participants' consciousness and so on.
Those situations are discussed by these four instruments that together make up *Instrument Ten*. Each has a paint catapult with a bespoke spoon to hold the paint, and a dedicated picture plane.
And the catapults throw paint from one instrument to another.
Each chair is occupied by paint deflectors (in place of a model person) to allow adjustment.

PERRY KULPER

And what are the underlying factors that form

the deflectors that receive the flying paint? What establishes their size and profile?

NAT CHARD

The deflectors have a scale that acknowledges the nature of the flying paint, which would be missed by a 1:6 model of a person. The figure of the picture plane is particular to the reception of the idea.
So, the uncertainty happens in both the throwing and the receiving of the splatter.

A subtext of the work is that these are instrumental instruments, but they also have the appearance of didactic instruments and use didactic techniques as a seduction to try and persuade people to take the strange things that happen with them seriously.
I am learning from didactic techniques associated with explicit knowledge to try and underpin my world of tacit knowledge.

I have been very interested in didactic instruments that seem paradoxical.
I spent quite a bit of time looking at habitat dioramas in the American Museum of Natural History, especially the background paintings by Belmore Browne and by James Perry Wilson.

I had made cameras to work out and to understand the projective technique Wilson was using on these dioramas at the time; I was really trying to understand the potential of a three-dimensional picture plane.
I learned a lot about a picture plane, the flat picture plane, anamorphic distortion, and so on – but what I also learned was about the uncertainty of the uncanny, and the power of the didactic instrument to produce a play between explicit and tacit knowledge. Curators and scientists have all this knowledge embodied in such a way through the diorama, that when the visitor comes, they can construct that explicit knowledge tacitly for themselves.
So, it seems to have this potential as a site for translation between these realms of knowledge.

PERRY KULPER

Nat, might there be cones which don't correspond with the mathematics of projection but rather with the constructed perception?
And things like peripheral vision and the gradients of distortion?
Can that be accounted for, or is it of interest in terms of the performance of a picture plane and what can be discussed situationally?

NAT CHARD

Yes, very much, not just the peripheral vision but also daydreaming, for example.
In essence, I'm interested in the realm of the uncertain.
A lot of ideas in architecture exist because they relate to things that can be articulated as explicit knowledge, rather than because they matter.
How the realm of tacit knowledge and personal experience can be discussed is something that interests me, but also I'm really attracted to it because it's an elusive subject to study and doesn't have an endpoint.

MICHAEL YOUNG

Now that I see these experiments explained in detail, I feel there's something incredibly weird about the fact that, for most of the last 500 years, we've been operating under the auspices that we can screw with what is catching vision, and we can screw with the subject.
And by manipulating them, we can create this either controlled and tyrannical – or perverse and distorted – relationship with anamorphosis, or curved domes and other kinds of projections. You're actually effing with the cone itself, turning its neutrality into a completely unstable zone.

NAT CHARD

It is in between being stable and unstable.

MICHAEL YOUNG

Yes, it's not quite completely out of control – it's not a chance generator, it's not random. But it's destabilising this thing we've been attached to, projective geometry. And I just think understanding that unlocked so much of what you've been up to.

NAT CHARD

Instrument Six, c.2008
Acrylic, glass, polarising filters, candles, screen material for retaining polarised light
Dimensions variable depending on configuration (fits within 1-metre cube)

NAT CHARD WITH PERRY KULPER

Instrument Eight, c.2012
High-speed flash photograph of Nat's instrument with
paint thrown by Perry's instrument in action

NAT CHARD
Instrument Ten, 2016
High-speed flash photograph of latex paint in flight

PERRY KULPER

But also, what I find interesting is, when you configure things like the picture plane, there is a 'beyond the picture plane' in your work as well, which there never is in the construction of the tyrannical. Because there are limits to that picture plane no matter what it can do, and it still has a backside and some other unknowable territory.

MICHAEL YOUNG

And then there's the uncanniness that goes on and on and on because the picture plane is folded a little bit like a baseball catcher's mitt that could unfold into the wall. So, it's a folded picture plane catching anamorphic projections from a semi-regular, part-controlled, projectile catapult of liquid.

NAT CHARD

That is starting to sound like a slightly promiscuous picture plane …

MICHAEL YOUNG

The glass bells of the 19th century, they are sort of anatomical studies holding little models of little people that were meant to then drop into the spaces if there are the people catapulting or getting catapulted, or getting catapulted on.

NAT CHARD

The little model people are implicated in the situation.

MICHAEL YOUNG

It makes perfect sense now – they're throwing stuff at each other. Do you launch the catapults simultaneously in *Instrument Ten*?

NAT CHARD

No … well …

MICHAEL YOUNG

That would be crazy, right? [Laughs]

NAT CHARD

Well, the nicest part of the instruments is using them.
And so, the most powerful form of representation is what I experienced when I'm worked with them rather than what they drew.
There's the anticipation of what they will do, and there's my desire of what I want them to do.
I set the thing up, I have an aim for it, and I have a hope for what it will do.
But I have a greater hope that it will do beyond what I hope it will do.
And then I have to set the camera up, and to fire the trigger manually. My remote cable for the camera is too short so I am stretching to control the catapult and camera. I capture maybe one in three throws, so, a whole load I just miss.
I didn't want to do the high-speed filming for years as this would undermine the whole experience and make it too reliable.
And so, there are all sorts of hopes and anxieties.
And then there's the pleasure. Did I catch the thing in flight?
And then the critical reception. Was it any good? What was the splash? And did it tell me anything?
So, I experience the very conditions that I'm trying to set up.

MICHAEL YOUNG

I'm also into the use of the rhetoric of didactic scientific mechanisms – maquettes, models and photography – to document something that is tacit or escapes that entirely.
I know it's not totally nefarious – you're not just using that rhetoric to make people believe you know what you're doing.
You know what you're doing, but there is something in the aesthetic tension between those two things – between the didactic mechanisms you use and the thing you're trying to document.
Like the early photographs of fluid dynamics – photographs of catching a drop, and all those things.

NAT CHARD

There is the discussion of Arthur Worthington in Lorraine Daston and Peter Galison's *Objectivity*[1] where the medium of recording the event is initially by drawing the after-image from a flash and subsequently through photography, and although both are made as

NAT CHARD

Pair of Chairs (the subject of Instrument Ten), c.2018
Inkjet, technical pen and airbrush, 120 × 90 cm (47 × 35½ in)
One of three simultaneous views (this one from below)

accurately as possible, their registrations of the same occurrence are significantly different. Operating between those conditions seems like a very nice place.

But also, with the advent of photography as a sort of didactic medium, the opportunism of spirit photographers to make their realms true … I'm finding that incredibly attractive.

MICHAEL YOUNG
And then there's just the purposeful aesthetic to the construction of the full-scale thing that makes it look like a model of the model … like the full-scale thing is still leaving its articulation, so it's not like the maquette is a model of the thing. That's the real thing that's holding it. They both look like models of each other.

WILLIAM MENKING
That takes it back to architecture as well, the maquette.

NAT CHARD
The instruments have a desire to go this way. I'm thinking of the conversation Perry and I have been having. When I send him a photograph of one of the instruments, he'll comment on how much closer they are becoming to architecture.
And they obviously want to get there. The chairs are a way of getting them out of being the instruments – to work out which bits of them become architecture …

MARK WEST
They actually want to be lunar modules.

NAT CHARD
The first time Mark saw one of my instruments is in the corridor of the school, and he just walked past and said: 'The eagle has landed!'

ANTHONY MOREY
When you're trying to rationalise and understand movements, also in terms of the spacing of the elements of an instrument itself, it's through trial and error?

NAT CHARD
Yes.

PERRY KULPER
But there is tacit knowledge built from your understanding of Newtonian fluids in relation to other fluids and trajectories.

NAT CHARD
Yes, what they do when they hit a deflector or model or something.
So that's why I have to keep on building new instruments.
I move on from the things that I know.

WILLIAM MENKING
The work seems intuitive to me. Is it?

NAT CHARD
A lot of is intuitive, and a lot of it is understood on reflection.

ANTHONY MOREY
Is that why you number them? I'm intrigued by you numbering them, because that takes it away from a performance. It becomes like an investigation like one, two, three instead of saying like, here's one thing and here's another. Instead, it becomes like an iterative process.

MICHAEL YOUNG
You move on to the next one, once one gets too paint-splattered to properly be a test case?

NAT CHARD
Well, it doesn't take so many throws to establish everything that can be learned from each instrument. I mean, for example, *Instrument Five*, probably had the most throws – there were probably a hundred throws or something.

MICHAEL YOUNG
I think in this there is a particularly British desire to take the kind of background everyday of machinery and sacralise it to the refined point of high tech – making the profane become sacred to the British refined steampunk high-tech thing. And then to profane it again by slamming the instrument with paint.
Over and over and over again.
And somehow, I think that there's a point of exhaustion when you might lose that tension

between the two. If something gets too covered by too many assaults, and it is no longer this pristine, boyish erector set that has every detail refined and getting assaulted. I think you need both, and maybe that's what then says: 'All right … I know we've covered everything … now … number 11!'

NAT CHARD
Yes, that's true.

ANTHONY MOREY
So what is the drawing in this setup? *Where* is your drawing, in light of understanding the picture plane as a participant, not as the end goal?
The actual aspect of you holding the space in the performance of the instrument, the placement and coordination of the preciousness – I think all those things are the drawing, in its entirety. Does the splatter photograph become the knowledge of what the performance is?

NAT CHARD
Well, they are very literal drawings on the picture plane, the splatter that lands on those surfaces. And the photographs of the flying paint, seeing the figure of the flying paint seems to be a really important image in the story.
But I think there's a sort of whole other world that is the model that gets hit by paint, where that paint has almost zero meaning in terms of the project after the event, other than where it has landed but where the coverage of paint on the thing changes its performance for subsequent throws. And then, there's also the room, which just gets really messed up.

Operating the instrument, I get the representation of the condition that I'm trying to discuss, because I experience it directly. That's the fullest version.
And then I get the representation of it in the photograph and the picture-plane splatter, which relies on me understanding what it is that I'm discussing when I'm making the throw.

PERRY KULPER
Feels like Matthew Barney in *Drawing Restraints*, in some way. It's restraining the development of tacit knowledge by constraining.

MICHAEL YOUNG
The thing I've been looping in my mind is this.
We can say that Jackson Pollock is not making drawings, he's making paintings.
And I don't think any of us here would say that. We need to have hands to make a drawing, right? And I don't think that anybody here would say that the only thing that is important for drawing is a line on paper.
So, then we start moving into other terms. You would also never describe Jackson Pollock in terms of projection, sectioning, picture plane unfolding or instruments. And yet, all four of those things we usually use with drawings, and all four of those things are essentially what your project is.
So, even though the paint as matter and in materiality and gravity hitting something, and being left there is similar to Pollock, the way in which you're constructing the didactic in the tacit world is a world of drawing, not the world of the painterly, if that makes any sense.
I think that framing is somehow crucial for us to keep, disciplinarily.

MARK WEST
It is also super boyish, it should be said. It has nothing to do with drawing, but it's just an observation that's so obvious and so powerful. Don't you think?

1 Lorraine Daston and Peter Galison, *Objectivity* (Princeton, NJ: Princeton University Press, 2010).

Keyword Phrases

MARK WEST

GETTING RIGHT WITH CHANCE

Prediction and control are highly prized. Yet, as Gregory Bateson reminds us, the new can be plucked from nowhere but the random.[1] If you are searching for something new, something beyond the ordinary, a good first step is to loosen your grip on control to allow chance into the mix. For those of us trained in architecture's culture of control, this can be unnerving. I know of no sweeter laboratory than collage for studying the fecundity and beauty of unpredictable events. The elegance of its method is stunning. Taken seriously, it models the core mechanism of creation – a recombination of fragments of known things to produce new, unknown things. This recombinant 'technology' relies largely on chance as its engine. Its practice frustrates control, opens one to serendipity, and teaches how to get right with chance. This involves subtle changes in state of mind in which, after one has left the table, the paper, and the glue, are carried on in the world at large. The habitual fiction of the world as a known and predictable space expands into a more complex and realistic rendition containing both named and nameless things.

[1] Gregory Bateson, *Mind and Nature: A Necessary Unity* (New York: E.P. Dutton, 1979), p. 45

DISTANCE/ CLOSENESS

The world, infinitely dense in scale and structure, reveals its internal structures differently depending on how close, or far away, you are when looking at it. We know this from microscopy, but something very similar is played out when one walks up to a painting by Rembrandt (for instance) and a nearly 'photographic' image resolves into individual brushstrokes and globs of paint, abstracting the thing seen into a kind of action painting. This way of painting presents an analogue of the scaled layers of structure found in the physical world. Or, an architectural example: the agrarian ornamentation of all 'classical' architectures mimics nature, not merely by its rendering of natural forms, but also in scalar density. But this scalar continuity was strangely abandoned by the architecture of machine modernism which presents, instead, vast, smooth, empty stretches in scale where nothing changes as one gets closer or moves farther away. These are physical things play-acting as platonic solids, perhaps pretending weightlessness … I suppose this is why cracks in a smooth blank wall are so disconcerting.

    I prefer a more complex press of matter with its many cracks, odours, perils, gravity and tragic beauty. We are trapped in matter. Everything is already full. There are no 'empty sites'. As you look at anything, closer, and closer again, new worlds emerge. As you step back farther, and farther, new worlds emerge. In a search for more realistic renditions of the physical world, I work to infuse this marvellous density into the images I make.

MICHAEL YOUNG

DIGITAL MOSAIC

All digital images are signals.
They are pulses of coloured light that must be continuously refreshed through electrical energy as signal pulses. Which means that all digital

images are temporally animate; they are performances. What a viewer sees and evaluates as a stable medium is not exactly stable. According to the media theorist Friedrich Kittler, the concept of medium is triple: storage, transmission, processing. Mineral pigments stored in a slow-drying oil-based liquid, adhered to a woven fabric canvas, tensioned flat to wooden bars, is commonly known by post-Renaissance Western European culture by the term 'painting'. The medium transmits this stored information, allowing an image to move from place to place without altering what is stored. Digital images are stored and transmitted as numeric information, their format and file size alter the visual performance, as does software, screen technologies, colour settings, display resolutions, etc. There is a tendency to treat digital images as if they are a medium akin to painting and photography. They are not. There are however two other aspects from the arts that provide interesting alignments.

All digital images are montages.
Montage functions in relation to the presence or absence of a disjunctive seam. This juncture is where the friction between two adjacent images alters the potential meanings constructed in the consciousness of the viewer. Each pixel of pulsed light in a digital image is independent of the pixel adjacent; they are montaged. The differences in hue between adjacent pulses is what becomes sensible to human perception. Most of these junctures happen below conscious attention; they are 'meaningless' because we cannot attend to them, yet they structure the digitally imaged world as a montage of discrete, independent signals.

All digital images are mosaics.
Mosaic tiles are discrete assemblages of independent pieces that group to form patterns or recognisable imagery as a collective. Where, when, how and why a pattern of pieces dissolves into seamless continuity or reveals its discrete elements is one of the fundamental questions of all mosaics. And is equally applicable to all digital images under the term 'resolution'. Resolution is the result of storage, transmission and processing. It is determined through an economic, technological and aesthetic negotiation.

REALISM

Realism as an aesthetic position is not the opposite of abstraction. In fact, over the past century abstraction has often been used in art to intensify realism. For example, a painting such as Kazimir Malevich's *Black Square* (1915) is abstract in that the reduced form and colour of the square resists any recognisable similarity to objects or events one would see in daily life. But because of this abstraction, the viewer no longer looks through the painting like a window towards the world; instead, it is a thing that one looks at. The viewer's attention is shifted to the cracking of paint, slight variations in pigment coverage, very real material aspects of decay in the world. Realism is the aesthetic tension between an object and its representation. The higher the tension, the greater the challenge to assumptions, the more intense the aesthetic as an affect. At particularly extreme moments, in the *Black Square* for example, the tension stretches to where image is material, where art and life collapse into each other.

What this means for architectural representation is more complicated than it is for art. An architectural representation is always assumed to represent something else, a past or future built environment, hence an architectural drawing can never simply be real in and of itself. Likewise, since it refers directly to the material realm it can never be fully abstract. This leads to an interesting dilemma. When architects call their images abstract it is because they look like something other than the building. When they use terms like realism, it is because the image looks like a photograph of a built reality. To further complicate this, a building can suppress its material, structure and assembly to appear abstract, or it can emphasise exactly these factors to appear 'more' real. And these aspects of a built construction do not have to match the abstraction or realism of the representations that the architect labours through in the production and evaluation of the design. Realism in architecture fluctuates between reality and its representation, never simply secure in one location.

Now, I suggested above that an architectural drawing can never be real in and of itself. This is not entirely true. In fact, there are architectural images that become worlds unto themselves. When this occurs, the architectural representation enters a delicate balance – it is a use of abstraction to frustrate or complicate easy assignation to a built world. This can be pushed to a point where the viewer begins to look at, not through, the image. In this, the image becomes the object; it is not representational of anything other than itself. These images are often derisively called 'paper architecture' and viewed as being by architects pretending to be artists. I have another interpretation. Realism redistributes the way in which reality becomes sensible, which is what the best architecture always does, whether it is built or not.

MARK DORRIAN AND ADRIAN HAWKER

GROUND SCORES

Marking the ground intensifies, or perhaps ambiguates, the relation between the drawing and the constructed project, granting things that gather and accumulate within the sequence of representations that make up a design process – things that might otherwise be viewed as inconsequential and thus dismissed – the possibility of some kind of materialisation and presence. One effect of this is to indicate a larger field of force or set of relations within which the project solidifies – seen in this way, architectural elements become situationally specific transformations or instantiations occurring within larger continuities.

In our projects, such markings might derive from representational documents such as city plans or aerial photographs, or from unintentional traces that seep into the field of the project through the process and materials of study (the glitch in the photocopied image, the rip in the paper, etc.), or from design moves that put all these into play in relation to programmatic demands and technical and material thinking. In *Cabinet of the City*, a municipal gallery project for Rome, the sequential stages of the hinging and unfolding map deposits a choreography of striations on the courtyard surface, which then twists and tilts in relation to them; in the Nam June Paik gallery, landscape contours, reread as an electromagnetic field, produce a pattern of topographic lines within which the project concretises; in the garden sector of the urban design project for Verona, linear scorings derived from the pattern of the disused railway lines interact with cuttings that act as constructed shadows of walls and with inscribed lines of projection that link things beyond the site to their doubles within it, defined according to the mimetic thinking that underpins the design; in the Egyptian museum project, the lines of Flinders Petrie's 19th-century trigonometrical survey of the pyramids becomes a net which, through a process of folding, traverses the arid landscape, catching shadows as it goes.

    The etymology of 'score' involves rifts in rock, and acts of incising and cutting, but also counting – the term meant 'twenty' in Icelandic and Old English, presumably due to that being the number reached when a notch was cut in a stick, or incised in a stone, when counting cattle. And it also, of course, comes, via music notation, to mean a graphic inscription that is to be performed. Thought in this way, a 'ground score' might be seen as something that potentialises differential series of performances – and the architectural object, as it's normally understood, might be just one of these. Through the ways that we trace or enact them, we become invested in the adventure of lines, which prompt and respond to us. When we made a drawing that could be walked on for our exhibition *On the Surface*, we hoped its marks and orientations would lead to new itineraries between the works that were on display. One day we were sent a recording of visitors who had begun to dance on it, making their own somatic drawings in space in response to what they found below their feet.

OPERATIVE, MOBILE, MATERIAL THING

It's an embarrassingly clumsy phrase to describe drawing, but it points to something important for us. The words in this sequence are not just qualifiers of one another but entwine and are interdependent – each of the ideas or terms is already within the others. The drawing is operative because it does a kind of work, one that is often beyond the intentions that guide its making – kinds of operativity can emerge from drawings even when, perhaps especially when, they appear to be detached from explicit instrumental ends, meaning that 'finality' is never a last word. Mobility is inherent in the diverse array of effects that drawings can produce and their variegated operativity. The drawing is never static and definitively concluded, but always open to being read and acted upon – or with – in unanticipated ways. These might derive from the displacement of familiar hierarchies by, for example, attending to different things – smudges, smears, spillages and other adventitious marks, or the wear and tear of material substrates. While what is material could seem in some way opposed to mobility, it is really the case that only those things that have some kind of material presence can be mobile. Even digital objects, often assumed to be exempt from this, are thoroughly material at all stages of their construction, storage and constitution as visible things.

    One aspect of our long-standing interest in maps is the way they tie together questions of mobility and materiality. Lots of drawings travel, but maps are special cases. On one hand, they are 'immutable mobiles' in Bruno Latour's phrase – they produce conditions of stability that allow information to be transported, and this gives them their normative utility. When we return to a map, we expect to see the same features in the same relation to one another. Yet, on the other, everything that is mobile is liable to change – perhaps through recontextualisation, but also through an array of material contingencies. Maps are blown by the wind, torn, rained upon, annotated and their legibility worn down by fingers, hasty refoldings, etc.

We imagined what different landscapes might be constructed from non-intentional marks, and also what accidents might have resulted in conventional symbols, whose 'official' status had now been drained away. We became interested in specific maps that played representationally and operatively with their material conditions – such as Jacques Callot's remarkable *Siege of Breda* (1627), in which the entire field of the image undergoes a continuous spatial warping, topographic prospect transforming into ichnographic plan and back again; or a 1950s Czechoslovakian concertina map book, bought from a Prague bookseller, a paper machine for producing unexpected juxtapositions.

And finally, there is the 'thing', with whose etymology as a 'gathering' we are familiar. Gathered by the drawing are what it brings to visibility by graphic inscription, relations with its author/s, its own conditions of production, and what came before and will come after – for we are always interested in where the drawing will lead us, and how it connects immanence to imminence.

NAT CHARD

TERRITORIES OF INDETERMINACY AND MISCHIEVOUS MATERIAL

In order to make sense of why we build architecture, we make programmes that predict how the architecture will support an imagined occupation. This is an essential part of architectural practice, yet it has awkward consequences. The programme is often reductive, missing out on all the unpredictable occurrences that make our lives so rich. By providing for the predicted (certain) occupation, the architecture tends to become prescriptive, narrowing the opportunity for uncertain or indeterminate occupation.

The predictions in the architectural programme are typically related to our explicit knowledge – perhaps to a vocation or ideas of domesticity. They are activities in which we can reliably predict the consequence of our architectural moves. Our knowledge of how to work with the unpredictable comes from our personal experience – from tacit knowledge. To ask the question of how we can address those occurrences we cannot predict, I have built a series of drawing instruments. The early versions worked optically with a folding picture plane to critically receive the projected image. The picture plane worked well but the optical projection made the combination of projection and reception too predictable – I was in total control of the whole process.

The solution was to find a more mischievous material to project than light, and I chose latex paint, a non-Newtonian fluid like blood. Forensic scientists have analogue and digital means of working back from blood splatter to divine the narrative that preceded the registration. When light is cast onto an object, its shadow is captive to the geometry of projection, whatever the angle at which one places the receptive screen. When paint is thrown at an object the splatter is less predictable, an outcome of that particular meeting between the flying paint (standing for an episode of occupation) and the model (standing for the architecture).

Another instrument's catapult throws the paint with an obedient trajectory of line and length, but the figure of each throw (witnessed by high-speed flash photography and later high-speed filming) is mischievously unique, providing each episode with an indeterminate character. A folding picture plane, at first behind the model but in later instruments alongside the trajectory of paint (to collect the splatter that comes off the model but not the rest of the paint), critically receives the consequence.

When working with these instruments I aim the catapult with an idea of what I want to happen. At the same time, I have the desire for it to do more than that. The biting point of the catapult's trigger is unpredictable and as soon as it lets go, I have to press the remote trigger for the camera and flash. After some practice I was able to catch about one in three throws of paint. When reviewing the photograph there is the question of whether I have caught the flying paint, and if so, whether the episode is of any interest. The cumulative experience of working with these instruments is feelings of anxiety and uncertainty that resonate with the condition their drawings represent.

THE FOLDED PICTURE PLANE AND THE SURFACE AS A CRITICAL RECEIVER

Since at least Leonardo, artists have curved the picture plane to overcome apparent distortions in one-point perspective. The problem is exemplified in Leonardo's three-column example, where three identical cylindrical columns, placed in a line, are viewed at right angles to that line, centred on the middle column. In one-point perspective the middle column appears narrower than its two outside neighbours, which are further away from the viewing position.

The picture plane is a surface that notionally sits between the observer and the thing being represented. This plane receives the image (whether as an observed situation or a constructed projection), makes any appropriate adjustments, and then projects that image on to the drawing surface. Typically, the adjustments are intended to make the image appear more true to life, but they can also be formed by the person making the drawing to produce a critical reception of the given image (as the form of the picture plane can change the figure and sometimes the nature of the projected content).

Initially in my work, the act of folding the picture plane was a means of taking possession of whatever was being projected upon the plane. This related to a series of projects for the human body to allow us to take possession of the given city on our terms. My first folding picture planes were a way of discussing such a relationship as critical receivers of projections, discussing where (if one were in possession of such an architecture) it would be possible to operate independently of some of the determining forces in the city.

From these lessons working with optical projection, all my subsequent drawing instruments employ folding picture planes to act as critical receivers of the splatter that comes from throwing latex paint at an architectural model. Each throw stands in for an episode of occupation, and while it can be aimed, each throw is unique and simulates the subtle indeterminacy of our engagements with architecture. Some of the splatter that comes off the model lands on the folded picture plane to record the consequence of the episode.

To understand the potential of the picture plane I studied the projection techniques of James Perry Wilson. Wilson studied architecture at Columbia and then worked for Bertram Goodhue until the Great Depression, when he became a diorama painter at the American Museum of Natural History in New York in 1934. Here he brought the rigour of architectural perspectival projection to diorama painting. He developed a 'dual grid' method of projecting the faceted geometry of panoramic survey photographs on to a semi-circular picture plane and then on to the particular form of the diorama shell. To fully understand this process, I built cameras particular to one of his dioramas where I could access the original site. These cameras made all of Wilson's adjustments in one photograph.

Bryan Cantley (USA)
Form:uLA is an experimental design practice owned by Bryan Cantley, which attempts to blur the indeterminate zone between architecture and its representation. An alumnus of UCLA, he has lectured at a number of architecture schools internationally, and has been visiting faculty at SCI-Arc and Woodbury. The San Francisco Museum of Modern Art purchased 11 of his models and drawings as a part of its permanent collection, and he was the recipient of a Graham Foundation Grant in 2002. Cantley has had a solo exhibition at the Bartlett School of Architecture, University College London (2008), as well as being the International Guest Lecturer at the Bartlett in 2008 and 2017. He has shown work in a number of other institutions, including SFMOMA, UNCC and UCLA. His solo exhibition *Dirty Geometries + Mechanical Imperfections* premiered at SCI-Arc in 2014, and his work was featured in *AD* 'Drawing Strength From Machinery' in 2008, and *AD* 'Drawing Architecture' in 2013. Bryan's first monograph, *Mechudzu*, was published by Springer Wien in 2011. His second book, *Speculative Coolness*, is forthcoming from Routledge in 2023.

Nat Chard (UK)
Nat Chard is Professor of Experimental Architecture at the Bartlett School of Architecture, University College London, following professorships at the Royal Danish Academy, Copenhagen, the University of Manitoba and the University of Brighton. He taught at the Bartlett throughout the 1990s. He is an architect registered in the UK and has practised in London. His work has been published and exhibited internationally. His research practice develops means of discussing uncertain conditions in architecture and the recent work has been acted out through a series of drawing instruments. With Perry Kulper he won the competition for Pamphlet Architecture 34 (*Fathoming the Unfathomable*).

Sir Peter Cook (UK)
Graduate of the Bournemouth College of Art and the Architectural Association in London, Peter Cook has been a pivotal figure within the architectural world for 50 years. A founder of the Archigram Group which was jointly awarded the Royal Gold Medal of the RIBA in 2004, he received a knighthood for his services to architecture in 2007, and in 2011 was granted an honorary Doctorate of Technology by Lund University. He is also a Commander of the Order of Arts and Letters of France and a member of the Royal Academy of Arts. His recent books include *Drawing: the Motive Force of Architecture* (Wiley) and *Peter Cook Architecture Workbook* (Wiley). A full catalogue of his work will be published by Circa Press. A former Director of the Institute of Contemporary Arts and the Bartlett, he is Emeritus Professor at University College London, the Royal Academy of Arts and the Frankfurt Städelschule. He was Kenzo Tange Visiting Professor at Harvard University's Graduate School of Design in 2015.

Metis: Mark Dorrian + Adrian Hawker (UK)
Metis is an atelier for art, architecture and urbanism founded by Mark Dorrian and Adrian Hawker at the University of Edinburgh in 1997 with the aim of connecting architectural teaching, research and practice. Their work focuses on the city and the complex ways in which it is imagined, inhabited and representationally encoded.

Mark Dorrian holds the Forbes Chair in Architecture at the University of Edinburgh. His work spans topics in architecture and urbanism, art history and theory, and media studies, and has appeared in journals such as *Cabinet*, *Chora*, *Cultural Politics*, the *Journal of Architecture*, the *Journal of Narrative Theory*, *Log*, *Parallax*, *Radical Philosophy*, and *Word & Image*. Mark's books include *Seeing From Above: The Aerial View in Visual Culture* (co-edited with Frédéric Pousin) and a volume of collected essays titled *Writing on the Image: Architecture, the City and the Politics of Representation*. Mark has been a visiting professor at schools in Europe, the USA and China and a visiting scholar at the Canadian Centre for Architecture in Montréal and in the Department of Prints and Drawings at the British Museum.

Adrian Hawker was educated at the Mackintosh School of Architecture, Glasgow School of Art and the Architectural Association, London. He is a Senior Lecturer at the Edinburgh School of Architecture and Landscape Architecture, the University of Edinburgh where, since 2017, he has been Master of Architecture Programme Director. His recent teaching and research operate under the term Island Territories, working with postgraduate students in architecture and landscape architecture to research, through design, the relationship between the island city and the landscape upon which it is founded. His writing and speculative architectural drawings have been published, exhibited and awarded internationally.

Riet Eeckhout (Belgium)
Riet Eeckhout is Guest Professor at the faculty of architecture of KU Leuven (Belgium). As a researcher she exhibits, publishes and writes about her drawings from within the discipline of architecture. She has been a guest speaker and teacher at a number of international universities

and conferences at which she has discussed her research in relation to the discipline of architecture. Her drawings have been exhibited internationally, including at the Venice Biennale, La Gallerie d'Architecture (Paris), Tchoban Foundation Museum of Architectural Drawing (Berlin), Architekturmuseum der TU Berlin, and Art Omi: Architecture (Ghent, NY).

Arnaud Hendrickx (Belgium)
Arnaud Hendrickx lives in Brussels and works in Brussels, Ghent and Leuven, Belgium. He trained as an architect at the School of Science and Art, Sint-Lucas Brussels. As an architect, he worked for Xaveer De Geyter architects and later founded RAUW Architects with Thierry Berlemont and Bart Callens, with whom he realised various buildings. In recent years, his spatial artistic practice has focused more and more on exhibition architecture, installations, public artworks and autonomous artefacts, rather than on buildings. He teaches and conducts research on the border area between art and architecture as an associate professor at the Faculty of Architecture at KU Leuven and as an adjunct professor at RMIT University, School of Architecture and Design (Melbourne, Australia). He is head of the Architecture and Art unit at the Department of Architecture at KU Leuven and a member of the research group 'Radical Materiality' at the Faculty of Architecture of the same university. He received his doctorate in 2012 at RMIT University with a thesis and exhibition project called *Substantiating Displacement.*

Thomas-Bernard Kenniff (Canada)
Thomas-Bernard Kenniff is a professor in the Environmental Design programme at the École de Design, Université du Québec à Montréal (UQAM), where he teaches design studio, theory and criticism and research by design. His work addresses the relationship between the built environment, design processes and society with a specific interest in public space and municipal architecture. Recent projects have focused on physical manifestations of the governmental apparatus in Québec and investigative approaches to architectural representation. He is the co-founder of the Bureau d'Étude de Pratiques Indisciplinées (BéPI, www.be-pi.ca), investigating hybrid and transversal modes of design and research, and co-editor of *Inventories: Documentation as Design Project* (BéPI, 2021). Thomas-Bernard holds a PhD in Architectural History and Theory from the Bartlett School of Architecture, University College London, and is a graduate of the University of Waterloo where he studied architecture and mathematics.

Perry Kulper (USA)
Perry Kulper is an architect and Associate Professor of Architecture at the University of Michigan. In a prior life he was a SCI-Arc faculty member for 17 years and held visiting teaching positions at Penn and ASU during that time. Subsequent to graduate studies at Columbia University he worked in the offices of respected mentors Eisenman/Robertson, Robert A.M. Stern and Venturi, Rauch and Scott Brown before moving to Los Angeles. His primary interests include: the roles and generative potential of architectural drawing; the outrageously different spatial opportunities offered by using diverse design methods in design practices; and in broadening the conceptual range by which architecture contributes to our cultural imagination. He was the Sir Banister Fletcher Visiting Professor at the Bartlett, 2018–19. In 2013 he published Pamphlet Architecture 34, *Fathoming the Unfathomable: Archival Ghosts and Paradoxical Shadows* with his friend and collaborator Nat Chard. They are at work on a new book to be published by UCL Press. Recently he optimistically ventured into the world of the digital, attempting to get a handle on a few operations in Photoshop. Fantastic beasts have also been on his mind.

Carole Lévesque (Canada)
Carole Lévesque's work explores the representation, temporality and practices of urban space and architecture. Through drawing and various modes of representation, her research investigates the processes of abandonment and renewal. Recent projects have specifically focused on *terrains vagues* in Beirut, Montréal and Rome. Co-founder of the Bureau d'Étude de Pratiques Indisciplinées (BéPI) and member of the Centre de Récherche Cultures – Arts – Sociétés (CELAT), she is a professor at the École de Design, Université du Québec à Montréal where she teaches studio, theory and criticism as well as research by design methods. She is co-editor of *Inventories: Documentation as Project* (BéPI, 2021) and author of *À Propos de l'Inutile en Architecture* (L'Harmattan, 2011) and *Finding Room in Beirut, Places of the Everyday* (Punctum Books, 2019). Carole holds a PhD in Aménagement, histoire et théorie de l'architecture from the Université de Montréal and a professional graduate degree in architecture from the University of British Columbia.

Johnny Leya (Belgium)
Johnny Leya graduated with Honours from the ULB Faculty of Architecture in Brussels in 2015. He is the founder of the architectural firm Traumnovelle and has worked in various architecture and urban planning offices, including the Charleroi Bouwmeester in Belgium, Ole Scheeren in Beijing, and Muoto in Paris. He presently teaches at the

Brussels Faculty of Architecture (ULB) and at the ERG, and is a regular guest critic at schools including Paris ENSA Versailles, EPFL Lausanne, and ETH Zürich.

C.J. Lim (UK)
C.J. Lim is Professor of Architecture and Urbanism at the Bartlett. He has held a long preoccupation with architectural storytelling, exploring how narratives from literature, history, politics and humanity can inform the innovation of resilient architecture and cities. He is the founding director of Studio 8 Architects in London – a multi-disciplinary and international award-winning practice. In 2006, the Royal Academy of Arts London awarded C.J. the Grand Architecture Prize. C.J.'s multi-disciplinary research and the resulting outputs have been internationally published, won numerous international awards, and are part of the permanent architectural collection of the Victoria and Albert Museum London, Fonds Regional d'Art Contemporain du Centre (FRAC) France, and RIBA British Architectural Library London. C.J. has authored 12 books and his work has appeared in numerous international solo and group exhibitions in galleries and museums around the world.

William Menking (USA)
William (Bill) Menking was an architectural historian, writer, critic, and curator of architecture and urbanism. He was professor of architecture, urbanism and city planning at Pratt Institute and lectured and taught at schools in the United States and Europe. He curated and organised international exhibitions on the visionary British architects Archigram, the Italian radical architects Superstudio, and contemporary English design, and his writing appeared in numerous architectural publications, anthologies and museum catalogues. Bill served as Commissioner of the US pavilion at the 2008 Venice Biennale. He died in 2020.

Anthony Morey (US)
Anthony Morey is a Los Angeles-based curator, writer, theorist and designer. He is the Executive Director and Curator at the A+D Museum in Los Angeles, along with being an editor-at-large of the website Archinect, founder of *M-A-S-K-S* journal, co-founder and Chief Curator of a One-Night Stand for Art and Architecture, Design Studio Faculty at USC and Creative Director of ynotWORKSHOP in Los Angeles. His work and research are invested in the tensions between text, psychology and image and their relationship to architecture and art.

Shaun Murray (UK)
Shaun Murray is a qualified architect and the director of ENIAtype, a transdisciplinary architecture practice founded in 2011. He gained his doctorate in architecture at the Planetary Collegium, University of Plymouth. He is a Senior Lecturer at the Department of Architecture and Landscape, University of Greenwich, Director of Architecture MArch (ARB RIBA Part 2) admissions and a unit leader on the engineering and architecture course at the Bartlett School of Architecture, UCL, and has been a unit master at the Architectural Association. He is the author of *Disturbing Territories* (Springer, 2006), which showcases his pioneering and widely published work in architectural drawing. He is the Editor-in-Chief of the international peer-reviewed design journal *Design Ecologies*, which was set up as a platform for the state-of-the-art experiments that link architecture, technology and philosophy, and is published biannually through Intellect Books. His current work on 'Abducted Ground: The Ineffaceable Beaduric's Island' is published in the 'Radical Drawings' issue of *Architectural Design*, (2022).

Mark Smout and Laura Allen (UK)
Mark Smout (Professor of Architecture and Landscape Futures) and Laura Allen (Professor of Architecture and Augmented Landscapes) are based at the Bartlett School of Architecture, UCL. Their practice concentrates on conceptual and theoretical design projects that operate with the ephemeral and enduring forces of change in our environment. Vernacular techniques and passive systems are reinvented to enhance the latent qualities of the site and the architecture that inhabits it. New strategies for inhabiting territories of change provide a model for an unfamiliar architecture that adapts with the restless and evolving landscape. Innovative techniques of architectural representation and the iterative process of design are particularly important. smoutallen.com

Neil Spiller (UK)
Neil Spiller is Editor of *Architectural Design* and is Founding Director of the AVATAR Group (Advanced Virtual and Technological Architectural Research). He has until recently been Hawksmoor Chair of Architecture and Landscape and Deputy Pro Vice-Chancellor of the University of Greenwich, London. Prior to this he was Vice-Dean and Graduate Director of Design at the Bartlett School of Architecture, University College London. His own work has been exhibited internationally and is in many collections worldwide. His books include *Cyberreader: Critical Writings of the Digital Era* (2002), *Digital Dreams* (1998), *Visionary Architecture: Blueprints of the Modern Imagination* (2006), *Digital Architecture Now* (2008) and *Surrealism and Architecture: A Blistering Romance* (2016). Spiller is also recognised internationally for his paradigm-shifting contribution to architectural drawing, discourse, research/experiment and teaching.

Prior to being appointed Editor of *AD,* he guest-edited eight issues including the influential and pioneering 'Architects in Cyberspace' (1995) and 'Architects in Cyberspace II' (1998).

Natalija Subotincic (Canada)
Natalija (Nada) Subotincic has been a professor of architecture for 32 years in Turkey, Denmark, Canada, and the USA. She most recently left MEF University in Istanbul to co-found a small museum in Montréal called Ceci n'est pas un musée. Since 2006 she has been collaborating with the Museum of Jurassic Technology in Los Angeles, designing exhibition spaces. Her creative research includes: 'Interpretation of Rooms', an ongoing spatial analysis of Sigmund Freud's consulting room and study; 'Incarnate Tendencies: An Architecture of Culinary Refuse', a social and architectural re-evaluation of food preparation and consumption in Jamie Horowitz and Paulette Singley (eds), *Eating Architecture* (MIT, 2004); 'Anaesthetic Induction', an enquiry into Duchamp's *Le Grand Verre* and *Étant Donnés*, in *Chora: Intervals in the Philosophy of Architecture* (McGill-Queen's University Press); and a photographic exploration of technology, architecture and the body in Alberto Pérez-Gómez's *Polyphilo or the Dark Forest Revisited: An Erotic Epiphany of Architecture* (MIT, 1992).

Michael Webb (USA)
Michael Webb is one of the original six members of the 1960s Archigram Group, a collection of radical young architects. They employed magazine-type formats, inflatable structures, clothing-like environments, bright colours and cartoon-like drawing techniques. Webb moved to the United States in 1965 to teach architecture at Virginia Tech, and has since taught at the Rhode Island School of Design, NJIT, Columbia University, Barnard College, Cooper Union, University at Buffalo, Pratt Institute and Princeton University. He has also mounted exhibitions in Europe and North America. His latest exhibition, *Two Journeys*, read like the pages of a book. It centred on two main themes: a train of thought deriving from the Reyner Banham article 'A Home is not a House' (1965) and a study of linear perspective projection. His monograph, *Michael Webb: Two Journeys*, was published in October 2018 by Lars Muller Publishers.

Mark West (Canada)
Mark West, is an artist, builder, professor of architecture, and inventor of numerous flexible-mould techniques for concrete construction. He is the author of *The Fabric Formwork Book* (Routledge, 2016), and was the founding Director of the Centre for Architectural Structures and Technology (CAST) at the University of Manitoba – the first academic laboratory/studio dedicated to fabric formwork technology. He has taught architecture at universities in the USA, Canada, Europe, Turkey and the UK since 1981, and his work has been widely published in art, architecture and civil engineering journals. He currently lives and works in Montréal, Canada at the newly opened Surviving Logic Atelier and the nascent Ceci n'est pas un musée. survivinglogic.ca

Michael Young (USA)
Michael Young is an architect and educator practising in New York City where he is a founding partner of the architectural design studio Young & Ayata. Young & Ayata have received a Progressive Architecture Award, the Design Vanguard Award, the Young Architects Prize, and a first-place prize for the design of the Bauhaus Museum in Dessau, Germany. Michael is currently an Assistant Professor at the Cooper Union. He was previously the Louis I. Kahn Visiting Assistant Professor at Yale University and has taught studios and seminars at Princeton, SCI-Arc and Columbia. He has published numerous essays, and the books *The Estranged Object* (Graham Foundation, 2015) and *Reality Modeled After Images* (Routledge, 2021). Michael was the 2019–20 Rome Prize Fellow at the American Academy in Rome.

MICHAEL WEBB
Car Ramp – Isometric View, c.1981
Graphite, coloured pencil, airbrush on board
39.7 × 53 cm (15½ × 21 in)

Drawing Matter Collections 1101.7
Reproduced courtesy of Drawing Matter and the architect

The image that appears on the cover of this book is a drawing by Michael Webb of the Sin Centre, a project that began over 60 years ago as his final-year thesis project at what was then the Regent Street Polytechnic School of Architecture in London. It is a project to which he has ever since continued to return. This drawing, which was likely produced in the early 1980s, is a cutaway view of one of the spiralling vehicle routes that organise the building. It is on a piece of illustration board that Webb had in his studio and had previously used for cutting on (some of the scratches became incorporated as joints in the depiction of the building's translucent cladding). We see the layers of aluminium-skinned ramps, tapered and marked with graphic codes like aircraft wings, and sectioned at points to show their interior structure. The drawing seems to glow with a soft and hallucinatory radiance that appears almost photographic in the way that it develops within its darkened ground. On the lower and left-hand sides, the image presses up close to the edge of the board on which it is drawn; at the other two it pushes beyond them. The curious interplay of flatness and depth in the drawing is partly to do with the image's spectral transparency, but also the way the vertical centreline that divides the panel acts as a section line for the cutaway of the uppermost ramp, meaning that – because we are not looking at the section obliquely – we have a non-volumetric view, seeing only the top surface which, as a result, ambiguously tends to flatten while at the same time being lifted away from what is below by a zone of shadow.

Although not exactly a 'recent' image, we have chosen it as a testimony to the significance and inspiration of Michael Webb's work for the contributors to this volume and to the importance of his extensive explorations through architectural drawing. In his work, encounters with, and (the often unexpected) effects of, specific media become opportunities for seeing things – or seeing something –afresh, whether this is occasioned by the discovery of how a diazo print has faded over time or, as in the cover image, the way that graphite, airbrush and board couple with a dream of metallic luminescence. When we engage with Webb's drawings we are engaging with complex forms of inquiry, processes of thinking that are sedimented in wondrous objects.
MD

First published in 2022 by Lund Humphries
Huckletree Shoreditch
Alphabeta Building
18 Finsbury Square
London
EC2A 1AH
www.lundhumphries.com

Drawing Architecture: Conversations on Contemporary Practice
© Mark Dorrian, Riet Eeckhout and Arnaud Hendrickx
All rights reserved

ISBN 978-1-84822-620-3

A Cataloguing-in-Publication record for this book is available from the British Library.

All rights reserved. No part of this publication may be reproduced, stored in a retrieval system or transmitted in any form or by any means, electrical, mechanical or otherwise, without first seeking the permission of the copyright owners and publishers. Every effort has been made to seek permission to reproduce the images in this book. Any omissions are entirely unintentional, and details should be addressed to the publishers.

Mark Dorrian, Riet Eeckhout and Arnaud Hendrickx have asserted their right under the Copyright, Designs and Patents Act, 1988 to be identified as the Editors of this Work.

Photograph p.201: Gert Skærlund Andersen
Photographs pp 10, 74, 76, 116, 164: Arnaud Hendrickx

Designed by Stefi Orazi Studio
Printed in Estonia

ACKNOWLEDGEMENTS

This book would not have come into existence without the shared commitment, trust and critical views of the Drawing Architecture group, whose members came together in many hours of generous conversation to show work and collectively think about architectural drawing: Laura Allen, Aaron Betsky, Bryan Cantley, Nat Chard, Peter Cook, Mark Dorrian, Riet Eeckhout, Adrian Hawker, Arnaud Hendrickx, Perry Kulper, Johnny Leya, C.J. Lim, Shaun Murray, William Menking, Anthony Morey, Mark Smout, Neil Spiller, Nataljia Subotincic, Michael Webb, Mark West and Michael Young.

We are grateful to the following university divisions and institutes for their material and financial support for this project, and for the invaluable assistance of individuals in them: KU Leuven Faculty of Architecture; Edinburgh College of Art, The University of Edinburgh; The Bartlett School of Architecture, University College London; the NY hub (New York, US); and the Belgian Academy in Rome, Dag Boutsen, Prof. Dr. Yves Schoonjans, Dr. Anneleen Van der Veken, Dr. Annette Kuhk, Prof. Dr. Kris Scheerlinck, Ben Robberechts.

We thank Louise Pelletier, Director of the Centre de design de l'UQAM in Montreal, Canada, for her encouragement in developing an exhibition from the project, which has been evolved under the curatorship of Carole Lévesque and Thomas-Bernard Kenniff, who have kindly co-authored an essay for this volume.

At Lund Humphries, Val Rose, our commissioning editor, received the proposal with enthusiasm and guided it through the acceptance process, before passing us on to Sarah Thorowgood, who has skilfully managed its production. We are grateful to Chris Schüler for his care and attention in copy-editing the text, and to Stefi Orazi for her beautiful book design.

Special thanks are given in acknowledgement of the patience and support of family throughout this project, in particular Ester Goris and Ephraim Joris.